ANALYSIS FOR FINANCIAL MANAGEMENT

ANALYSIS FOR FINANCIAL MANAGEMENT

ROBERT C. HIGGINS
The University of Washington

1984

RICHARD D. IRWIN, INC.
Homewood, Illinois 60430

A professional edition of this book is available
through Dow Jones-Irwin.

ISBN 0-256-03004-9
Library of Congress Catalog Card No. 83–80590

Printed in the United States of America

1 2 3 4 5 6 7 8 9 0 ML 0 9 8 7 6 5 4 3

In memory of Alex Robichek,
teacher, colleague and friend.

Preface

Analysis for Financial Management is my conception of what today's manager needs to know about financial management. Written with the conviction that finance is too important to be left to specialists, its purpose is to present standard techniques and modern developments in a practical, intuitively accessible way. The book is intended for nonfinancial managers and business students interested in the practice of financial management, and it assumes no prior background beyond a rudimentary and perhaps rusty familiarity with financial statements. Emphasis throughout is on the managerial implications of financial analysis.

Analysis for Financial Management is an attempt to translate into another medium the enjoyment and challenge I have faced the past 15 years teaching executives and college students. From this experience I have come to believe that recent developments in the field, such as market efficiency and β-risk, are important to practitioners, that financial techniques and concepts need not be abstract or obtuse, and that finance has much to say about the broader aspects of company management. At no time in recent memory have the financial shoals been more treacherous for business or have the rewards to creative financial management been higher.

I wish to express my gratitude to Yoshi Tsurumi for originally suggesting this project, to Linda Denton and Debbie Malestky for preparing the manuscript, to George McCain for reading an earlier version of the text, to my children, Sara and Steve, for providing the financial incentive, and most importantly to my many students and colleagues at the University of Washington, The Management Studies Centre, Macquarie University, The Intensive Management Development Institute, and the Pacific Coast Banking School for creating the hothouse in which the ideas expressed here took root.

Introduction

Analysis for Financial Management is a practical introduction to a topic of broad managerial concern. The perspective throughout is on the effective management of company resources, beginning in Part I with the management of existing resources. The focus here is on the assessment of the financial health of a company, its strengths, weaknesses, recent performance, and future prospects. This involves a review of financial statements followed by careful consideration of their use in evaluating financial performance. A recurring theme is that business must be viewed as an integrated whole and that effective financial management is possible only within the context of a company's broader operating characteristics and strategies.

The remainder of the book deals in one way or another with the acquisition and management of new resources. Part II begins with a look at the planning of future performance, including financial forecasting and managing growth. Growth management addresses the problem of keeping company capital requirements within the resource constraints imposed by high interest rates and unsettled financial markets. Part III looks at financing operations. This includes examination of the principal security types, the markets in which they trade, and the proper choice of security type by the issuing firm. The latter topic requires a close look at financial leverage, its impact on the firm, and shareholders. Evaluation of investment opportunities is the topic of Part IV. Included here is the use of discounted cash flow techniques—such as the net present value and the internal rate of return—as figures of investment merit. Also included is a look at the difficult task of incorporating risk analysis into decision making. In order to concentrate more fully on topics of primary significance, tangential material and extensions appear in end-of-chapter appendixes.

A word of warning: *Analysis for Financial Management* emphasizes the application and interpretation of analytic techniques in decision making. These techniques have proved useful for putting financial problems into perspective and for helping managers anticipate the consequences of alternative actions. But techniques can never substitute for thought. Even with the best techniques it is still necessary to define and prioritize issues, to modify the techniques appropriately for specific circumstances, to strike the proper balance between quantitative analysis and more qualitative concerns, and to evaluate alternatives insightfully and creatively. Mastery of technique is only a necessary first step toward effective management.

Contents

Determining the Relevant Cash Flows: *Depreciation. Working Capital. Allocated Costs. Sunk Costs. Excess Capacity. Financing Costs.* Appendix: *Mutually Exclusive Alternatives and Capital Rationing.*

Appendixes

PART I

Assessing the Financial Health of a Firm

1 | Interpreting Financial Statements

Financial statements are like fine perfume;
to be sniffed but not swallowed.
Abraham Brilloff

Accounting can usefully be thought of as the scorecard of business. It translates the activities of a company into a set of objective numbers which provide information about the firm's performance, problems, and prospects. Finance involves the interpretation of these accounting numbers for the assessment of performance and the planning of future actions.

The skills of financial analysis are important to a wide range of people, including investors, creditors, and regulators. Nowhere are they more important than within the company. Regardless of functional specialty or company size, managers who possess these skills are able to diagnose their firm's ills, prescribe useful remedies, and anticipate the financial consequences of their actions. Like a ball player who cannot keep score, an operating manager who does not fully understand accounting and finance works under an unnecessary handicap.

This chapter and the two that follow look at the use of accounting information for the assessment of financial health. We begin with an overview of the accounting principles governing financial statements and a discussion of one of the most abused and confused notions in all of finance—cash flow. Chapter 2 looks at measures of financial performance and ratio analysis; and the third chapter examines the added problems inflation creates in assessing financial health.

The Cash Flow Cycle

Finance can seem arcane and complex to the uninitiated. There are, however, a comparatively few basic principles which should guide your thinking. One is that *a company's finances and its operations are integrally connected.* A company's activities, method of manufacture, and competitive strategy all fundamentally shape its financial structure. The reverse is also true. Decisions which appear primarily financial in nature can significantly affect company operations. For example, the way a company finances its assets can affect the nature of the investments it is able to undertake.

The cash flow–production cycle appearing in Figure 1–1 illustrates the

Figure 1–1. The Cash Flow–Production Cycle

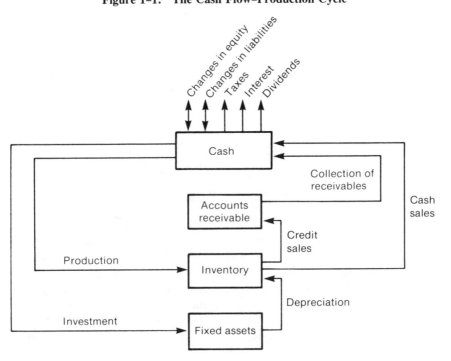

close interplay between company operations and finances. For simplicity, suppose the company shown is a new one which has raised money from owners and creditors, has purchased productive assets, and is now ready to begin operations. To do so the company uses cash to purchase raw materials and hire laborers; they make the product and store it temporarily in inventory. What began as cash is now physical inventory. When the company sells an item, the physical inventory changes once again into cash. If the sale is for cash, this occurs immediately; otherwise cash is not realized until some time later when the account receivable is collected.

This simple movement of cash to inventory, to accounts receivable, and back to cash is the firm's *working capital cycle*. Another ongoing activity represented in Figure 1–1 is investment. Over time the company's fixed assets are consumed, or worn out, in the manufacture of products. It is as if every item passing through the factory takes with it a small portion of the value of fixed assets. The accountant recognizes this process by continually reducing the accounting value of fixed assets and increasing the value of merchandise flowing into inventory by an amount known as depreciation. To maintain productive capacity, the company must invest part of its newly received cash in new fixed assets. The object of the exercise, of course, is to assure that the cash returning from the working capital cycle and the investment cycle exceeds the amount that started the journey.

We could complicate Figure 1–1 further by including accounts payable and by expanding on the use of debt and equity to generate cash, but the figure already demonstrates two basic principles. First, as already noted, a company's operating policies, production techniques, and inventory and credit-control systems fundamentally determine its financial profile. If, for example, a company requires prompter payment on credit sales, its financial statements will reveal a reduced investment in accounts receivable and possibly a change in its revenues and profits. This linkage between a company's operations and its finances is our rationale for studying financial statements. We seek to understand company operations and to predict the financial consequences of changing operations.

The second principle illustrated in Figure 1–1 is that *profits do not equal cash flow*. Cash, and the timely conversion of cash into inventories, accounts receivable, and back to cash, is the lifeblood of any company. If this cash flow is severed or significantly interrupted, insolvency can occur. Yet the fact that a company is profitable and perhaps growing is no assurance that its cash flow will be sufficient to maintain solvency. To illustrate, suppose a company is losing control of its accounts receivable by allowing customers an increasingly long time to pay, or suppose the company consistently makes more merchandise than it sells. Then even though the company is selling merchandise at a profit in the eyes of an accountant, its sales may not be producing enough cash inflows to replenish the cash outflows required for production and investment. When a company has insufficient cash to pay its maturing obligations, it is insolvent. As another example, suppose the company is managing its inventory and receivables carefully, but that rapid sales growth is forcing an ever-larger investment in these assets. Then as before, despite the fact that the company is profitable, it may have too little cash to meet its obligations. The company will literally be "growing broke." These brief examples illustrate why a manager must be concerned at least as much with cash flows as with profits.

We will return to these themes repeatedly in later chapters and will consider cash flow analysis in some detail in a few pages. But first it is necessary to review the basics of financial statements.

The Balance Sheet

The most important source of information for evaluating the financial health of a company is its financial statements, consisting of a balance sheet, an income statement, and a statement of changes in financial position. The statement of changes in financial position is largely a forgotten stepsister of the other two, and we can safely ignore it.

A balance sheet is a financial snapshot, taken at a point in time, of all the assets owned by the company and all the liabilities and equity claims against these assets. The balance sheet formula is:

$$\begin{matrix} \text{Total money} \\ \text{invested in company} \end{matrix} = \begin{matrix} \text{Money supplied} \\ \text{by creditors} \end{matrix} + \begin{matrix} \text{Money supplied} \\ \text{by owners} \end{matrix}$$

$$\text{Assets} = \text{Liabilities} + \text{Shareholders' equity}$$

The term *shareholders' equity* is also known as net worth or frequently just equity.

To illustrate the techniques and concepts presented throughout this book, I will refer whenever possible to Tektronix, Inc. (TEK), a large, rapidly growing manufacturer of sophisticated electronic test equipment located in Oregon. Tables 1–1 and 1–2 present TEK's fiscal year 1978 and 1979 financial statements. The asset and liability categories shown in Table 1–1 should be self-explanatory except possibly current assets and current liabilities.

Table 1–1
TEKTRONIX, INC.
Balance Sheets
Fiscal Years 1978, 1979
($ millions)

Assets	1978	1979	Change in Account
Current assets:			
Cash and securities	$ 66	$ 42	−24
Accounts receivable	115	153	38
Inventories	163	215	52
Prepaid expenses	13	19	6
Total current assets	357	429	
Plant and equipment	198	287	
Accumulated depreciation	85	101	
Net plant and equipment	113	186	73
Land	7	8	1
Other long-term assets	14	20	6
Total assets	$491	$643	

Table 1-1 *(concluded)*

Liabilities and Shareholder's Equity	1978	1979	Change in Account
Current liabilities:			
Short-term debt.........................	$ 11	$ 29	18
Accounts payable	33	42	9
Income taxes due	18	20	2
Incentives and retirement................	23	32	9
Payroll due	23	30	7
Total current liabilities	108	153	
Long-term debt.........................	37	62	25
Deferred tax liability	16	19	3
Other long-term liabilities	4	6	2
Total liabilities	165	240	
Shareholders' equity:			
Common shares	24	32	8
Retained earnings	302	371	69
Total shareholders' equity	326	403	
Total liabilities and shareholders' equity	$491	$643	

Table 1-2
TEKTRONIX, INC.
Income Statements
Fiscal Years 1978, 1979
($ millions)

	1978	1979
Net sales	$599	$787
Cost of sales	266	360
Gross profit...........................	333	427
Operating expenses:		
Engineering expense....................	50	61
Selling expense	87	113
Administrative expense..................	53	68
Profit sharing	49	64
Operating income	94	121
Nonoperating income....................	6	12
	100	133
Interest expense	4	6
Income before tax.......................	96	127
Income tax............................	39	50
Earnings	$ 57	$ 77
Dividends	11	8
Additions to retained earnings..............	46	69
Common shares outstanding	17.8	18.0
Earnings per share	$3.20	$4.28

The accountant defines any asset or liability which will be converted into cash within one year as current; all other assets or liabilities are long term. Inventory is a current asset because it is reasonable to assume it will be sold and will generate cash within the year. Accounts payable is a short-term liability because it must be paid within the year. Note that even though TEK is a manufacturing firm, over two thirds of its assets are current. We will have more to say about this in the next chapter.

One common source of confusion is the many accounts appearing in the shareholders' equity portion of the balance sheet. TEK has two: common shares and reinvested earnings. Other frequently used accounts include paid-in capital and retained earnings. My advice is to forget these distinctions. They keep lawyers and accountants employed, but seldom make any practical difference. Just add up everything that is not a liability and call it shareholders' equity.

A Word to the Unwary

Nothing puts a damper on a good financial discussion (if such exists) faster than the suggestion that if a company is short of cash, it can always spend some of its shareholders' equity. Shareholders' equity is on the liabilities side of the balance sheet not the asset side. It represents money already spent.

The Income Statement

The income statement measures a company's sales, expenses, and earnings over a specified time period, usually one year. The income statement formula is:

$$\text{Earnings} = \frac{\text{Net}}{\text{sales}} - \frac{\text{Cost of}}{\text{goods sold}} - \frac{\text{Other}}{\text{expenses}} - \text{Taxes}$$

To complicate matters, earnings are also commonly referred to as profits or income and sales are frequently called revenues. I have never found a meaningful distinction between these alternatives.

Measuring Earnings

This is not the place for a detailed discussion of accounting. However, because earnings, or lack of same, are a critical indicator of financial health, several technical aspects of earnings measurement deserve mention.

The measurement of accounting earnings involves two steps: the identification of revenues for the period and the matching of corresponding costs to revenues. Looking at the first step, it is important to note that revenue is not the same as cash received. According to the *accrual principle* (a cruel principle?) of accounting, revenue is recognized as soon as the effort required to generate the sale is substantially complete and there is a reasonable certainty that payment will be received. The accountant sees the timing of the actual cash receipts as only a technicality. For credit sales the accrual principle means that revenue is recognized when the customer is billed, not when he pays. This can result in a significant time lag between the generation of revenue and the receipt of cash. Looking at TEK, for instance, we see that revenue in 1979 was $787 million but that accounts receivable increased $38 million over the year. We conclude that cash received from sales during 1979 was only $749 million ($787 million − $38 million); the other $38 million of revenue still awaits collection.

Depreciation. Fixed assets, and associated depreciation, present the accountant with a particularly thorny problem in matching. Suppose in 1980 a company purchases for $5 million a machine which has an expected productive life of 10 years. The machine will contribute to revenue generation for the next decade; so rather than assign the entire $5 million cost to the 1980 income statement, the accountant spreads it over the machine's useful life in the form of depreciation. The only cash outlay associated with the machine occurs in 1980, so the annual depreciation listed as a cost on the company's income statement is not a cash outflow. It is a *noncash charge* used to match the 1980 expenditure with resulting revenue. TEK buries its annual depreciation charge in cost of goods sold, but elsewhere in its financial statements we learn that depreciation was $15 million and $16 million in 1978 and 1979, respectively.

To determine the amount of depreciation to be taken on a particular asset, three estimates are required: the asset's useful life, its salvage value, and the method of allocation to be employed. All of these estimates should be based on economic and engineering information, experience, and on any other objective data about the asset's likely performance. Broadly speaking, there are two methods of allocating an asset's cost over its useful life. Under the *straight-line* method, the accountant depreciates the asset by a uniform amount each year. If an asset costs $5 million, has an expected useful life of 10 years, and an estimated salvage value of $1 million, straight-line depreciation would be $400,000 per year [($5 million − $1 million)/10].

The second method of cost allocation is really a family of methods known as *accelerated depreciation*. Each technique charges more depreciation in the early years of the asset's life and correspondingly less in later years. Accelerated depreciation does not enable a company to take more depreciation in total; instead it alters the timing of the recognition. While the specifics of the various accelerated techniques need not detain us here, you should recognize that the life expectancy, the salvage value, and the allocation method used by a company can fundamentally affect reported earnings.

In general, if a company is conservative and depreciates its assets rapidly, it will tend to understate current earnings, and vice versa.

Taxes. A second noteworthy dimension of depreciation accounting involves taxes. Most companies, except the very small, keep at least two sets of financial records: one for managing the company and reporting to shareholders and another for determining its tax bill. The objective of the first set is, or should be, to portray accurately the financial performance of the company. The objective of the second is much simpler: to minimize taxes. Forget objectivity and minimize taxes. These differing objectives mean that the accounting principles used to construct the two sets of books differ substantially. Depreciation accounting is a case in point. Regardless of the method used for reporting to shareholders, company tax books will minimize current taxes by employing the most rapid method of depreciation over the shortest useful life allowed by the tax authorities.

This dual reporting creates some complications on a company's published financial statements. To illustrate, the income taxes of $50 million appearing on TEK's 1979 income statement are the taxes due according to the accounting techniques used in constructing TEK's published statements. Since TEK used different accounting techniques when reporting to the tax authorities—techniques intended to defer the recognition of tax liabilities until future years—$50 million is not the amount acutally owed by TEK in 1979. To confirm this, note on TEK's balance sheet that deferred tax liability, a long-term liability, rose $3 million in 1979 and income taxes due, a short-term liability, rose $2 million. Here's what happened: Using legal tax-deferral techniques, TEK was able to delay payment of $5 million of tax liabilities from 1979 to future years. Because these taxes are only postponed, not eliminated, they are a liability, of which $2 million is payable in the coming fiscal year and $3 million is a longer-term liability. In the meantime, TEK has use of the money. In essence, tax-deferral techniques create the equivalent of an interest-free loan from the government.

Cash Flow Analysis

Having now completed our brief review of financial statements, let's use the statements to learn more about company cash flows. As noted earlier, it is frequently important to distinguish between cash flow and profit when assessing the financial health of a company. The income statement is of some help in this regard, but it does not tell the whole story for two reasons: First, it includes accruals that are not cash flows and, second, it only records the cash flows associated with the sale of goods or services during the accounting period. There are a whole host of other cash receipts and expenditures occurring which do not appear on an income statement. To illustrate, Table 1–1 shows that TEK added $52 million to inventories during

1979. Yet there is no sign of this substantial expenditure on the company's income statement. TEK also raised $25 million in cash by increasing long-term debt, and again there is no trace of this transaction on the income statement except for a modest increase in interest expense. Clearly, an income statement does not tell the whole cash flow story.

Changes in Balance Sheet Accounts

To create a more complete picture of how a company spent its money and where the money came from, it is necessary to reorganize the balance sheet and income statement information to create a *cash flow statement*. This is easily done. The first step is to place balance sheets for two dates side by side and note all the changes in balance sheet accounts that occurred over the accounting-period. The right-most column in Table 1–1 contains the requisite changes for TEK during 1979. The second step is to divide the changes into those which generated cash and those which consumed cash.

A company generates cash in two ways: by reducing an asset or by increasing a liability. For example, the sale of used equipment, the liquidation of inventories, and the reduction of accounts receivable are all reductions in asset accounts and are all sources of cash to the company. On the liabilities side of the balance sheet, an increase in a bank loan or the sale of common stock are increases in liabilities which again generate cash.

A company also uses cash in two ways: to increase an asset account or to reduce a liability account. To illustrate, adding to inventories or accounts receivable or building a new plant all increase assets and all use cash. Conversely, the repayment of a bank loan, the reduction of accounts payable, and an operating loss all reduce liabilities and all use cash. Naturally, total

---

Cash Flow from Operations

Companies also generate cash from operations. Such cash appears in two forms: (1) earnings and (2) noncash charges, like depreciation, which the accountant deducts from revenue but which are not cash outflows.

Cash flow from operations = Earnings + Noncash charges

Cash flow from operations is automatically included in our analysis when we say that the only two sources of cash are a reduction in assets or an increase in liabilities. Thus, the portion of earnings retained by the company adds to shareholders' equity (increase in a liability account), and depreciation reduces net fixed assets (reduction of an asset account). In similar fashion, deferred taxes increase a liability account and are thus a source of cash.

uses of cash over an accounting period must equal total sources; otherwise, the company would be spending cash it didn't have.

The Sources and Uses Statement

The third step in cash flow analysis is to segregate the changes in balance sheet accounts into those which are sources of cash and those which are uses. The result is a *sources and uses statement*. Table 1–3 presents a

Table 1–3
TEKTRONIX, INC.
Sources and Uses Statement
Fiscal year 1979 ($ millions)

Sources:

Reduction in cash	$ 24
Increase in short-term debt	18
Increase in accounts payable	9
Increase in income taxes due	2
Increase in incentives and retirement	9
Increase in payroll due	7
Increase in long-term debt	25
Increase in deferred tax liability	3
Increase in other long term liabilities	2
Increase in common shares	8
Increase in retained earnings	69
Total sources	$176

Uses:

Increase in accounts receivable	$ 38
Increase in inventories	52
Increase in prepaid expenses	6
Increase in net plant and equipment	73
Increase in land	1
Increase in other long term assets	6
Total uses	$176

sources and uses statement for TEK during 1979. A sources and uses statement makes explicit a good deal of information about the cash flowing through a company, which is only implicit in published financial statements. For example, the statement reveals that the largest sources of money to TEK during 1979 were an increase in retained earnings, an increase in long-term debt, and a reduction in cash; the major uses were an increase in net plant and equipment, an increase in inventories, and an increase in accounts receivable. Note that over one half of the money spent went to increase receivables and inventory.

How can a reduction in cash be a source of cash? It is the same as when you withdraw money from a checking account. You reduce your bank balance but generate cash to spend.

The Cash Flow Statement

To squeeze more information out of the sources and uses statement, it is common to expand and rearrange the statement in several respects. There are a number of different formats for doing this, but one of the best is that used by Wells Fargo Bank, a simplified version of which will be presented here. The first step is to disaggregate two of the terms appearing in the sources and uses statement to capture a little more detail. Replace change in net plant and equipment with its equal, investment minus depreciation.

$$\text{Change in net plant and equipment } = \text{ Investment } - \text{ Depreciation}$$
$$\$73 = \$89 - \$16$$

Investment is obviously a use of cash and depreciation is a source.[1] The second change is to replace increase in retained earnings with its equal, earnings minus dividends.

$$\text{Increase in retained earnings } = \text{ Earnings } - \text{ Dividends}$$
$$\$69 = \$77 - \$8$$

Here, earnings are obviously a source of cash and dividends a use.

Table 1–4 presents a rearrangement of the expanded sources and uses statement for TEK, referred to as a *cash flow statement*. Note that no new information appears here. The table is just a regrouping of the data in Table 1–3 under some convenient headings. The first part of this statement, cash provided by operations, can be thought of as a restructuring of TEK's income statement from an accrual accounting basis to one of cash accounting. Beginning with earnings, the restructuring goes as follows: Depreciation is a noncash charge which should be added back to earnings to calculate cash provided. Next, in accordance with the matching principle, the accountant records a number of expenses in 1979 that do not involve cash outlays in that year. These are reflected on the balance sheet as increases in liability accounts. For TEK, they include increases in accounts payable, taxes due, incentives and retirement, payroll due, and deferred tax liability. Since these are not cash outlays in 1979, we add them back to earnings. On the other side of the coin, the accountant following the matching principle ignores a number of cash outlays which did occur in 1979. These appear on the balance sheet as increases in asset accounts. For TEK, they include increases

---

[1]Technically, depreciation is not an independent source of cash, but rather is part of cash flow from operations. Although accountants turn blue when depreciation is called a source of cash, the distinction need not concern us.

Table 1–4
TEKTRONIX, INC.
Cash Flow Statement
Fiscal Year 1979 ($ millions)

Cash provided by operations:

Earnings for 1979	$ 77
Depreciation	16
Increase in accounts payable	9
Increase in income taxes due	2
Increase in incentives and retirement	9
Increase in payroll due	7
Increase in deferred tax liability	3
Increase in inventories	(52)
Increase in prepaid expenses	(6)
Increase in accounts receivable	(38)
Total	27

Plus cash provided by external financing:

Increase in short-term debt	18
Increase in long-term debt	25
Increase in other long-term liabilities	2
Increase in common shares	8
Total	53

Less financing costs:

Dividends	8
Total	8

Less new investment:

Investment in plant and equipment	89
Increase in land	1
Increase in other long-term assets	6
Total	96

Equals change in cash:

Reduction in cash	$ 24

in inventories and prepaid expenses. Since the accountant missed these cash outlays, we subtract them from earnings to calculate cash provided. Finally, the accountant does not distinguish between cash sales and credit sales when measuring earnings; and since credit sales generate no cash until collected, we must subtract the increase in accounts receivable to calculate cash provided by operations.

Table 1–4 indicates that operations in 1979 contributed $27 million to TEK's cash balances. Although the accountant says TEK earned $77 million in 1979, the actual amount of cash which fell into the till was fully $50 million less. As noted earlier, earnings do not equal cash flow.

The remainder of the table should be self-explanatory. We could expand the analysis further, as Wells Fargo does, by acknowledging that the in-

---

Does the Increase in Retained Earnings Always Equal Earnings Minus Dividends?

No! Gains or losses which are judged by the accountant to be nonrecurring are charged directly to retained earnings. Examples of nonrecurring gains or losses include sale of an asset at a price other than its value on the financial statements, casualty losses, losses incurred in the termination of a business, and gains or losses incurred in the consolidation of foreign assets and liabilities. Any gains or losses posted directly to retained earnings cause the change in retained earnings to differ from earnings minus dividends.

---

crease in long-term debt is the net effect of new borrowings and the repayment of maturing obligations, and by pulling interest expense out of earnings and including it with debt repayments under the heading of financing costs. However, even without these refinements, Table 1–4 is sufficient to highlight the differences between accrual accounting and cash accounting.

What insights can we gain about TEK from examining its cash flow statement? The most apparent is that despite TEK's substantial earnings in 1979, cash provided by operations was a much more modest figure. The difference can be attributed chiefly to the fact that rapidly increasing sales forced TEK to invest more cash into inventories and accounts receivable. The implication of this comparatively modest generation of cash from operations is that TEK was heavily dependent on external financing sources, especially debt, to pay for its significant plant and equipment investment.

In sum, we can draw several conclusions from our discussion of cash flow. One is that earnings are not cash. A second is that several types of cash flow are relevant to managers. *Cash flow from operations,* defined as earnings plus noncash charges, measures the additions to cash generated by operations, ignoring any changes in assets or liabilities required to support operations. A company is in serious trouble if its cash flow from operations is negative, because it is not generating enough operating cash even to pay for production costs, to say nothing of recouping its investment in fixed assets. *Cash provided by operations,* as shown in Table 1–4, provides a broader look at cash flow by including changes in those assets and liabilities most closely tied to operations. It is *incorrect* to say that a company with negative cash provided by operations is necessarily in trouble. When a company like TEK is growing rapidly, the buildup in inventories and receivables which accompanies increased sales can make cash provided by operations negative. However, if the added sales are profitable, if management is controlling its investment in inventories and receivables, and if it has arranged for sufficient outside financing, the situation need not be a dangerous one.

Quoth the Banker, "Watch Cash Flow"
Once upon a midnight dreary as I pondered weak and weary
Over many a quaint and curious volume of accounting lore,
Seeking gimmicks (without scruple) to squeeze through some new
  tax loophole,
Suddenly I heard a knock upon my door,
    Only this, and nothing more.

Then I felt a queasy tingling and I heard the cash a-jingling
As a fearsome banker entered whom I'd often seen before.
His face was money-green and in his eyes there could be seen
Dollar-signs that seemed to glitter as he reckoned up the score.
    "Cash flow," the banker said, and nothing more.

I had always thought it fine to show a jet black bottom line,
But the banker sounded a resounding, "No,
Your receivables are high, mounting upward toward the sky;
Write-offs loom. What matters is cash flow."
    He repeated, "Watch cash flow."

Then I tried to tell the story of our lovely inventory
Which, though large, is full of most delightful stuff.
But the banker saw its growth, and with a mighty oath
He waved his arms and shouted, "Stop! Enough!
    Pay the interest, and don't give me any guff!"

Next I looked for non-cash items which could add ad infinitum
To replace the ever-outward flow of cash,
But to keep my statement black I'd held depreciation back,
And my banker said that I'd done something rash.
    He quivered, and his teeth began to gnash.

When I asked him for a loan, he responded, with a groan,
That the interest rate would be just prime plus eight,
And to guarantee my purity he'd insist on some security—
All my assets plus the scalp upon my pate.
    Only this, a standard rate.

Though my bottom line is black, I am flat upon my back,
My cash flows out and customers pay slow.
The growth of my receivables is almost unbelievable;
The result is certain—unremitting woe!
And I hear the banker utter an ominous low mutter,
    "Watch cash flow."

Herbert S. Bailery, Jr.

Source: Reprinted from *Publishers Weekly,* January 13, 1975, published by R. R. Bowker Company. Copyright © 1975 by Xerox Corporation.

But these "ifs" are big ones, and unless management understands the nature of its cash flows, trouble lies ahead. We will talk more about the problems of managing growth in Chapter 5.

Financial Statements and the Value Problem

To this point we have reviewed the basics of financial statements and have seen how they can be rearranged to provide information about the cash flowing through a company. As a further perspective and in anticipation of later materials, I want to conclude by examining a recurring problem in the use of accounting data for financial decision making.

Market Value versus Book Value

Part of what I will call the value problem involves the distinction between the market value and the book value of shareholders' equity. TEK's 1979 balance sheet states that the value of shareholders' equity is $403 million. This is known as the *book value* of TEK's equity. However, TEK is not worth $403 million to its shareholders or to anyone else, for that matter. There are two reasons why. One is that financial statements are *transactions based*. If a company purchased an asset in 1950 for $1 million, this transaction provides an objective measure of the asset's value, which becomes the value of the asset on the company's balance sheet. Unfortunately, it is a 1950 value that may or may not have much relevance today. Moreover, to further confound things, the accountant attempts to reflect the gradual deterioration of an asset over time by periodically subtracting depreciation from its balance sheet value. TEK's total accumulated depreciation for 1979 and previous years was $101 million. This practice makes sense as far as it goes, but depreciation is the only change in value recognized by the accountant. The $1 million asset purchased in 1950 may be technologically obsolete and therefore virtually worthless today; or due to inflation, its current value may be much higher than its original purchase price. This is especially true of land where current value can be many times the original cost.

It is tempting to argue that accountants should forget the original cost of long-term assets and provide a more meaningful current value. The problem, however, is that objectively determinable current values of many assets do not exist. Faced with a trade-off, accountants have opted for objective historical cost values over subjective estimates of current value.

To understand the second, more fundamental reason TEK is not worth $403 million, we need recall that equity investors buy shares for the future income they hope to receive, not for the value of the firm's assets. The problem with the accountant's measure of shareholders' equity is that it bears little relation to future income. The chief reason is that companies have many assets and liabilities which do not appear on their balance sheets, but which, nonetheless, affect future income. Examples of unrecorded assets include patents and trademarks limiting competition for the firm's products, loyal customers fostered by a reputation for quality and service, entrenched market position created by effective advertising or superior technology, and, of course, better management. It is said that in many companies the most valuable assets go home to their spouses in the evening. Examples of unrecorded liabilities include pending lawsuits, inferior management, and obsolete production processes. The accountant's inability to measure assets and liabilities such as these means that book value is customarily a highly inaccurate measure of the value seen by shareholders.

For a publicly traded company, it is a simple matter to calculate the value of equity as seen by shareholders: Just multiply the number of common shares outstanding by the market price per share. On the last day of its fiscal year 1979, TEK's common shares closed on the New York Stock Exchange at $49 per share. With 18 million shares outstanding, this yields a value of $882 million. In total, equity shareholders valued their investment in TEK at $882 million, over twice the book value. This figure is known as the *market value* of equity.

Table 1–5 presents the market and book values of equity for five representative companies. It demonstrates clearly that book value is a poor proxy for market value.

Table 1–5. The Book Value of Equity Is a Poor Proxy for the Market Value of Equity

Company	Date	Book Value of Equity	Market Value of Equity	Ratio Market Value to Book Value
Amdahl Corporation	12/25/81	$ 266 million	$ 517 million	1.9
Bendix Corporation	9/30/81	1.5 billion	1.1 billion	0.7
Bethlehem Steel Corporation	12/31/81	2.8 billion	1.1 billion	0.4
IBM Corporation	12/31/81	18.2 billion	33.7 billion	1.9
Mobil Corporation	12/31/81	14.7 billion	10.3 billion	0.7

Economic Income versus Accounting Income

A second dimension of the value problem has its roots in the accountant's distinction between *realized* and *unrealized* income. To an economist, income is what you could spend during the period to end up as well off at the end as you were at the start. For example, suppose a woman's assets, net of liabilities, are worth $100,000 at the start of the year and rise to $120,000 by the end of the year. Suppose further that she received $30,000 as wages during the year, all of which she spent. The economist would say this individual earned $50,000 that year ($30,000 wages + $20,000 increase in net assets).

The accountant, on the other hand, would say this individual earned only $30,000. The accountant would not recognize the $20,000 increase in the market value of assets as income because the gain was not *realized* by the sale of the assets. Because the market value of the assets could fluctuate in either direction before the assets are sold, the gain is only on paper; and accountants do not recognize paper gains or losses. Accountants consider *realization* the necessary objective evidence required to record the gain.

It is easy to criticize accountants' conservatism when measuring income. Certainly the amount the woman could spend, ignoring inflation, and be as well off as at the start of the year is the economist's $50,000, not the accountant's $30,000. Moreover, if the woman were to sell her assets for $120,000 and immediately repurchase them for the same price, the $20,000 gain would become realized in the accountant's eyes, and he would include it as part of income. That income could depend upon a sham transaction like this is enough to raise suspicions about the accountant's definition.

However, two points should be noted in the accountant's defense. First, if the woman described above holds her assets for several years before selling them, the gain or loss recognized by the accountant on the sale date will just equal the sum of the annual gains and losses recognized by the economist. So it's really not total income that is at issue here but just the timing of its recognition. A second point in the accountant's favor is that it is extremely difficult to measure the periodic change in the value of many assets unless they are actively traded. So even if an accountant wanted to include paper gains and losses in income, he would often have great difficulty doing so. In the corporate setting, this means the accountant must be content to measure what we can call income from operations rather than economic earnings.

To summarize, the value problem means that financial statements will customarily provide distorted information about company earnings and market value. This limits their applicability for many important managerial decisions. However, financial statements are frequently the best information available, and if their limitations are borne in mind, can be a useful starting point for analysis. In the next chapter, we consider the use of accounting data for evaluating financial performance.

Chapter Summary

1. The purpose of this chapter has been to review the accounting principles governing financial statements and to describe the relationship between earnings and cash flow.

2. A company's finances and its business operations are integrally related. We study a company's financial statements because they are a window on its operations.

3. Earnings are not cash flow. The financial executive must watch both.

4. A balance sheet is a snapshot of a company's assets and liabilities at a point in time. An income statement records sales, related expenses, and earnings over a period. Both documents are transactions based and use the accrual principle. Because accounting statements are transactions based, long-term assets and depreciation are listed at historical cost, and paper gains and losses are ignored. Use of the accrual principle means that revenues and expenses do not always coincide with cash inflows and outflows.

5. Three steps are required to translate an income statement and balance sheet into a cash flow statement: (*a*) calculate changes in balance sheet accounts over the accounting period, (*b*) determine which changes used cash and which provided cash, and (*c*) segregate the sources from the uses. Cosmetic modifications to the resulting sources and uses statement change it into a cash flow statement.

6. There are two recurring problems in the use of accounting statements for financial analysis: (*a*) accounting book values seldom equal market values and (*b*) the accountant's refusal to recognize unrealized gains and losses makes accounting income differ from economic income.

Additional Reading

Graham, Benjamin, and Charles McGolrick. *The Interpretation of Financial Statements*. 3d ed. New York: Harper & Row, 1975. 120 pages.
First published in 1937 by a recognized leader in the investment community. Tightly written, but a bit dry.

Tracy, John A. *How to Read a Financial Report*. New York: John Wiley & Sons, 1980. 154 pages.
Subtitled "Wringing Cash Flow and Other Vital Signs out of the Numbers . . . for Managers, Entrepreneurs, Lenders, Lawyers, and Investors," this is a lively practical introduction to the nuances of financial statements and their interpretation.

Chapter Problems

1. Table 4–1 presents financial statements over the period 1978–1981 for R&E Supplies, Inc.

a. Construct a sources and uses statement for the company from 1978 through 1981 (one statement for all three years).

b. Assume that dividends over the four years were $185,000, $199,000, $191,000, and $145,000 and that annual depreciation was $30,000, $25,000, $50,000, and $40,000. Construct a cash flow statement for the company from year-end 1978 through 1981.

c. What was R&E Supplies' cash flow from operations from year-end 1978 through 1981?

d. What was the company's cash provided by operations over the same period?

e. What insights, if any, do the above calculations give you about the financial position of R&E Supplies, Inc.?

2. Explain briefly how each of the following transactions would affect a company's financial statements.

    a. Purchase of a new building for $1 million cash.

    b. Purchase of a new $1 million building, financed 20 percent with cash and 80 percent with a bank loan.

    c. A $100,000 payment to trade creditors.

    d. Sale of $1 million of merchandise for cash.

    e. Sale of $1 million of merchandise for credit.

3. Why do you suppose financial statements are constructed on an accrual basis rather than a cash basis when cash accounting is so much easier to understand?

2 Evaluating Financial Performance*

The cockpit of a 747 airliner, if you have never seen one, looks like a three-dimensional video game. It is a sizable room crammed with meters, switches, lights, and dials requiring the full attention of three highly trained pilots. When compared to the cockpit of, say, a Piper Cub, it is tempting to conclude that the two planes are different species rather than distant cousins. Yet at a more fundamental level, the similarities probably exceed the differences. Despite the complexity and the technology, the 747 pilot controls his plane in the same way as the Piper Cub pilot: with a stick, a throttle, and flaps. And if either pilot wants to change the attitude of his plane, he does so by making simultaneous adjustments to the same few levers he has for controlling the plane.

Much the same is true of companies. Once you strip away the facade of apparent complexity, the levers by which managers affect the financial performance of their firm are comparatively few and are similar among firms. The executive's job is to control these levers to assure a safe and efficient flight. And like the pilot, he or she must remember that the levers are interrelated; so that one cannot change the business equivalent of the flaps without also adjusting the stick and the throttle.

The Levers of Financial Performance

Our goal in this chapter will be to analyze financial statements for the purpose of evaluating performance and for understanding the levers of management control. We begin by studying the ties between a company's operating decisions—such as pricing policy, inventory control practices, and financing

---

*I owe a special thanks to George Parker for help on this chapter.

strategies—and its financial performance. These operating decisions are the levers by which management controls financial performance. Then we will broaden the discussion to consider the uses and limitations of ratio analysis as a tool for evaluating performance. To retain a practical perspective, we will again use the financial statements for Tektronix, Inc., presented in Tables 1–1 and 1–2 of the last chapter, to illustrate the techniques. The chapter will conclude with an evaluation of TEK's financial performance relative to its competition.

Return on Equity

By far the most popular yardstick of financial performance among practicing managers is the return on equity (ROE), defined as:

$$\text{Return on equity} = \frac{\text{Earnings}}{\text{Shareholders' equity}}$$

Referring to Tables 1–1 and 1–2 in the last chapter, TEK's ROE for 1979 was:

$$\text{ROE} = \frac{\$77}{\$403} = 19.1\%$$

It is not an exaggeration to say that the careers of many senior executives rise and fall in harmony with their firm's ROE. ROE is accorded such importance because it is a measure of the *efficiency* with which the firm employs owners' capital. It is an estimate of the earnings per dollar of invested equity capital, or alternatively, the percentage return to owners on their investment in the firm.

Later in this chapter we will consider some significant problems with ROE as a measure of financial performance, but for now let us accept it provisionally as at least widely used and see what we can learn.

Three Determinants of ROE

To see how a company can increase its ROE, let us restate the ratio in terms of its three principal components.

$$\text{ROE} = \frac{\text{Earnings}}{\text{Shareholders' equity}}$$

$$= \frac{\text{Earnings}}{\text{Sales}} \times \frac{\text{Sales}}{\text{Assets}} \times \frac{\text{Assets}}{\text{Shareholders' equity}}$$

In words,

$$\frac{\text{Return on}}{\text{equity}} = \frac{\text{Profit}}{\text{margin}} \times \frac{\text{Asset}}{\text{turnover}} \times \frac{\text{Financial}}{\text{leverage}}$$

We find that TEK's ROE in 1979 was generated as follows:

$$\frac{\$77}{\$403} = \frac{77}{787} \times \frac{787}{643} \times \frac{643}{403}$$

$$19.1\% = 9.8\% \times 1.2 \times 1.6$$

This expression says that management has three levers for controlling ROE. They are (1) the earnings squeezed out of each dollar of sales, or the *profit margin,* (2) the sales generated from each dollar of assets employed, or the *asset turnover,* and (3) the amount of debt used to finance the assets, or the *financial leverage.* With limited exception, whatever management does to increase these ratios increases ROE.

Table 2–1 presents ROE decomposed into its three principal components for 11 widely diverse companies. It shows clearly that there are many paths to heaven: The ROE's of the companies are quite similar, but the combinations of profit margin, asset turnover, and financial leverage which produce this end result vary widely. Thus ROE ranges from a high of 19.5 percent for Exxon to a low of 9 percent for K mart, while the range for the profit margin, to take one example, is from a low of 0.7 percent for Safeway to a high of 11.4 percent for IBM. ROE differs by a factor of about 2 to 1, while the profit margin differs by a factor of over 16 to 1.

To understand why such diversity exists and how managerial decisions and a company's competitive environment combine to affect ROE, let us examine ROE's principal determinants in more detail. In anticipation of our

Table 2–1. ROE and Its Principal Components for 11 Diverse Firms (1981 unless otherwise noted)

	Return on Equity (ROE) (percent)	=	Profit Margin (percent)	×	Asset Turnover (times)	×	Financial Leverage (times)	Return on Assets (percent)
Citicorp	12.4	=	2.9	×	0.15	×	27.85	0.44
IBM	18.2	=	11.4	×	0.98	×	1.63	11.17
Safeway Stores	10.4	=	0.7	×	4.49	×	3.32	3.14
Xerox	16.0	=	6.9	×	1.13	×	2.06	7.80
Exxon	19.5	=	4.8	×	1.39	×	2.91	6.67
Revlon	17.8	=	7.4	×	1.02	×	2.36	7.55
Pacific Gas and Electric*	14.1	=	10.0	×	0.47	×	3.03	4.70
Southern Railway*	13.5	=	10.7	×	0.54	×	2.36	5.78
Delta Air Lines*	10.0	=	3.1	×	1.45	×	2.22	4.50
K mart	9.0	=	1.3	×	2.48	×	2.72	3.22
Tektronix†	19.1	=	9.8	×	1.20	×	1.60	11.76

*1980.
†1979.

discussion of ratio analysis which follows, it will also be useful to devote some attention to related, commonly used financial ratios.

The Profit Margin

The profit margin measures the portion of each dollar of sales that trickles down through the income statement to profits. The ratio is of particular importance to operating managers because it reflects the company's pricing strategy and its ability to control operating costs. As Table 2–1 indicates, profit margins differ greatly among industries and companies within an industry, depending on the nature of the product sold and the company's competitive strategy.

Note from the table that profit margin and asset turnover tend to vary inversely. This is no accident. In the manufacturing sector, companies like IBM, with unique products, or companies which add significant value to a product, can demand high profit margins. However, because maintaining unique products and adding significant value to a product usually require lots of assets, these same firms tend to have lower asset turns. Much the same is true at the retail level. Grocery stores like Safeway, which add little to product value and which minimize selling costs, have very low profit margins but high asset turns. At the other extreme, jewelry stores that carry expensive inventories and spend heavily on display and selling have low asset turns but much higher profit margins. It should be apparent, therefore, that a high-profit-margin company is not necessarily better than a low-margin company. It all depends on the combined effect of the profit margin and the asset turnover.

Return on Assets. The product of these two ratios is known as the *return on assets (ROA)*.

$$\text{ROA} = \frac{\text{Profit}}{\text{margin}} \times \frac{\text{Asset}}{\text{turnover}}$$

$$= \frac{\text{Earnings}}{\text{Sales}} \times \frac{\text{Sales}}{\text{Assets}}$$

$$= \frac{\text{Earnings}}{\text{Assets}}$$

TEK's ROA in 1979 was:

$$\text{ROA} = \frac{77}{643} = 12\%$$

This means that TEK earned an average of 12 cents on each dollar invested.

ROA is a basic measure of the efficiency with which a company allocates and manages its resources. It differs from ROE because ROA measures profit as a percent of total assets while ROE measures profit as a percent of shareholders' equity only.

Some companies, like IBM, produce their ROA by combining a high profit margin with a moderate asset turn, while others, like Safeway, adopt the reverse strategy. A high profit margin *and* a high asset turn is ideal, but can be expected to attract considerable competition which will eventually drive the ROA down to a more normal level. Conversely, a low profit margin and a low asset turn will attract only bankruptcy lawyers.

Gross Margin. When analyzing a company's profit margin, it is often interesting to distinguish between variable costs and fixed costs of manufacture. Variable costs are those which change as sales vary, fixed costs are those which remain constant. Companies with a high proportion of fixed costs are more vulnerable to sales declines than other firms because it is impossible to reduce fixed cost as sales fall. This means that falling sales will produce major profit declines.

The gross margin distinguishes, as far as possible, between fixed and variable costs. It is defined as:

$$\text{Gross margin} = \frac{\text{Gross profit}}{\text{Sales}} = \frac{\$427}{\$787} = 54.3\%$$

The accountant does not differentiate between fixed and variable costs when constructing an income statement. However, most items in cost of goods sold are variable, while most of the other operating costs are fixed. Roughly speaking then, 54.3 percent of TEK's sales dollar is a *contribution to fixed cost and profits*. 54.3 cents of every sales dollar is available to pay for fixed costs and to add to profits.

Asset Turnover

The second principal determinant of ROE is the sales generated by each dollar of assets, or the asset turnover. TEK's asset turnover of 1.2 means that TEK generated $1.20 of sales for each dollar invested in assets. This ratio is a measure of capital intensity, with a low asset turnover signifying a capital-intensive business and a high turnover the reverse.

The nature of a company's products and its competitive strategy contribute significantly to the asset turnover it achieves. However, the process is not a mechanical one. Management diligence and creativity in controlling assets is also vital. When technology is similar among competitors, control of assets is often the margin between success and failure.

Control of current assets is especially critical. It may appear at first glance that distinguishing between current and fixed assets based solely on whether the asset will revert to cash within one year is artificial. But there is more involved than this. Current assets, especially accounts receivable and inventory, have several unique properties which should be recognized. One is that if something goes wrong—if sales decline unexpectedly, if customers delay payment, or if a critical part fails to arrive—a company's investment in current assets can grow very rapidly. When you observe that even manufacturing companies routinely have one half or more of their money invested in current assets, it is easy to appreciate that even modest alterations in the management of these assets can significantly affect company finances.

A second distinction is that unlike fixed assets, current assets can become a source of cash during downturns in the business cycle. As sales decline, a company's investment in accounts receivable and inventory should decline as well, thereby freeing cash for other uses. The fact that in a well-run company current assets move in accordionlike fashion with sales is appealing to creditors. For they know that during the upswing of a business cycle rising current assets will require loans, while during a downswing falling current assets will provide the cash to repay the loans. In bankers' jargon such a loan is said to be *self-liquidating* in the sense that the use to which the money is put creates the source of repayment.

Because control of current assets is so important in generating an acceptable ROE, it is useful to analyze each type of asset individually. This gives rise to what are known as *control ratios*. Although the form in which each ratio is commonly expressed varies, any control ratio is really just an asset turnover for a particular type of asset. In each instance, the firm's investment in an asset is compared to net sales, or a closely related figure.

Why compare current assets to sales? The fact that a company's investment in, say, inventories has risen over time could be due to two forces: (1) perhaps sales have risen and simply dragged inventories along or (2) management may have slackened its control of inventories, allowing excess quantities to accumulate. Relating inventory to sales in a control ratio adjusts for changes in sales, enabling the analyst to concentrate on the more important effects of changing management control. Thus the control ratio distinguishes between sales-induced changes in investment and other, perhaps more sinister, causes. Below are presented a number of standard control ratios.

Inventory Turnover. The inventory turnover ratio is defined as:

$$\text{Inventory turnover} = \frac{\text{Cost of goods sold}}{\text{Ending inventory}} = \frac{\$360}{\$215} = 1.7 \text{ times}$$

An inventory turn of 1.7 times means that an average item in TEK's inventory turns over 1.7 times per year; or said differently, the average item sits in inventory about seven months before being sold (12 months ÷ 1.7 times = 7 months).

Several alternative definitions of the inventory turnover ratio exist, including sales divided by ending inventory, and cost of goods sold divided by average inventory. Cost of goods sold is a more appropriate numerator than

---

A Problem

Sales of XYZ Company are up 20 percent over the last year. Meanwhile inventories have risen from $25,000 to $35,000. What portion of this increase in inventories would you say is due to sales growth and what portion to changing inventory control?

Answer: Sales are up 20 percent, so it is reasonable to expect that inventories will also increase 20 percent to $30,000 [$25,000 + (20% × $25,000)]. The remaining $5,000 increase, or 50 percent of the total, must be due to slackening management control.

---

sales because sales include a profit markup which is absent from inventory. But beyond this, there is little to choose from among the various definitions.

The Collection Period. The collection period provides information about a company's accounts receivable management. It is defined as:

$$\frac{\text{Collection}}{\text{period}} = \frac{\text{Accounts receivable}}{\text{Credit sales per day}} = \frac{\$153}{\$787 \div 365} = 71.9 \text{ days}$$

Credit sales rather than net sales are used here because only credit sales generate accounts receivable. As a manufacturer, virtually all of TEK's sales are on credit, so we can use net sales in place of credit sales in this instance. Credit sales per day is defined as credit sales for the accounting period divided by the number of days in the accounting period. Using TEK's annual statements, the divisor is 365 days.

It is possible to interpret TEK's 71.9 day collection period in either of two ways: We can say that TEK has an average of 71.9 days worth of credit sales tied up in accounts receivable, or we can say that the average time lag between sale and receipt of cash from the sale is 71.9 days.

If we liked, we could define a more conventional asset turnover ratio for accounts receivable as credit sales/accounts receivable. However, the collection-period format is more informative because it is possible to compare a company's collection period with its terms of sale. Thus if TEK sells on 60-day terms, a collection period of 71.9 days may not be bad, but if the terms of sale are 30 days, our interpretation would be quite different.

Days Sales in Cash. This ratio is defined as:

$$\frac{\text{Day sales}}{\text{in cash}} = \frac{\text{Cash and securities}}{\text{Net sales per day}} = \frac{\$42}{\$787 \div 365} = 19.3 \text{ days}$$

TEK has 19.3 days worth of sales in cash and securities.

A Word of Warning on Seasonal Companies
Interpreting many ratios of companies with *seasonal sales* can be quite difficult. For example, suppose a company's sales are seasonal, with a large peak at the end of the year. The sales peak will result in a high year-end accounts receivable balance. Yet in calculating credit sales per day, using annual financial statements, this peak will be averaged with periods of low sales. The result will be an apparently very high collection period. To avoid being misled, a better way to calculate the collection period for a seasonal company is to relate end-of-year accounts receivable to credit sales per day, based on the prior 60–90 days sales. This matches the accounts receivable to the credit sales which actually generated those receivables.

Payables Period.   The payables period is a control ratio for a liability. It is just the collection period applied to accounts payable.

$$\frac{\text{Payables}}{\text{period}} = \frac{\text{Accounts payable}}{\text{Credit purchases per day}} = \frac{\$42}{\$360 \div 365} = 42.6 \text{ days}$$

The proper definition of the payables period is in terms of credit purchases because this is what generates accounts payable. However, credit purchases are seldom available to the outside analyst, so it is frequently necessary to settle for the closest approximation—cost of goods sold. This is what we have done in the above figures for TEK. The $360 million is TEK's cost of goods sold, not its credit purchases. Cost of goods sold can differ from credit purchases for two reasons. First, the company is producing, and hence purchasing material at a rate which differs from its sales rate; and second, the company adds labor and depreciation to material in the production process, thereby making cost of goods sold much larger than purchases. Because of these differences, it is not meaningful to compare a manufacturing company's payables period, based on cost of goods sold, to its purchase terms.

Financial Leverage

The third principal lever by which management affects ROE is financial leverage, defined as the substitution of debt for equity in company financing. Determining the appropriate degree of financial leverage for a particular company is a major responsibility of corporate financial officers (to which we will later devote a full chapter). Here it is sufficient to recognize that while companies have considerable latitude in selecting a leverage amount, there are economic and institutional constraints on their discretion. As Table 2–1 suggests, the nature of a company's business and its assets influence the financial leverage it can employ. In general, businesses which have highly predictable and stable operating cash flows can safely undertake more financial leverage than firms facing a high degree of market uncertainty. Public utilities like Pacific Gas and Electric in Table 2–1 are an example of such stable, highly levered firms. In addition, enterprises such as commercial banks, which have a diversified portfolio of liquid assets, can also safely use more financial leverage than the typical firm. By *liquid assets,* I refer to assets which can be readily sold without significant loss of value.

Another pattern evident in Table 2–1 is that ROA and financial leverage tend to be inversely related. Companies with low ROA generally employ more debt financing, and vice versa. This is consistent with the previous paragraph. Safe, stable, liquid investments tend to generate low returns but substantial borrowing capacity. Commercial banks are extreme examples of this pattern. Citicorp, as an example, combines what by manufacturing standards would be a horrible ROA of 0.44 percent with an astronomic leverage ratio of 27.85 to generate a representative ROE of 12.4 percent. The key to this pairing is the safe, liquid nature of Citicorp assets.

In following paragraphs we will discuss the more common ways to measure financial leverage and the related concept of liquidity. These ratios are useful to managers and creditors in appraising a company's debt capacity.

A Problem

The equation ROE = ROA × Financial leverage suggests that debt financing transforms—or levers—ROA into a higher ROE. Can you think of a situation in which more debt would lower ROE?

Answer: Suppose the firm's earnings are so low or the interest rate on the new debt so high that the percentage decline in earnings due to the increased interest expense more than offsets the increase in leverage. Then increasing leverage would reduce ROE. We will explore the relation between ROE and financial leverage in considerable detail in Chapter 7.

Balance Sheet Ratios.   The most common way to measure financial leverage is to compare the book value of a company's liabilities to the book value of its assets or of its shareholders' equity. This gives rise to the debt-to-assets ratio and the debt-to-equity ratio, defined as:

$$\text{Debt-to-assets ratio} = \frac{\text{Total liabilities}}{\text{Total assets}} = \frac{\$240}{\$643} = 37.3\%$$

$$\text{Debt-to-equity ratio} = \frac{\text{Total liabilities}}{\text{Shareholders' equity}} = \frac{\$240}{\$403} = 59.6\%$$

The first ratio says that 37.3 percent of TEK's capital, in book-value terms, comes from creditors of one kind or another. The second ratio says the same thing in a slightly different way: Creditors supply TEK with 59.6 cents for every dollar supplied by shareholders.[1]

Coverage Ratios. There exist a number of variations on these balance sheet ratios. However there is conceptually no reason to prefer one over the other, for they all focus on the balance sheet value of liabilities and, hence, all suffer from the same weakness. The financial burden imposed on a company by the use of debt financing ultimately depends not on the size of the liability relative to assets or to equity but on the ability of the company to meet the annual cash payments required by the debt. A simple example will illustrate the distinction. Suppose two companies have the same debt-to-assets ratio, but one is very profitable, while the other is losing money. The company which is losing money will probably have difficulty meeting the annual interest and principal payments required by its loans; yet the profitable company with the same debt-to-assets ratio may have no such difficulties.

To measure the financial burden placed on a company by its use of leverage, it is useful to calculate what are known as coverage ratios. The two most common coverage ratios, times interest earned and times burden covered, are defined as:

$$\text{Times interest earned} = \frac{\text{Earnings before interest and taxes}}{\text{Interest expense}}$$

$$= \frac{\$133}{\$6} = 22.2 \text{ times}$$

$$\text{Times burden covered} = \frac{\text{Earnings before interest and taxes}}{\text{Interest} + \dfrac{\text{Principal repayment}}{1 - \text{Tax rate}}}$$

$$= \frac{\$133}{\$6 + \dfrac{\$2.7}{1 - 0.39}} = 12.8 \text{ times}$$

Both ratios compare income available to some annual measure of financial obligation. For both ratios the income available is *earnings before interest*

---

[1]The leverage ratio used earlier, Assets/Shareholders' equity, is just the Debt-to-equity ratio plus one:

$$\frac{\text{Assets}}{\text{Equity}} = \frac{\text{Liabilities} + \text{Equity}}{\text{Equity}} = \frac{\text{Liabilities}}{\text{Equity}} + 1$$

and taxes (EBIT). This is the earnings generated by the company that can be used to make interest payments. EBIT is before tax because interest payments are a before-tax expenditure and we want to compare like quantities. TEK's times-interest-earned ratio of 22.2 means that the company earned its interest obligation 22.2 times over in 1979; EBIT was 22.2 times as large as interest.

The times-burden-covered ratio expands the definition of annual financial obligation to include debt principal repayments as well as interest. If a company fails to make a principal repayment when due, the outcome is just as if it had failed to make an interest payment. In both cases, the company is in default and creditors can force it into bankruptcy. When including principal repayment as part of the company's financial burden, we must remember to express the figure on a before-tax basis comparable to interest and EBIT. Unlike interest payments, principal repayments are not a tax-deductible expense. This means that if a company is in, say, the 50-percent tax bracket, it must earn $2 before taxes to have $1 after taxes to pay creditors. The other dollar goes to the tax collector. For other tax brackets, the before-tax burden of a principal repayment is found by dividing the repayment by one minus the company's tax rate. Looking at the supplementary information in TEK's annual report, we find that the company's principal repayments in 1979 were $2.7 million, while its tax rate was 39 percent ($50 million income tax/$127 million income before tax). The before-tax burden of TEK's principal repayment, therefore, was $4.4 million [$2.7/(1 − .39)]. Adding this to TEK's $6 million interest obligation yields a times-burden-covered ratio of 12.8 times. The company earned its interest and repayment obligation 12.8 times over in 1979.

An often-asked question is, Which of these coverage rates is more meaningful? The answer is that both are important. If a company could always roll over its maturing obligations by taking out new loans as it repaid old ones, the *net* burden of the debt would be just the interest expense. The problem with this logic is that the replacement of maturing debt with new debt is not an automatic feature of capital markets. In some instances, when capital markets are unsettled or the fortunes of a company decline, creditors may refuse to renew maturing obligations. In these cases, the burden of the debt is interest plus principal payments. This is what happened to Burmah Oil, a large British company, in 1974. Burmah took out a large, short-term Eurodollar loan to finance acquisition of Signal Oil Company in the United States, thinking they could roll over the maturing short-term debt into more permanent financing as it came due. However, before Burmah was able to roll over the debt, Herstatt Bank in Germany failed, creditors became very conservative, and no one was willing to lend money to Burmah. A crisis was averted only when the British government bailed Burmah out by purchasing for cash a large block of British Petroleum stock owned by Burmah. In sum, it is fair to conclude that the times-burden-covered ratio is too conservative, assuming the company will pay its existing loans down to zero; but the times-interest-earned ratio is too liberal, assuming the company will roll over all its obligations as they mature.

Another frequent question is, How much coverage is enough? This question cannot be answered precisely, but several generalizations are possible. If a company has ready access to cash in the form of unused borrowing capacity or sizable cash balances or readily salable assets, it can operate safely with lower coverage ratios than competitors without such sources of cash. The ready access to cash gives the company a means of payment it can use whenever operating earnings are insufficient to cover financial obligations. A second generalization is that coverage should increase with the *business risk* faced by the firm. TEK is in a very dynamic environment characterized by rapid technological changes and high rates of product obsolescence. In view of this high business risk, TEK would be ill-advised to take on the added financial risk that accompanies low coverage ratios. Said another way, an electric utility which has very stable, predictable cash flows can operate safely with much lower coverage ratios than a company like TEK which has trouble forecasting more than three or four years into the future.

Liquidity Ratios. As noted earlier, one determinant of a company's debt capacity is the liquidity of its assets. An asset is liquid if it can be readily converted to cash, while a liability is liquid if it must be repaid in the near future. As the Burmah Oil debacle illustrates, it is risky to finance illiquid assets like fixed plant and equipment with liquid, short-term liabilities because the liabilities will come due before the assets generate enough cash to pay them. A company which mismatches the maturity of its assets and liabilities in this manner must roll over, or refinance, maturing liabilities to avoid insolvency.

Two common ratios intended to measure the liquidity of a company's assets relative to its liabilities are the *current ratio* and the *acid test,* defined as:

$$\text{Current ratio} = \frac{\text{Current assets}}{\text{Current liabilities}}$$

$$= \frac{\$429}{\$153} = 2.8 \text{ times}$$

$$\text{Acid test} = \frac{\text{Current assets} - \text{Inventory}}{\text{Current liabilities}}$$

$$= \frac{\$429 - \$215}{\$153} = 1.4 \text{ times}$$

The current ratio compares the assets that will turn into cash within the year to the liabilities that must be paid within the year. A company with a low current ratio lacks liquidity in the sense that it cannot reduce its current asset investments to supply cash to meet maturing obligations. It must rely instead on operating income and outside financing.

You should recognize that this is a rather crude definition of liquidity for at least two reasons. First, rolling over some obligations, such as accounts payable, involves virtually no insolvency risk provided the company is at least marginally profitable; second, the size of a company's investment in current assets and its ability to reduce this investment to pay its bills are two different things. Unless sales decline, cuts in accounts receivable and inventory will usually have a negative impact on profits, sales, and production efficiency. Except in liquidation, companies do not customarily sell off large portions of their current assets to meet maturing obligations.

The acid-test ratio, or what is sometimes called the *quick ratio,* is identical to the current ratio except that the numerator is reduced by the value of inventory. The reason for subtracting inventory is that it frequently is illiquid. Under distress conditions, a company or its creditors may not be able to realize much cash from the sale of inventory. In liquidation sales, the typical experience is that sellers receive 40 percent or less of the book value of inventory.

Is ROE a Reliable Financial Yardstick?

Until now we have assumed that management wants to increase its ROE, and we have analyzed three important levers of financial performance: profit margin, asset turnover, and financial leverage. We concluded that regardless of whether a company is General Motors or the corner drugstore, careful management of these levers can positively affect ROE. We also saw that determining and maintaining appropriate values of the levers is a challenging managerial task involving an understanding of the nature of the company's business, the way it competes, and the interdependencies among the levers themselves.

It is time now to ask how reliable ROE is as a measure of financial performance. If Company A has a higher ROE than Company B, is its financial performance necessarily superior? If Company C increases its ROE, is this unequivocal evidence of improved financial performance?

As a measure of financial performance, ROE is prone to three problems: the timing problem, the risk problem, and the value problem. Seen in proper perspective, these potential difficulties mean that ROE is seldom an unambiguous measure of performance. ROE remains a useful and important indicator, but it must be interpreted in light of its limitations and should never be used mechanistically to suggest that a higher ROE is always better than a lower one.

The Timing Problem

Many business opportunities require the sacrifice of present earnings in anticipation of enhanced future earnings. This is true when a company introduces a new product involving heavy start-up costs. If we calculate the company's ROE just after introduction of the new product, it will appear depressed. But rather than suggesting poor performance, the low ROE is just the result of the company's new product introduction. Because ROE necessarily includes earnings for only one year, it frequently fails to capture the full impact of longer-term decisions.

The Risk Problem

Most business decisions involve the classic "eat well–sleep well" dilemma. If you want to eat well, you had best be prepared to take risks in search of higher returns. If you want to sleep well, you will likely have to forgo high returns in search of safety. Seldom will you find high returns *and* safety. (And when you do, please give me a call.)

The problem with ROE in this regard is that it says nothing about what risks a company has taken to generate its ROE. Consider a simple example. Take-a-Risk, Inc., earns an ROA of 6 percent from its investment in South African gold mines which it combines with an assets-to-shareholders'-equity ratio of 5.0 to produce an ROE of 30 percent (6% × 5.0). Never-Dare, Ltd., meanwhile, has an ROA of 10 percent on its investment in government securities which it finances with equal portions of debt and equity to produce an ROE of 20 percent (10% × 2.0). Which company is the better performer? My answer is Never-Dare. Take-a-Risk's ROE is high, but its high business risk and extreme financial leverage make it a very uncertain enterprise. I would prefer the more modest but eminently safer ROE of Never-Dare. Even if I preferred eating well to sleeping well, I would still choose Never-Dare and finance my purchase with a little personal borrowing to lever my return on the investment. In sum, because ROE looks only at return while ignoring risk, it can be an inaccurate yardstick of financial performance.

The Value Problem

ROE measures the return on shareholders' investment; however, the investment figure used is the *book value* of shareholders' equity, not the *market value*. This distinction is an important one. TEK's ROE in 1979 was 19.1 percent and, indeed, this is the annual return you could have earned had you been able to buy TEK's equity for its book value of $403 million. But that would have been impossible, for as noted in the previous chapter, the market value of TEK's equity was $882 million. At this price, your annual return would have been only 8.7 percent, not 19.1 percent ($77/$882 = 8.7%). The market value of equity is more significant to shareholders because it measures the current, realizable worth of the shares, while book value is only history. We conclude that because of possible divergence between the market value of equity and its book value, a high ROE may not be synonymous with a high return on investment to shareholders.

The Earnings Yield and the P/E Ratio.   It might appear that we can circumvent the value problem by just replacing the book value of equity with its market value in the ROE. Such a ratio is known as the *earnings yield.*

$$\text{Earnings yield} = \frac{\text{Earnings}}{\text{Market value of shareholders' equity}}$$

$$= \frac{\text{Earnings per share}}{\text{Price per share}} = \frac{\$4.28}{\$49} = 8.7\%$$

Is it logical to say that earnings yield is a useful measure of performance and that managers should try to increase their earnings yield? No! The difficulty with earnings yield as a performance measure is that price per share is very sensitive to investor expectations about the future. A share of stock entitles its owner to a portion of *future* earnings as well as present earnings. Naturally, the higher the investor's expectations of future earnings, the more he will be willing to pay for the stock. This means that a bright future, a high stock price, and a *low* earnings yield go together. Clearly, a high earnings yield is not a useful measure of performance. Said another way, the earnings yield suffers from a severe timing problem of its own which invalidates it as a performance measure.

Turning the earnings yield on its head produces the price-to-earnings ratio, or the P/E ratio.

$$\text{Price-to-earnings ratio} = \text{P/E ratio}$$

$$= \frac{\text{Price per share}}{\text{Earnings per share}} = \frac{\$49}{\$4.28}$$

$$= 11.5 \text{ times}$$

The P/E ratio adds little to our discussion of performance measures, but due to its wide usage among investors, it deserves comment. The P/E ratio measures the amount of money investors are willing to pay for one dollar of current earnings. It is a means of standardizing stock prices to facilitate comparison among companies with different earnings. In May 1979, investors were paying $11.50 for each dollar of TEK current earnings. Speaking broadly, a company's P/E ratio depends on two things: its future earnings prospects and the risk associated with those earnings. As noted in the previous paragraph, stock price, and hence the P/E ratio, rises as a company's prospects for future growth improve. Risk has the opposite effect. A high degree of uncertainty about a company's future earnings prospects will result in a low P/E ratio. In general, the P/E ratio tells you little about a company's current financial performance, but it is a useful indicator of what investors feel about the company's future prospects.

ROE or Market Price?

For years academicians and practitioners have been at odds over the proper measure of financial performance. Academicians criticize ROE for the reasons cited above and argue instead that the correct measure of financial performance is the firm's stock price. Moreover, they contend that managements' goal should be to maximize stock price. Their logic is persuasive: Stock price represents the value of the owners' investment in the firm. Assuming the objective of managers is to further the interests of owners, managers should take actions which increase value to owners.

Can ROE Substitute for Share Price?

The accompanying graphs (Figures 2–1, 2–2, and 2–3) provided by Mitchell and Company, a Cambridge consulting firm, suggest that the differences between academicians and practitioners over the proper measure of financial performance may be more apparent than real. The graphs plot the market value of equity divided by book value of equity against ROE for three representative industries. ROE is measured as a weighted average of recent annual ROE's. The strong positive relationship visible in each graph suggests that high-ROE firms tend to have high stock prices relative to book value.

The graphs also indicate that the ROE-market value relation differs among industries. Of the three industries shown, it is most pronounced for basic chemicals and least pronounced for cosmetics and toiletries, indicating that an increased ROE will have the most impact on share price among chemical firms and the least among cosmetics and toiletries. The proximity of the company dots to the fitted line is also interesting. It shows the importance of factors other than ROE in determining a company's market-to-book ratio. The company dots are very close to the fitted line in the chemical industry, suggesting that other factors are comparatively unimportant. The opposite conclusion applies in the brewing industry, where the company dots are more widely dispersed about the line.

As one of its services, Mitchell and Company helps clients analyze the impact of operating decisions on stock price. They report that the graphs have proven useful for this purpose and have also served as a starting point for more detailed examinations of prospective corporate restructurings. From our perspective, the graphs offer tantalizing, preliminary evidence that despite its weaknesses, ROE may be a useful proxy for share price in measuring financial performance.

Practitioners acknowledge the logic of this reasoning but maintain that it is not practical. One problem is the difficulty of specifying precisely how operating decisions affect stock price. If we cannot say what impact a change in financial leverage will have on a company's stock price, the goal of increasing price becomes ambiguous. A second problem is that managers

**Figure 2–1.   Relative Equity Valuation, Cosmetics and Toiletries
(1981 sales over $230 million)**

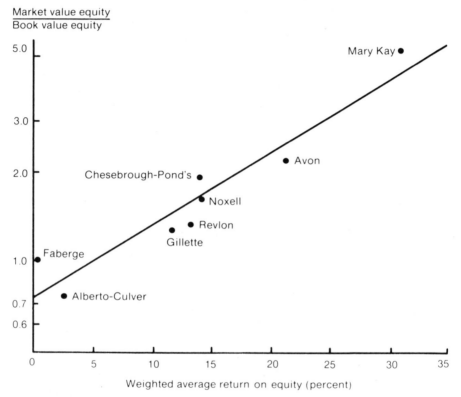

Source: © 1982 Mitchell and Company. Used with permission.
Note: Vertical axis is log scale.

typically know more about their company than outside investors. Why then should managers consider the assessments of less-informed investors when making business decisions? Yet another practical problem with stock price as a performance measure is that it depends on a whole array of factors outside the company's control. One can never be certain whether an increase in stock price reflects improving company performance or an improving external economic environment. For these reasons, practitioners have continued using ROE as an admittedly imperfect measure of financial performance.

Figure 2–2. Relative Equity Valuation, Basic Chemical Industry, 1981

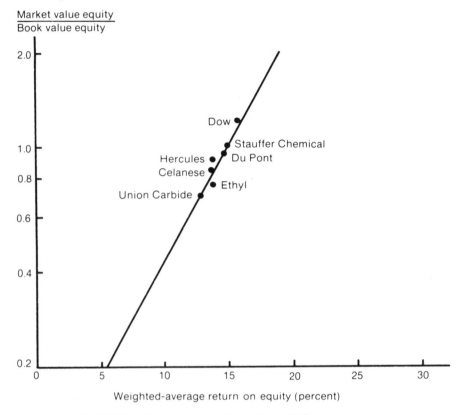

Source: © 1982 Mitchell and Company. Used with permission.
Note: Vertical axis is log scale.

Ratio Analysis

In the course of our discussion of the levers of financial performance, we defined a number of financial ratios. It is time now to broaden the discussion to consider the systematic use of such ratios to analyze financial performance. This involves nothing more than calculating a number of diverse ratios and comparing them to certain standards, in search of insights into the company's operations and its financial health.

Ratio analysis is widely used by managers, creditors, regulators, and investors. Used with care and imagination, the technique can reveal much about a company and its operations. But there are a few things to bear in mind about ratios. First, a ratio is just one number divided by another, so it is unreasonable to expect that the mechanical calculation of one ratio, or even several ratios, will automatically yield important insights into anything

Figure 2–3. Relative Equity Valuation, Brewing Industry, 1981

Source: © 1982 Mitchell and Company. Used with permission.
Note: Vertical axis is log scale.

as complex as a modern corporation. It is useful to think of ratios as clues in a detective story. One or even several ratios might be misleading, but when combined with other knowledge of a company's management and economic circumstances, ratio analysis can tell an interesting story.

A second point to bear in mind is that there is no single correct value for a ratio. The observation that the value of a particular ratio is too high, too low, or just right depends on the perspective of the analyst and on the company's competitive strategy. As an example, consider the current ratio, previously defined as the ratio of current assets to current liabilities. From the perspective of a short-term creditor, a high current ratio is a positive sign because it suggests ample liquidity and a high likelihood of repayment. Yet an owner of the company might look on the same current ratio as a negative sign suggesting that the company's assets are too conservatively deployed. Moreover, from an operating perspective, a high current ratio could be a sign of conservative management or it could be the natural result of a competitive strategy that emphasizes liberal credit terms and sizable inventories.

In this case, the important question is not whether the current ratio is too high, but whether the chosen strategy is best for the company.

Using Ratios Effectively

Having calculated a number of ratios, the natural question is what to do with them. If there are no universally correct values for ratios, how do you interpret them? How do you decide whether a company is healthy or sick? There are three approaches: compare the ratios to rules of thumb, compare them to industry averages, or look for changes in the ratios over time. Comparing a company's ratios to such rules of thumb has the virtue of simplicity, but has little to recommend it conceptually. The appropriate value of ratios for a company depends too much on the analyst's perspective and on the company's specific circumstances for rules of thumb to be very useful. The most positive thing to be said in their support is that over the years, companies conforming to these rules of thumb tend to go bankrupt somewhat less frequently than those that do not.

Comparing a company's ratios to industry ratios provides a useful feel for how the company measures up to its competitors. But, it is still true that company-specific differences can result in entirely justifiable deviations from industry norms. There is also no guarantee that the industry as a whole knows what it is doing. The knowledge that one railroad was much like its competitors was cold comfort in the depression of the 1930s, when virtually all railroads got into financial difficulties.

The most useful way to evaluate ratios uses trend analysis. Calculate ratios for a company over several years and take note of how they change over time. Trend analysis eliminates company and industry differences, enabling the analyst to draw firmer conclusions about the company's financial health and its variation over time.

Ratio Analysis of Tektronix

As a practical demonstration of ratio analysis, let us see what the technique can tell us about Tektronix, Inc. Table 2–2 presents what are known as *common-size* financial statements for TEK for the years 1976–79 as well as industry averages for 1979. The comparison industry is engineering and scientific instruments. A common-size balance sheet simply presents each asset and liability as a percent of total assets. A common-size income statement is analogous except that all items are scaled in proportion to net sales instead of total assets. The motivation for scaling financial statements in this fashion is to concentrate on underlying trends by abstracting from changes in the dollar figures caused by growth or decline. In addition, common-size statements are useful in removing simple scale effects when comparing companies of differing size.

Looking first at the balance sheet, note that although TEK is a manufacturing company, two thirds of its assets are short term—primarily accounts

Table 2–2
TEKTRONIX, INC.
Common-Size Balance Sheets
1976–1979 and Industry Averages for 1979*

	1976	1977	1978	1979	Industry Average
Current assets:					
Cash and securities	20.4	22.9	13.5	6.5	6.2
Accounts receivable...........	20.6	21.2	23.4	23.9	33.2
Inventories	28.7	28.5	33.3	33.4	33.3
Prepaid expenses	2.5	2.3	2.6	2.9	2.3
Total current assets........	72.0	74.7	72.8	66.7	75.0
Net plant and equipment.........	24.0	21.4	23.0	29.0	{ 19.6
Land	1.7	1.6	1.3	1.3	
Other long-term assets	2.3	2.3	2.8	3.1	5.4
Total assets....................	100.0	100.0	100.0	100.0	100.0
Current liabilities:					
Short-term debt	0.9	1.3	2.1	4.5	7.7
Accounts payable.............	5.2	5.8	6.7	6.5	13.5
Income taxes due	3.9	4.7	3.8	3.2	{
Incentives and retirement	3.7	4.5	4.6	4.9	{ 15.2
Payroll due..................	3.8	4.0	4.7	4.7	
Total current liabilities	17.5	20.3	21.9	23.8	36.4
Long-term debt	11.2	9.6	7.6	9.6	18.2
Deferred tax liability............	4.0	3.4	3.3	3.0	{ 2.9
Other long-term liabilities........	0.0	0.7	0.8	0.9	
Total liabilities	32.7	34.0	33.5	37.3	57.4
Shareholders' equity	67.3	66.0	66.5	62.7	42.6
Total liabilities and equity........	100.0	100.0	100.0	100.0	100.0

TEKTRONIX, INC.
Common-Size Income Statements
1976–1979 and Industry Averages for 1979*

	1976	1977	1978	1979	Industry Average
Net sales......................	100.0	100.0	100.0	100.0	100.0
Cost of sales.................	46.2	43.1	44.5	45.7	60.7
Gross profit	53.8	56.9	55.5	54.3	39.3
Operating expenses:					
Engineering expense	8.1	8.5	8.3	7.7	{
Selling expense...............	14.1	14.1	14.5	14.4	{ 30.7
Administrative expense	8.6	8.9	8.9	8.6	{
Profit sharing	7.2	8.9	8.9	8.6	
Operating income	15.8	16.8	15.7	15.4	8.6
Nonoperating income..........	0.6	0.7	1.0	1.5	NA
	16.4	17.5	16.7	16.9	8.6
Interest expense	1.3	0.9	0.7	0.8	1.2
Income before tax	15.1	16.6	16.0	16.1	7.5
Income tax	6.9	7.0	6.5	6.3	NA
Earnings......................	8.2	9.7	9.5	9.8	NA

Note: All values are given as percentage of total. Some columns may not add due to rounding.

*One hundred firms in the engineering, laboratory, scientific and research instruments industry. Copyright Robert Morris Associates, *1980 Annual Statement Studies* (Philadelphia, 1980), p. 109 for the period 6/30/78—3/31/79. Used with permission. See note on pp. 53–54 of this text.

receivable and inventories. Moreover, the portion of total assets committed to these accounts has risen steadily over the years. We will have more to say about TEK's control of current assets in a few pages. Offsetting this buildup in accounts receivable and inventory has been a sharp decline in cash and securities as a percentage of total assets, especially in the last two years. When compared to industry figures, however, this trend should not yet cause concern because the proportion of TEK's assets in cash and securities still exceeds the industry average.

Looking at the liability side of TEK's balance sheet, we see a steady, modest substitution of short-term-debt financing for equity. However, again in comparison with industry percentages, TEK is still conservatively financed.

The most noteworthy thing about TEK's common-size income statements is their stability over the years. Despite the company's rapid growth, costs as a proportion of sales have changed very little. We see no evidence of economies of scale or of escalating costs. Looking at the industry figures, we see that TEK's gross profit as a percentage of sales, or gross margin, is well above average, but that its operating income is about equal to the average. The high gross margin suggests that TEK has a considerably lower variable manufacturing cost per sales dollar than its competitors. The fact that TEK's earnings as a percentage of sales, or profit margin, is more nearly equal to its competitors, however, indicates that most of this advantage is offset by TEK's higher engineering, selling, and administrative costs. This is consistent with the company's competitive strategy. It spends large sums to develop the best products and provide superior field services, and it makes up for these expenditures by charging higher price markups over manufacturing cost than competitors.

Continuing our ratio analysis of TEK, Table 2–3 presents 17 previously discussed ratios for TEK over the period 1976–77. For most of the ratios, the table also contains 1979 average values for the engineering and scientific instruments industry. Where possible, the industry figures include the median value of the ratio, the upper quartile, and the lower quartile.[2] Table 2–4, at the end of the chapter, presents similar ratios for other representative industries.

Looking at the first ratio, we see that TEK's ROE has risen steadily over the years from 12.9 percent to 19.1 percent, but that it is marginally below

---

[2]If we were to array all of the ratios for the companies in the industry from the highest value to the lowest, the figure falling in the middle of the series is the *median;* the ratio halfway between the highest value and the median is the *upper quartile;* while the ratio halfway between the lowest value and the median is the *lower quartile.* Industry ratios (see pp. 53–54) are from Robert Morris Associates, *1980 Annual Statement Studies* (Philadelphia, 1980), and Dun & Bradstreet, *Key Business Ratios* (New York, 1979).

Table 2–3. Ratio Analysis of Tektronix, Inc.

	1976	1977	1978	1979	Upper Q	Median	Lower Q
					Industry Values		
Profitability ratios:							
Return on equity (percent)	12.9	16.1	17.4	19.1	37.0	20.8	12.0
Return on assets (percent)	8.2	10.6	11.6	12.0		11.8	
Profit margin (percent)	8.2	9.7	9.5	9.8	10.2	6.0	3.5
Gross margin (percent)	53.7	56.9	55.4	54.3		37.9	
Price to earnings (times)	17.6	13.6	12.7	11.5			
Leverage and liquidity ratios:							
Assets to equity (times)	1.5	1.5	1.5	1.6	2.4	1.8	1.3
Debt to assets (percent)	32.8	34.0	33.4	37.3		57.7	
Debt to equity (percent)	48.7	51.5	50.2	59.6	142.5	76.9	30.4
Times interest earned (times)	12.6	19.3	25.0	22.2	10.9	4.6	2.4
Times burden covered (times)	9.0	9.4	20.1	12.8			
Current ratio (times)	4.1	3.7	3.3	2.8	4.1	2.4	1.6
Acid test (times)	2.5	2.3	1.8	1.4		1.0	
Turnover-control ratios:							
Asset turnover (times)	1.1	1.1	1.2	1.2	2.2	1.7	1.4
Inventory turnover (times)	1.7	1.7	1.6	1.7		2.6	
Collection period (days)	70.3	70.6	70.7	71.9	74	51	36
Days sales in cash (days)	69.8	75.9	40.4	10.3		13.3	
Payables period (days)	38.7	44.6	45.3	42.6		64.4	

the industry median. To see why, look at ROE's principal components. The profit margin is high by industry standards and is rising, so this is not the culprit. All of the leverage and liquidity ratios indicate TEK is conservatively financed. Financial leverage is rising, but income is rising even faster, so coverage is quite healthy. And while the current ratio and acid test are falling, suggesting diminishing liquidity, they remain well above the industry median.

The comparatively modest use of debt financing contributes in part to TEK's below-median ROE, but the real divergence from industry norms appears in the turnover-control ratios. TEK's asset turnover places it solidly in the lower quartile of the industry. In each asset category, TEK has considerably more invested per dollar of sales than the industry median. The differences are most glaring for inventories, where TEK's turnover is only 1.7 times compared to an industry median of 2.6, and for accounts receivable, where TEK's collection period is 71.9 days versus an industry median of 51 days. Looking at TEK's ROA, we see that the low asset turn offsets almost completely the company's attractive profit margin, resulting in an ROA

Table 2–4. Selected Ratios for Representative Industries

Line of Business and Number of Firms Reporting	Current Ratio (times)	Total Liabilities to Net Worth (percent)	Collection Period (days)	Net Sales to Inventory (times)	Total Assets to Net Sales (percent)	Profit Margin (percent)	Return on Assets (percent)	Return on Equity (percent)
Agriculture, Construction, Mining								
Dairy farms (102)	5.7	30.0	7.3	22.1	91.5	14.8	10.1	16.1
	1.7	56.3	16.4	6.8	170.8	8.1	5.2	9.0
	0.9	107.3	30.6	3.4	350.5	4.7	3.1	4.6
Drilling oil and gas wells (112)	2.3	26.0	—	—	59.1	17.1	19.0	42.3
	1.4	82.7	—	—	105.3	11.1	10.2	27.4
	0.8	226.7	—	—	184.3	7.1	5.4	14.0
General contractors, houses (105)	4.6	26.6	—	—	40.2	18.3	11.1	25.6
	2.1	61.7	—	—	70.2	6.1	6.9	17.5
	1.3	151.7	—	—	120.1	2.2	3.2	8.6
Manufacturing								
Electronic components and accessories (108)	3.8	32.9	36.1	12.9	39.2	14.3	18.2	30.0
	2.5	62.7	47.8	7.4	50.1	7.6	10.6	19.3
	1.7	168.3	58.4	4.6	67.1	4.4	6.5	12.1
Household furniture (116)	3.9	31.3	18.2	13.2	29.0	6.1	13.5	25.9
	2.5	71.3	34.1	9.4	42.2	3.0	7.0	13.3
	1.8	148.4	47.4	5.2	51.8	0.9	2.6	4.2
Mens and boys apparel (114)	3.5	43.4	23.3	10.8	27.8	5.5	10.2	23.3
	2.4	97.2	43.8	6.3	42.1	3.0	5.1	11.4
	1.7	180.9	66.0	4.2	56.1	1.6	2.4	6.2
Motor vehicle parts and accessories (121)	4.0	35.5	30.6	9.1	39.3	10.2	11.9	25.7
	2.7	72.3	39.0	7.3	54.0	4.0	5.5	12.0
	1.9	132.8	50.7	4.5	73.2	1.4	0.5	1.2

Retailing

Department stores (102)	5.1	33.3	—	6.9	35.7	5.7	11.8	21.4
	3.1	**61.5**	—	**4.7**	**44.4**	**2.6**	**5.9**	**11.2**
	2.1	137.0	—	3.8	59.6	1.0	2.9	5.0
Grocery stores (105)	3.9	27.9	—	25.8	12.6	3.6	15.1	20.6
	2.3	**61.4**	—	**17.7**	**16.8**	**1.8**	**8.8**	**17.6**
	1.5	124.0	—	12.4	25.3	1.0	6.1	10.7
Jewelry stores (101)	5.9	27.0	14.2	2.9	57.9	15.6	16.2	27.0
	3.6	**44.5**	**32.4**	**2.3**	**79.5**	**8.0**	**10.2**	**16.6**
	2.2	88.3	56.5	1.5	107.1	4.6	6.4	11.6

Services

Automotive rental and leasing (114)	2.5	73.1	20.0	—	112.4	19.0	11.3	26.4
	1.1	**149.2**	**40.5**	—	**172.3**	**6.2**	**5.0**	**14.9**
	0.6	532.1	68.2	—	287.7	2.4	2.0	7.0
Computer and data processing services (109)	3.7	34.4	38.3	—	38.8	12.7	19.1	45.3
	1.8	**79.3**	**55.1**	—	**47.4**	**7.0**	**11.0**	**26.1**
	1.1	186.3	80.8	—	77.3	2.0	6.2	14.8

Wholesaling

Electrical appliances, TV and radio sets (116)	2.7	55.6	24.1	10.0	26.3	3.7	9.8	25.4
	1.9	**105.6**	**34.3**	**5.8**	**34.3**	**2.2**	**4.8**	**11.2**
	1.5	210.1	46.3	4.1	51.8	0.8	2.2	5.0
Hardware (107)	4.5	34.7	30.8	8.8	32.6	6.9	14.0	25.4
	2.5	**70.4**	**39.4**	**6.0**	**37.8**	**3.6**	**7.3**	**15.0**
	1.7	142.2	49.2	3.6	50.0	1.9	2.8	7.8
Petroleum and petroleum products (105)	3.2	37.1	16.4	46.4	13.4	3.3	13.4	35.3
	1.9	**109.6**	**24.4**	**27.9**	**20.2**	**2.0**	**8.4**	**23.4**
	1.3	226.6	38.6	11.3	32.7	1.2	5.9	13.3

Note: Ratio values listed are for upper, median, and lower quartiles. Number in ( ) indicates number of companies surveyed.
Reprinted with special permission of *Dun's Business Month* (formerly *Dun's Review*), November 1981, copyright 1981, Dun and Bradstreet Publications Corporation.

about equal to the industry median. (Remember: ROA = Profit margin $\times$ Asset turnover.)

There are two possible explanations for TEK's low asset turnover. One is that it is the natural result of a company's competitive strategy calling for ample inventory selection and liberal credit terms. Perhaps the high profit margin is due to such a strategy. If so, the low turnover can be forgiven. The other explanation is that TEK has inadequate inventory-control and credit-administration systems. If this is true, improving these systems would lead to a significant improvement in ROE. To illustrate, if TEK improved its asset turnover from 1.2 to the industry median of 1.7, and if its profit margin did not fall as a result, its ROE would rise from 19.1 to 26.7 percent, a resounding improvement ($26.7\% = 9.8\% \times 1.7 \times 1.6$).

In sum, ratio analysis indicates that TEK is a profitable, conservatively financed company. Debt levels are rising slowly over time and liquidity is declining, but neither trend yet appears to be dangerous. Its one potential problem area is the management of current assets, where the inventory turnover and the collection period are markedly worse than median industry experience and are failing to improve.

Appendix

Evaluating Divisional Performance

A number of large corporations today employ over 100,000 people. To reduce the bureaucracy which typically accompanies size and to motivate middle-level executives, many companies have decentralized by dividing the company into divisions, or profit centers. The profit centers are under the direction of headquarters, but insofar as possible, each profit center is responsible for managing its own operations as if it were an independent company.

Senior executives in decentralized companies face the recurring problem of evaluating profit-center performance. To appreciate the magnitude of the problem, it is useful to note that ITT has over 100 profit centers in Europe alone.

Management has at least three objectives in mind when evaluating profit-center performance: to learn which centers need help and what type of help is required, to learn which profit centers are doing exceptionally well so that investment in these activities can be increased, and to learn which profit-center managers are doing well so their superior achievement can be rewarded. Rewarding superior performance motivates all managers to work harder and to make decisions which are in the best interests of the corporation.

The evaluation of profit-center performance is obviously closely related to the topics discussed in this chapter. Both a company and a profit center involve the investment of resources in anticipation of earnings, and the problem is to measure return on the investment. There are, however, some differences. One is that profit centers seldom have debt or equity of their own. Instead, all financing is done at the corporate level; so it is impossible to define an ROE for a profit center. A second difference is that in profit-center evaluation, the managerial incentives created by the evaluation are usually a more prominent concern.

Return on Investment.   It should come as no surprise to learn that the most common technique for profit-center evaluation is a variation of ROE known as return on investment, or ROI.

$$\frac{\text{Return on}}{\text{investment}} = \text{ROI} = \frac{\text{Profit-center earnings}}{\text{Profit-center assets}}$$

Alternative definitions of earnings and assets exist among companies using the ROI. Some use profit-center earnings before the subtraction of corporate overhead expenses, while others use earnings after overhead. For assets the most common alternatives are total assets after depreciation or gross assets before depreciation.

ROI as a Measure of Profit-Center Performance. Just as with ROE, ROI suffers from timing, risk, and value problems when used as a performance measure. The timing problem is especially critical because it encourages managers to take a short-run focus. If you anticipate being a profit-center manager for only five years, the natural incentive is to do whatever you can to boost near-term ROI and to ignore everything beyond this horizon. American industry has received considerable criticism recently for just such a myopia, and perhaps an over-reliance on ROI is one of the root causes of this problem.

Residual Profits. A second incentive problem with ROI involves new investment. Suppose division managers are rewarded according to their divisions' ROI and that division A has an ROI of 25 percent, while division B's is only 5 percent. Now assume that each division is presented with an opportunity to invest in a project yielding a 20 percent return.

Although 20 percent is a rather attractive return, the manager of division A will likely reject the investment because it will reduce his ROI, while the manager of B will jump at the chance to make the investment because it will increase his ROI. In fact, he'll undertake any investment promising more than 5 percent. The net effect of this distortion is that successful divisions will tend to underinvest and unsuccessful ones will overinvest.

There is no simple way to circumvent the timing, risk, and value problems inherent in the use of accounting ratios, but it is possible to eliminate the distortion described above by using what is known as residual profits rather than ROI as the performance measure. It is defined as:

$$\frac{\text{Residual}}{\text{profits}} = \frac{\text{Profit-center}}{\text{earnings}} - K \times \frac{\text{Profit-center}}{\text{assets}}$$

where K is a percentage number representing the minimum acceptable rate of return on investment in the profit center, as defined by senior management. In later chapters we will refer to K as the cost of capital and will explain how it can be estimated.

To illustrate the use of residual profits, consider again divisions A and B faced with an investment promising a 20 percent return. If both divisions have assets of $100 and if K equals 15 percent, then residual profits are:

Division A	*Division B*
$\frac{\text{Residual}}{\text{profits}} = \$25 - 15\% \times 100$	$\frac{\text{Residual}}{\text{profits}} = \$5 - 15\% \times 100$
$= \$10$	$= -\$10$

Then, supposing the new 20 percent investment costs $50, its contribution to residual profits will be +$2.50 regardless of which division makes the investment ($2.50 = 20% × $50 − 15% × $50). Now, both division managers will want to make any investment promising a return greater than 15 percent regardless of their existing ROI or residual profits.

A closing comment regarding the evaluation of profit center performance: U.S. managers appear to be relearning an important lesson these days. It is short-sighted to manage anything strictly by the numbers. Executives need to take a broader, more qualitative view of the evaluation process, even when such a perspective reduces objectivity and dilutes incentives. Corporations are too complicated to allow the substitution of mechanical rules for creative thought. Numerical measures of performance are valuable tools, but their use must be kept in perspective.

Chapter Summary

1. Although a major corporation and the corner drugstore may seem vastly different, the levers by which managers in both firms affect performance are similar and few in number. The purpose of this chapter has been to study the ties between these levers and the firm's financial performance.

2. Return on equity is the most popular single yardstick of financial performance. However, it does suffer from timing, risk, and value problems.

3. The primary components of return on equity are the profit margin, the asset turnover ratio, and financial leverage. The profit margin summarizes income statement performance; the asset turnover ratio focuses on the left-hand side of the balance sheet and indicates how efficiently management has used the firm's assets; financial leverage looks at the right-hand side of the balance sheet and how the company has financed its assets.

4. Control ratios are very important for operating managers. They indicate the efficiency with which the company uses a specific type of asset, such as accounts receivable or inventories.

5. More financial leverage is not always better than less. Financial leverage can be measured using balance sheet ratios or coverage ratios. The latter are usually superior for long-term debt.

6. Ratio analysis is the systematic examination of a number of company ratios in search of insights into the firm's operations and its financial vitality. Used creatively, ratios are useful tools, but can be misleading if applied mechanically.

Sources for Business Ratios

Check your library for:

Robert Morris Associates. *Annual Statement Studies.* Philadelphia, published annually.

Common-size financial statements and widely used ratios in many business lines. Ratios broken out into four size ranges by total assets. Also contains comparative historical data. Excellent bibliography entitled "Sources of Composite Financial Data."

RMA cannot emphasize too strongly that their composite figures for each industry may *not* be representative of that entire industry (except by coincidence), for the following reasons:

1. The only companies with a chance of being included in their study in the first place are those for whom their submitting banks have recent figures.

2. Even from this restricted group of potentially includable companies, those which are chosen, and the total number chosen, are not determined in any random or otherwise statistically reliable manner.

3. Many companies in their study have *varied* product lines; they are "mini-conglomerates," if you will. All they can do in these cases is categorize them by their *primary* product line, and be willing to tolerate any "impurity" thereby introduced.

In a word, don't automatically consider their figures as representative norms and don't attach any more or less significance to them than is indicated by the unique aspects of the data collection.

Leo Troy. *Almanac of Business and Industrial Financial Ratios.* 1981/1982 edition. Englewood Cliffs, N.J.: Prentice-Hall, 1982.
   Common-size income statements and selected ratios for many business lines. Ratios broken out into 12 size ranges. Based on IRS data for 1977–78 period.

Dun & Bradstreet Corporation. *Key Business Ratios.* New York, published annually.
   Fourteen ratios for over 800 lines of business. Median-, upper-, and lower-quartile values. Ratios broken out into four size ranges by net worth for each business line.

Schonfeld & Associates, Inc. *IRS Corporate Financial Ratios.* Chicago, 1982.
   Detailed financial ratios for many business lines based on IRS data for 1976–77.

Additional Reading

Altman, Edward I. "Financial Ratios, Discriminant Analysis, and the Prediction of Corporate Bankruptcy." *Journal of Finance,* September 1968, pp. 589–609.
   An academic study using financial ratios and a statistical technique called discriminant analysis to predict corporate bankruptcy. Author concludes that ratios can accurately predict bankruptcy up to two years prior to the event.

Bernstein, Leopold A. *Financial Statement Analysis: Theory, Application, and Interpretation.* Rev. ed. Homewood, Ill.: Richard D. Irwin, 1978. 784 pages.
   A detailed examination of financial statements and their uses from an accounting perspective. Not what I would call exciting reading, but particularly levelheaded and thorough.

Chapter Problems

1. Table 4-1 presents financial statements over the period 1978-1981 for R&E Supplies, Inc.

   a. Calculate the return on equity, the profit margin, the asset turnover ratio, and the financial leverage for each year.

   b. What insights, if any, do these figures provide about R&E Supplies' recent performance? As a shareholder or manager, would you be concerned?

2. Table 2-1 indicates that Exxon's ROE in 1981 was 19.5 percent and K mart's was only 9 percent.

   a. Does this suggest that Exxon is a better-managed company than K mart? Why or why not?

   b. From an equity investor's perspective do these differing ROEs suggest that Exxon's common stock is a better buy than K mart's? Why or why not?

3. Acorn Manufacturing's sales (all on credit) for the just-completed year were $250 million, year-end accounts receivable were $41 million, the gross margin was 16 percent, and the payables period (based on cost of goods sold) was 28 days.

   a. What was Acorn's collection period?

   b. If Acorn wants to reduce its collection period to 10 days, to what would accounts receivable have to fall at the current sales level?

   c. Looking at this changing collection period in isolation, find out how much money Acorn would have to raise to finance the reduced collection period.

   d. What were Acorn's accounts payable at year-end?

4. Given the following information, complete the balance sheet shown below.

Collection period	70 days	Days sales in cash	20
Current ratio	2.8	Inventory turnover	9
Total debt to assets	71%	Payables period	14 days
Acid test	1.73		

   (All sales are on credit. All calculations assume a 365-day year.)

   Handwritten annotations: Accts Rec / Credit Sales @ day; cur. As. / curr. liab.; TOTAL LIAB / TOTAL ASSETS; incorrect; CASH + Sec. / Net Sales @ day; COGS / Ending Inventory; Accts Pay; Credit Purch. @ day or COGS @ day

Assets	
Current:	
Cash...................	$ 100,000
Accounts receivable	_____
Inventory.............	300,000
Total current assets...	_____
Net fixed assets........	_____
Total assets	$1,500,000

Liabilities and Equity	
Current liabilities:	
Accounts payable ......$	_____
Short-term debt........	_____
Total current liabilities	_____
Long-term debt.........	_____
Shareholders' equity.....	_____
Total liabilities and equity	_____

3

Inflation and the Assessment of Company Performance

Assessing the financial performance of a company during inflation is like measuring the width of a table with a rubber band. The size of the yardstick keeps changing. In this chapter, we will consider the ways in which inflation distorts historical-cost financial statements, and we will look briefly at inflation accounting techniques designed to minimize these distortions. An important conclusion of this inquiry will be that inflation has not been as detrimental to companies as many financial experts would lead us to believe.

What Is Inflation?

Intuitively, everyone knows that inflation involves a general increase in prices. If inflation were *uniform* so that all prices rose by the same percentage, the rate of inflation would obviously be the rate of change of the general price level. But inflation is *differential* rather than uniform. At any one time, the prices of many things, like oil and meat, are rising rapidly; while the prices of other things, like hand calculators and computers, may actually be declining. With the prices of different things changing at different rates over time, the meaning of inflation and the rate of inflation are less clear. Economists solve this problem by defining a price index, which is a weighted average of the prices of a number of different items. For example, the consumer price index is a weighted average of the prices of a typical "market basket" of consumer purchases, where the weights are the proportion of the typical consumer's budget spent on each item in the basket. The inflation rate is then the rate of change of this price index.

Anticipated and Unanticipated Inflation

There is an old saying in finance that during inflation it is good to be a debtor because the debtor borrows expensive dollars today and repays cheap dollars in the future. However, if you think about this saying a minute, you will realize that whatever a debtor gains as a result of inflation the creditor must lose, and even creditors are not so dumb as to consistently lose money on their loans. The truth is that if creditors anticipate inflation over the term of their loan, they will increase the interest rate charged to compensate for the declining value of the currency. This is the single most important reason interest rates have risen so dramatically over the past decade. Increasing inflation expectations have caused creditors to increase interest rates.

The focus of this chapter is on the impact of inflation on firm financial performance. From the preceding paragraphs, two effects of inflation should already be clear. First, if inflation is differential and a company's revenues are rising at a different rate than its costs, the company can gain or lose from inflation, depending on whether its revenues are rising faster than its costs. There can also by cyclical effects of differential inflation. During the upswing in the business cycle, inflation can be of the demand-pull type and profit margins can increase. But during the downswing, attempts on the part of labor to increase wages can create cost-push inflation which lowers profit margins.

The second obvious effect of inflation relates to whether the inflation is anticipated or unanticipated. If it is unanticipated, those companies which had the good fortune to borrow money before the inflation increased will gain from the inflation. They borrowed the money at low interest rates and will now be able to repay the debt with cheap dollars. Of course, the opposite is also true. If a company has the misfortune to borrow money just before the inflation rate unexpectedly declines, it will lose from inflation. It will have borrowed the money at a high, inflation-adjusted interest rate and will now have to repay the debt with unexpectedly valuable dollars.

There will be times when differential inflation and unanticipated inflation significantly affect a company's financial performance. However, from the viewpoint of industry as a whole, these instances will be more the exception than the rule. It is not likely that industry costs will systematically rise at a rate different from industry revenues for any lengthy period. Nor is it likely that companies as a whole will systematically gain or lose from unanticipated changes in the rate of inflation. The broader question of interest is, *What happens to company financial performance when inflation is uniform and anticipated?* This will be the focus of the remainder of the chapter.

Nominal versus Real

To discuss inflation intelligibly, it is necessary to distinguish between *nominal* and *real* quantities. A nominal number is simply one which might appear in a newspaper or a company's financial statement; it is *not* adjusted for the changing price level. A real number is expressed in *units of constant purchasing power;* it is adjusted for the changing price level.

The important thing about a sum of money is not the number of zeros after the last digit, nor the number of pieces of paper it represents, but what the money will buy. I would rather earn $10 and have the market basket of goods I consume cost $9 than earn $100,000 and have the market basket cost $200,000. In other words, under inflation the important information about a sum of money is not its nominal amount, but its purchasing power, or real amount.

To illustrate the difference between real and nominal dollars, suppose for simplicity that our consumer's market basket contains only bread. Table 3–1

Table 3–1.   Converting Nominal Earnings to Real Earnings

	1970	1980
Nominal earnings	$1 million	$2.4 million
Cost of one loaf of bread	$1.00	$2.00
Real earnings in bread units	1 million loaves	1.2 million loaves
Real earnings in 1970 dollars	$1 million	$1.2 million
Real earnings in 1980 dollars	$2 million	$2.4 million

shows the nominal earnings of a company which have grown from $1 million in 1970 to $2.4 million in 1980. This appears to be a healthy gain, but during the same period the price of a loaf of bread has doubled from $1 to $2. So in terms of the purchasing power of earnings, the company could buy 1 million loaves in 1970 and 1.2 million loaves in 1980, a much more modest increase. These are the real earnings of the company.

It is not common to state real earnings in terms of loaves of bread, so let's go through the same exercise using dollars of constant purchasing power. First, we will use constant 1970 dollars. In 1970, 1 million loaves of bread cost $1 million, while 1.2 million loaves cost $1.2 million; so these are the respective earnings figures in constant 1970 dollars. In 1980, the same number of bread loaves cost $2 million and $2.4 million, respectively. These are the company's earnings in constant 1980 dollars. Note that while the constant-dollar earnings differ depending on which year we use as the base, the percentage change in the earnings is the same. Real earnings increased 20 percent over the decade.

The notion that 1970 dollars are different from 1980 dollars is confusing, but it is central to understanding inflation. Dollars in 1970 were worth more than dollars in 1980 because the same number of dollars had greater purchasing power.

Calculating Constant-Dollar Amounts.   Mechanically the adjustment for the declining purchasing power of the currency is quite simple. Suppose the consumer price index (CPI) for three years is:

Year	1979	1980	1981
CPI	0.98	1.14	1.27

and you want to calculate the constant 1980 dollar value of $100 in each year. The first step is to divide each CPI number by the 1980 CPI. This yields:

Year	1979	1980	1981
CPI	0.86	1.00	1.11

Then, divide the nominal $100 amount by the revised CPI. This yields the following constant 1980 dollar values:

Year	1979	1980	1981
Value of $100	$116	$100	$90

One hundred dollars in 1979 was comparable to $116 in 1980 purchasing power, while $100 in 1981 is worth only $90 in 1980 dollars.

Inflation and Company Profits

Inflation distorts the reported earnings of a company in three distinct ways. One involves the valuation of inventory, another the use of historical-cost depreciation, and the third, the accounting for interest cost under inflation. The first two sources of distortion are well known, while the third is less well known and frequently misunderstood.

The Inventory Valuation Adjustment

There are two widely used methods of inventory accounting in the United States: first-in, first-out (FIFO) and last-in, first-out (LIFO). In an inflationary environment, a company's reported earnings and its tax bill depend on which method a company uses. To illustrate, suppose a company manufactures and sells boxes and that it keeps its inventory of finished boxes in a stack as shown in Figure 3–1. Each time a new box is completed, it is added to the top of the pile. The dollar amounts to the left of the boxes are the cost incurred by the company in making each box. Since prices are rising, the cost of each successive box is higher, starting with the oldest box in inventory at $1 and rising to the most recently produced box at a cost of $1.50.

Figure 3-1. Inventory Valuation, Taxes, and Earnings under Inflation

Cost of Production	Finished boxes		FIFO Accounting	LIFO Accounting
$1.50		Selling price	$2.00	$2.00
1.40		Cost of goods sold	1.00	1.50
1.30		Taxable income	1.00	.50
1.20		Tax @ 50%	.50	.25
1.10		Earnings after tax	$ .50	$ .25
1.00				

When the company sells a box for, say, $2, the accountant must match the cost of the box sold against the revenue. If the company uses FIFO, the assigned cost of goods sold will be $1; while if LIFO accounting is employed, the cost of goods sold will be $1.50. (Here, we ignore all practical problems associated with removing a box from the bottom of the stack.) As shown in the figure, the choice of the inventory valuation method significantly affects the company's tax liability and its reported earnings. In our numerical example, FIFO accounting produces earnings and taxes of $0.50 as opposed to $0.25 for LIFO accounting.

Why LIFO Is Superior.   Which earnings figure is correct? Since the current cost of manufacturing one box is much closer to $1.50 than to $1.00, the LIFO earnings figure is the more accurate measure of true earnings under inflation.

Why Is FIFO More Popular than LIFO?   Inasmuch as LIFO accounting presents a more accurate picture of company earnings under inflation and reduces the firm's tax bill, it may come as a surprise to learn that FIFO is presently the more popular method of inventory accounting in the United States. There are two possible explanations for the popularity of FIFO, neither of which is very convincing. One is that while LIFO accounting produces a more accurate income statement, it also produces a less accurate balance sheet. Looking again at Figure 3-1, observe that as the company using LIFO accounting continues to sell boxes off the top of the stack, the boxes remaining in inventory get older and older, and the recorded value of the inventory falls increasingly below its true value. As a result, the recorded value of finished-goods inventory on the company's balance sheet will be below its true value. The question faced by management then is where the inflation distortion should best appear. FIFO distorts the income statement, but LIFO distorts the balance sheet. The appropriate answer is that LIFO is superior to FIFO because the balance sheet distortion only confuses readers of the company's annual reports, while the income statement distortion results in higher taxes. Better confused readers than higher taxes.

A second possible explanation for the popularity of FIFO accounting is based on the premise that shareholders value the higher reported earnings which accompany FIFO accounting even though taxes are higher and the added profits are illusory. The problem with this justification is that it implies a very low opinion of the analytical abilities of shareholders and security analysts—much lower, I think, than can be justified.

It may appear that one solution to the LIFO–FIFO dilemma would be to use LIFO accounting for tax purposes and FIFO for reporting purposes. In this way, the company would minimize its tax bill while maximizing reported earnings. The problem with this strategy is that, contrary to other accounting options, the tax authorities require companies to use the same system of inventory valuation for tax and reporting purposes.

Historical-Cost Depreciation

The second well-known distortion in reported earnings caused by inflation exists because accounting principles require the use of historical-cost depreciation. The problem is much like that of FIFO inventory accounting just discussed. Because depreciation must be based on the original cost of an asset, the amount charged against income during inflation understates the true decline in the value of assets. Or said differently, historical-cost depreciation is not sufficient to maintain the value of company assets during inflation. The understatement of annual depreciation causes an overstatement of reported earnings and an increase in taxes paid.

To see the difficulty with historical-cost depreciation under inflation, look at Table 3–2. Suppose in 1975 a company purchased an asset for $10,000 and it began depreciating on a straight-line basis of $1,000 per year over 10 years to a zero salvage value. Five years later, in 1980, the remaining book value of the asset is $5,000, its life expectancy is five years, and the annual depreciation is still $1,000.

However, suppose that due to a 50 percent inflation over the period 1975–80, the nominal value of the asset is now $7,500. That is, suppose it would cost the company $7,500 in 1980 to replace the asset with one of identical productive capacity and life expectancy. This 50 percent inflation is reflected in a rise in the consumer price index from 1.00 in 1975 to 1.50 in 1980. With a remaining five-year life expectancy, an annual nominal depreciation of $1,500 is now required to reduce the asset to a zero salvage value in 1985 ($1,500 = $7,500 ÷ 5 years). Consequently, historical-cost depreciation understates the warranted nominal depreciation by $500.

In real terms, the 1980 value of the asset, *in constant 1975 dollars,* is still $5,000 ($5,000 = $7,500 ÷ 1.5), but the value of the $1,000 historical-

**Table 3–2.   Under Inflation, Historical-Cost Depreciation Is Insufficient
to Maintain Value of Assets**

1975		*1980 Book Values*	
Original cost	$10,000	Remaining book value	$5,000
Expected life	10 years	Expected life	5 years
Annual depreciation	$1,000	Annual depreciation	$1,000
Consumer price index (CPI)	1.00	CPI	1.50
1980 Nominal Values		*1980 Real Values in 1975 Dollars*	
Nominal value	$7,500	Real value in 1975 dollars	$5,000
Expected life	5 years	Expected life	5 years
Warranted nominal annual		Warranted real annual	
depreciation	$1,500	depreciation	$1,000
Nominal book-value annual		Real book-value annual	
depreciation	$1,000	depreciation	$667
Understatement of nominal		Understatement of real	
depreciation	$500	depreciation	$333

cost depreciation is only $667 ($1,000 ÷ 1.5). In *real* terms, the company
has realized no gain as a result of holding the asset during inflation, but
annual depreciation has declined by one third.

Gains to Net Debtors

The third distortion to reported income created by inflation involves the
way accountants measure interest on a loan. Consider the following fanciful
example. In early 1980, the SLH Company needs $100 for one year to
make an attractive investment, and the treasurer visits the company's principal bank to negotiate a loan. The banker is pleased to lend $100 but is
concerned about inflation, which the treasurer and the banker agree will
probably be 100 percent next year. The banker states that he only wants to
maintain the purchasing power of the money he lends and to earn a modest
4 percent return. Using bread as a representative commodity, he tells the
treasurer, "Bread costs $1 a loaf today; so, in effect, you want to borrow
100 loaves. I want you to repay enough money in one year to purchase 104
loaves so I can earn a real return of 4 percent on the loan. Since we expect
bread to cost $2 a loaf in one year, you will need to repay $208 ($2 per loaf
× 104 loaves). This works out to an interest rate of 108 percent."

In economic terms, the banker has invoked the well-known Fisher Effect,
after the American economist Irving Fisher. In symbols, the Fisher Effect
says:

$$i_n = (1 + i_r)(1 + \bar{p}) - 1$$

where i_n is the nominal rate of interest, i_r is the real rate of interest, and $\bar{p}$ is
the expected rate of inflation. From the above example,

$$108\% = (1 + 4\%)(1 + 100\%) - 1$$

The accounting for this loan appears in Table 3–3. In bread accounting terms—that is, in *real* terms—SLH Company borrows enough money to buy 100 loaves and one year later repays enough to buy 104 loaves; so the real interest rate is 4 percent. In nominal dollars, as it would appear on the company's income statement, SLH borrows $100 and repays $208 for a whopping 108 percent interest rate. The constant 1980 and 1981 dollar figures are consistent with the bread accounting: SLH borrows at a real interest rate of 4 percent.

Table 3–3. Measuring Interest under Inflation

	Bread Accounting	Nominal Dollars	Real 1980 Dollars	Real 1981 Dollars
Borrow in 1980	100 loaves	$100	$100	$200
Repay in 1981	104 loaves	$208	$104	$208
Principal payment	100 loaves	$100	$100	$200
Interest payment	4 loaves	$108	$ 4	$ 8
Interest rate	4%	108%	4%	4%

Why must SLH pay a nominal interest rate of 108 percent? When SLH repays the loan in 1981, the accountant will call $100 of the payment return of principal and $108 interest. But most of what the accountant calls interest is no such thing. Let's look at the transaction in constant 1981 dollars. In 1980, SLH borrows money which has a purchasing power equal to $200 in 1981 dollars (100 loaves × $2 per loaf). In 1981, the company owes the bank only $100 in 1981 dollars, plus interest. The effect of inflation has been to reduce the *real* value of the principal owed by $100. This is the notion of borrowers repaying with cheaper dollars during inflation. From SLH's perspective, it is just as if one half the liability had been forgiven. But from the bank's perspective, the real value of the loan principal has fallen $100 without the bank receiving a payment. To compensate, the bank charges $108 plus the $100 principal due. The accountant calls the $108 "interest," but in economic terms, only $8 is interest and the rest is principal repayment.

Net Monetary Credtiors and Debtors. To decide what effect this overstatement of interest expense will have on reported earnings, we must determine whether a company is a net monetary creditor or debtor. An asset is said to be *monetary* if it is denominated in units of currency and *physical* if it is not. Cash, marketable securities and accounts receivable are monetary assets because when the assets mature, the company will receive a specified amount of currency. Inventories, plant, equipment, and land are physical assets whose ultimate value in units of currency depends, at least in part, on the future inflation rate. Most liabilities are monetary, while net worth is physical.

The great majority of companies are net monetary debtors; their monetary liabilities exceed their monetary assets. For these companies, the overstatement of nominal interest expense described above causes an understatement of reported earnings and a decrease in taxes paid. For net monetary creditors, the distortions will be just the reverse.

The Net Effect of Inflation on Reported Earnings.   In this chapter, we have seen that FIFO inventory accounting, historical-cost depreciation, and the mislabeling of interest expense each distort reported earnings under inflation. The overstatement of reported earnings caused by FIFO accounting and historical-cost depreciation is well known. In fact, for several years the U.S. government has published, as part of the national income accounts, the adjustments to aggregate reported income of U.S. companies required to remove the distortions. They are known as the inventory valuation adjustment (IVA) and the capital consumption adjustment (CCA).

As noted above, the third distortion to reported earnings, caused by the mislabeling of interest expense, *understates* reported earnings under inflation. The size of this understatement is not known precisely, but one recent study suggests that the *average* understatement of U.S. firms is about equal in magnitude, but opposite in sign, to the *total* overstatement due to FIFO accounting and historical-cost depreciation.[1] This means that for the average firm, the three distortions to income created by inflation may almost offset one another, leaving reported income about equal to true income. This does not suggest that such a conclusion applies to every company. For depending on the nature of the company, its accounting system, and its capital structure, reported income can differ substantially from true income. The conclusion is appropriate only on average, and it is helpful to recall the tale of the man who drowned while fording a river because he had heard it was only five feet deep on average.

Our discussion has focused on inflation-induced biases in reported income. Inflation also distorts a company's balance sheet in important ways. One mentioned briefly is the understatement of inventory value inherent in LIFO accounting. A second is the overstatement of liabilities. Consistent with the idea that borrowers repay debts with cheaper dollars during inflation, the real value of liabilities declines during inflationary periods. However, this change in value is ignored by the accountant, with the result that the apparent indebtedness of the company overstates reality. Companies

---

[1] F. Modigliani and R. Cohn, "Inflation, Rational Valuation and the Market," *Financial Analysts Journal,* March/April, 1979.

have not increased their true financial leverage over the last decade as much as standard balance sheet ratios suggest. The appendix to this chapter contains a numerical example illustrating this conclusion.

Let me caution again: I am *not* saying it is necessarily good to be a debtor during inflation. The real value of liabilities does decline, but if inflation is anticipated, the interest rate rises to counteract the decline. The accountant's error is that he includes the higher interest rate but fails to include the fall in the value of the liabilities.

Inflation Biases and Company Earnings: A Problem

During a period of rapid inflation, Companies A and B both report earnings of $100 million. Company A uses LIFO accounting, has primarily current assets, and makes extensive use of debt financing. Company B uses FIFO accounting, has primarily fixed assets, and is very conservatively financed. Which company, in truth, is probably the more profitable?

Answer: Company A. FIFO accounting and historical-cost accounting cause reported earnings to exceed true earnings during inflation. Company A suffers comparatively little from these biases. Debt financing and the resulting misstatement of interest expense cause reported earnings to understate true earnings. Company A does suffer from this bias. Hence, true earnings are probably above $100 million. By the same reasoning, Company B's true earnings are probably below $100 million.

Inflation Accounting

As a partial remedy to the problems cited in this chapter, the Financial Accounting Standards Board (FASB) in the United States has recently begun requiring large companies to report the effects of inflation in their financial statements. All public U.S. companies having either $1 billion in total assets or $125 million in inventories and gross properties must present the supplemental information. It is presented using two formats: *constant*-dollar accounting and *current*-dollar accounting. As used above, constant-dollar accounting adjusts for changes in the *general* price level by restating historical-cost figures in units of constant purchasing power. Current-dollar accounting recognizes that different asset prices inflate at different rates and adjusts for changes in specific price levels. In current-dollar accounting, the accountant uses a different price index to calculate the current value of each category of assets. There is general agreement that, of the two techniques, current-dollar accounting is conceptually superior. The difficulty with it is that suitable price indices for many types of assets are unavailable. More conservative accountants and financial analysts feel that if managers are given too much latitude in selecting which indices to use, objectivity will suffer.

The inflation accounting data required by the FASB is a major help in assessing firm financial performance under inflation. It continues to suffer from two weaknesses, however. One is that only selected balance sheet information is provided, and the other is that gains to net debtors, while reported, are not shown clearly as part of income.

How Much Difference Does Inflation Accounting Make?

To grasp the magnitude of the differences which can arise between historical-cost and constant-dollar financial statements, look at the following table. It shows 1980 historical-cost and constant-dollar income statements and balance sheets for three diverse firms, Southern Railways, Hewlett Packard and Safeway Stores. Southern Railways is capital intensive; Hewlett Packard is a high technology, rapidly growing firm; and Safeway Stores is a highly levered retail operation.

Looking first at the income statements, we see that constant-dollar accounting increases Safeway's net income a whopping 35 percent, increases Southern Railway's 26 percent, and *decreases* Hewlett Packard's by 39 percent. Inflation adjustments clearly matter. The principal difference among the companies is "gains to net debtors." Because of its high financial leverage, Safeway has a gain to net debtors well in excess of its historical cost income; while Hewlett Packard is a net creditor and consequently reports a loss.

The major balance sheet impact of constant-dollar accounting is to increase nonmonetary assets and shareholders' equity. The mechanism is straightforward: If an individual bought a home in 1970 for $30,000, and in 1982 it has a mortgage with a remaining principal of $10,000, the historical-cost balance sheet for the home, ignoring depreciation, would be:

Nonmonetary asset	$30,000	Liabilities	$10,000
		Equity	20,000
Total	$30,000	Total	$30,000

But if inflation has pushed the constant 1982 dollar value of the home to $100,000, the constant-dollar balance sheet would be:

Nonmonetary asset	$100,000	Liabilities	$ 10,000
		Equity	90,000
Total	$100,000	Total	$100,000

As in the table, constant-dollar accounting produces an increase in nonmonetary assets and shareholders' equity.

The question of which balance sheet is more accurate naturally hinges on the current *market* value of the asset. For homes and many other assets, there is strong reason to believe that the constant-dollar figure is a closer approximation to market value than is historical cost. For other assets, such as little-used railroad track or obsolete production equipment, the answer is less clear-cut.

The impact of the increase in nonmonetary assets on the firms' debt-to-asset ratios is apparent in the table: Southern Railway's ratios improve from 59 to 33 percent; Hewlett Packard's, from 34 to 31 percent; and Safeway's, from 68 to 52 percent.

The combined income statement and balance sheet impact of constant-dollar accounting is reflected in the return-on-equity ratios at the bottom of the table. Although net income rises for two companies, the increase in equity predominates, and constant-dollar ROE falls significantly for every firm.

To summarize, the intent here is *not* to ridicule historical-cost financial statements but simply to demonstrate that the differences between historical-cost and constant-dollar accounting are large and pervasive. Historical-cost accounting certainly has its weaknesses; however, inflation accounting is new and still highly controversial. One debate involves the extent to which it is proper to write up fixed assets with inflation, while another surrounds the question of whether gains to net debtors should appear on the income statement. Until these and related controversies are resolved, many executives are prepared to acknowledge that inflation distorts historical-cost statements but remain skeptical about the objectivity and usefulness of current inflation accounting techniques.

Historical-Cost and Constant-Dollar Financial Statements
Fiscal Year 1980 ($ millions except per share)

Income Statement

	Southern Railway	Hewlett Packard	Safeway Stores
Net income as reported in historical cost financial statement...	$ 178	$ 269	$ 119
Decrease for additional depreciation	(88)	(22)	(100)
Decrease for additional cost of goods sold	0	(62)	(72)
Increase from gains to net debtors	134	(22)	214
Constant dollar net income	$ 224	$ 163	$ 161
Increase in net income (percent)	26%	− 39%	35%

Balance Sheet

	Southern Railway		Hewlett Packard		Safeway Stores	
	Historical Cost	Constant Dollar	Historical Cost	Constant Dollar	Historical Cost	Constant Dollar
Monetary assets	$ 501	$ 501	$ 946	$ 946	$ 257	$ 257
Nonmonetary assets	2,664	5,122	1,391	1,618	3,082	4,107
Total assets	$3,165	$5,623	$2,337	$2,564	$3,339	$4,364
Liabilities	$1,878	$1,878	$ 790	$ 790	$2,275	$2,275
Shareholders' equity	1,287	3,745	1,547	1,774	1,064	2,089
Total liabilities and equity	$3,165	$5,623	$2,337	$2,564	$3,339	$4,364
Debt-to-assets ratio (percent)	59%	33%	34%	31%	68%	52%
Return-on-equity ratio (percent)	13.8%	6.0%	17.4%	9.2%	11.2%	7.7%

Appendix

Overstating Interest Expense during Inflation:
A Numerical Example

To see what happens to standard, historical-cost financial statements under inflation, and in particular to see what happens when the accountant mislabels interest expense, consider the following example. For simplicity, we will assume uniform, fully anticipated inflation; we will ignore the distorting effects of FIFO accounting and historical-cost depreciation. In addition, we will ignore taxes. Table 3A–1 shows the financial statements of the XYZ Company under the following conditions:

I.   No inflation, historical-cost accounting.
II. 100 percent inflation, historical-cost accounting.
III. 100 percent inflation, constant-dollar accounting.

In the no-inflation case, XYZ has operating income of $7, pays interest of 4 percent on its $50 debt, and earns $5. At the end of the year, XYZ buys $10 of new plant which it pays for with earnings plus $5 of new debt. We assume XYZ pays no dividend and that depreciation is just sufficient to maintain the real value of assets. Throughout the year, XYZ's debt-to-equity ratio stays constant at 1.00.

In the case of 100 percent inflation and historical-cost financial statements, two important changes occur: All prices double on the first day of the year; and to maintain their real return of 4 percent, creditors increase the interest rate on XYZ's debt to 108 percent. XYZ behaves just as it did in the first case, except now the year is apparently a disaster. Nominal operating income doubles to $14 due to inflation, but interest expense rises 27-fold, and the company incurs an apparent operating loss of $40. To cover this loss and to pay for the new plant cost of $20, XYZ must now borrow $60. Due to inflation, XYZ's year-end debt-to-equity ratio soars to 11 to 1, and its times-interest-earned ratio falls from 3.5 ($7 ÷ $2) to only 0.26 ($14 ÷ $54). Analysis of XYZ's historical-cost financial statements suggests that inflation has all but ruined the company, despite the fact that XYZ was able to raise its prices to maintain *real* operating income. And the company's creditors are still earning the same 4 percent real return. How can this happen? The answer lies in the treatment of interest expense.

The third case restates the second in terms of constant 1981 dollars. Look first at the income statement. Everything is the same as in the second case except now we add another quantity—*gain to net debtor*. This is the decline in the real value of XYZ's liabilities as a result of inflation. Alternatively, we can say it is the principal repayment disguised as interest in the discussion

Table 3A–1. Financial Statements of XYZ Company under Three Conditions

I. No inflation, historical-cost accounting

Income Statement, 1981	
Operating income	$ 7
Interest expense @ 4%	(2)
Earnings	$ 5

Sources and Uses of Cash

Sources:		Uses:	
New debt	$ 5	New plant . . .	$10
Retained earnings . . .	5		
Totals	$10		$10

Balance Sheet, 1980			
Net plant	$100	Debt	$ 50
		Net worth	50
Totals	$100		$100

Balance Sheet, 1981			
Net plant	$110	Debt	$ 55
		Net worth	55
Totals	$110		$110

II. 100 percent inflation, historical-cost accounting

Income Statement, 1981	
Operating income	$ 14
Interest expense @ 108%	(54)
Earnings	$(40)

Sources and Uses of Cash

Sources:		Uses:	
New debt	$60	Loss	$40
		New plant . . .	20
Totals	$60		$60

Balance Sheet, 1980			
Net plant	$100	Debt	$ 50
		Net worth	50
Totals	$100		$100

Balance Sheet, 1981			
Net plant	$120	Debt	$110
		Net worth	10
Totals	$120		$120

III. 100 percent inflation, 1981 constant-dollar accounting

Income Statement, 1981	
Operating income	$ 14
Interest expense @ 108%	(54)
Gain to net debtor	50
Earnings	$ 10

Sources and Uses of Cash

Sources:		Uses:	
New debt	$60	"Principal repayment" . .	$50
Earnings	10	New plant . . .	20
Totals	$70		$70

Balance Sheet, 1980, in 1981 Dollars			
Net plant	$200	Debt	$100
		Net worth	100
Totals	$200		$200

Balance Sheet, 1981, in 1981 Dollars			
Net plant	$220	Debt	$110
		Net worth	110
Totals	$220		$220

above. A principal repayment is *not* a cost and should not appear on an income statement. To confirm this, recall that a company does not include new borrowings as revenue; and, in turn, it should not include debt repayments as an expense. Technically, principal repayments are a *return of capital*.

By adding gains to net debtors back to operating income, we are correcting the mistake made by the accountant when he or she called the entire $54 interest expense. Note that this is *not* equivalent to suggesting that it is good to be a debtor during inflation. The gain to net debtors offsets $50 of interest expense, leaving the debtor with the same real debt cost as in the no-inflation case. Note, too, that the earnings of $10 is the same in real terms as the $5 earned in the first case.

The 1980 balance sheet is a restatement of the balance sheet shown in the first two cases in constant 1981 dollars. Net plant on these earlier statements is $100 in 1980 dollars. Since the purchasing power of one 1980 dollar equals two 1981 dollars, the constant purchasing-power equivalent in 1981 dollars is $200. The same is true of debt. At the start of the year, $50 in 1980 dollars would have paid off XYZ's liabilities. In terms of purchasing power, this is equal to $100 in 1981 dollars.

The values on the 1981 balance sheet follow directly from the income statement and the 1980 constant-dollar balance sheet. Observe that in *real* terms the 1981 balance sheets for the *first* and the *third* case are identical. In particular, the debt-to-equity ratio and the times-interest-earned ratio, counting interest as $4, are back to their no-inflation values of 1.00 and 3.5, respectively. In this example, anyway, uniform, fully anticipated inflation acts as a veil obscuring our assessment of company performance; but it has no lasting economic impact.

While inflation is to a large degree only a veil, this conclusion overstates the case in several important respects. One is that inflation is seldom uniform or fully anticipated. And when it is not, real economic gains and losses can occur. A second problem, even with the idealized inflation considered here, appears in XYZ's sources and uses statement for case III. While gains to net debtors are appropriately an addition to earnings, they are *not* a source of cash. The cash generated by operations is negative $40, as shown in the second case. Looking at the case III sources and uses statement, if earnings are $10, we must record an offsetting use of $50 for principal repayment. This is the $50 which the accountant erroneously calls interest. To balance sources and uses, XYZ must borrow $60. If the creditor understands that the $54 interest payment included an implicit $50 principal payment, he or she will look on the new loan as a net increase of only $10, and XYZ should encounter no difficulty borrowing the money. If the creditor does not understand inflation and bases the credit decision on the historical-cost financial statements of case II, XYZ may have real difficulty financing operations—even though inflation has had no real impact on profitability.

Taxes and Gains to Net Debtors.   Another effect of inflation apparent from the above example involves income taxes. Interest payments are a tax-deductible business expense, but principal repayments are not. They must be paid out of aftertax earnings. When the tax authorities look at XYZ's reported earnings as shown in case II, it will appear that the company has incurred a sizable loss; so rather than owing taxes, XYZ will be eligible for a rebate. In effect, inflation enables XYZ to disguise a $50 principal repayment as interest and to convert it into a tax-deductible expense. But do not fear for the tax authorities. What is an expense for XYZ is income to the creditors, and taxable as such. The lender must pay income taxes on the full $54 interest received, even though $50 is return of principal.

Whether the tax treatment of interest and principal repayments under inflation creates incentives for companies to borrow more is an open question. If borrowers and lenders were in the same tax bracket and the economy worked just the way theoreticians say it should, we would see no effect. Lenders would increase interest rates to maintain the same *aftertax* return, and this would just offset the borrower's ability to convert principal repayments into interest. In actuality, inflation probably creates incentives for companies to borrow.

Chapter Summary

1. The purpose of this chapter has been to understand the ways in which inflation distorts historical cost financial statements and to consider ways to reduce these distortions.

2. The important fact about a sum of money is not its nominal amount but what it will buy.

3. Under inflation, dollars at different dates have different purchasing powers and hence are not directly comparable. To compare them, it is necessary to restate one or both amounts in dollars of constant purchasing power.

4. Inflation affects reported company profits in three ways: (*a*) if the firm uses FIFO accounting, cost of goods sold is understated and earnings are overstated, (*b*) historical cost depreciation also overstates earnings, and (*c*) the accountant's overstatement of interest expense produces an understatement of earnings of net monetary debtors.

5. On average these three biases appear to cancel one another out; however, this need not be true for individual businesses.

6. Inflation significantly distorts company balance sheets by understating assets and equity. This overstates return on equity and financial leverage.

7. Inflation accounting promises a partial correction of inflation-induced biases but is still in its infancy and not universally understood or accepted.

Additional Reading

Flynn, Thomas D. "Why We Should Account for Inflation." *Harvard Business Review,* September–October 1977, pp. 145–57.

Written for the general manager, this article reviews the alternative approaches to inflation accounting and discusses the benefits to business of inflation accounting.

Kaplan, Robert S. "Purchasing Power Gains on Debt: The Effect of Expected and Unexpected Inflation." *The Accounting Review,* April 1977, pp. 369–78.

A careful look at what the chapter calls *gains to net debtors,* an important and often neglected effect of inflation.

Chapter Problems

1. In 1975 Jay Kittle earned $25,000. In 1980 he earned $32,000. The consumer price index (CPI) was 100.0 in 1975 and 153.1 in 1980.
   a. What was the percentage increase in Mr. Kittle's nominal earnings?
   b. What were Mr. Kittle's earnings in constant 1975 dollars? In constant 1980 dollars?
   c. What was the percentage increase in Mr. Kittle's real earnings?

2. The consumer price index for 1974 through 1980 was:

	1974	1975	1976	1977	1978	1979	1980
CPI	91.6	100.0	105.8	112.7	121.2	134.9	153.1

   a. In purchasing power terms, how much was $100 in 1974 worth in 1980?
   b. In purchasing power terms, how much was $100 in 1980 worth in 1974?
   c. What has been the constant 1977 dollar value of $100 in each year 1974 through 1980?

3. a. Looking at Table 1–1, find Tektronix's net monetary debtor (creditor) position at year-end 1979. (Assume prepaid expenses and other long-term liabilities are monetary and other long-term assets are physical.)
   b. If the company maintained this position throughout 1980, what gain or loss would TEK report on its 1980 constant-dollar financial statements as a result of its net monetary debtor or creditor position? (You may want to use the CPI figures presented in question 2 in your calculations.)

4. What impact would allowing companies to base depreciation on the current value of long-term assets, rather than the original cost, have on earnings during inflation? In what sense, if any, would companies benefit from such a change?

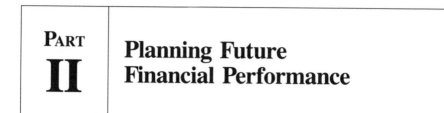

PART II

Planning Future Financial Performance

4 Financial Forecasting

Planning is the substitution of error for chaos.
Anonymous

To this point we have looked at the *past,* evaluating existing financial statements and assessing past performance. It is time now to look toward the *future.* We begin in this chapter with an examination of the principal techniques of financial forecasting and a brief consideration of planning and budgeting as practiced by modern, large corporations. The following chapter will look at planning problems unique to the management of company growth. Throughout this chapter our emphasis will be on the *technique* of forecasting and planning; so as a counterweight, it will be important for you to bear in mind that proper technique is only a part of effective planning. At least as important is the development of creative market strategies and operating policies which underlie the financial plans.

Pro Forma Statements

Finance is central to a company's planning activities for at least two reasons. One is that much of the language of forecasting and planning is financial. Plans are stated in terms of financial statements, and many of the measures used to evaluate the plan are financial. Second, and more importantly, the financial executive is responsible for an increasingly scarce resource: money. Because virtually every corporate action has financial implications, a critical part of any plan is the determination of whether it is attainable given the company's limited resources.

Companies typically prepare a wide array of plans and budgets. Some, like production plans and staff budgets, focus in detail on a particular aspect of the firm, whereas others, like pro forma statements, are much broader in scope. Our strategy in this chapter will be to begin with the broader techniques and to talk briefly about more specialized procedures later when we address planning in the large corporation.

Pro forma financial statements are the most widely used technique for financial forecasting. A pro forma statement is nothing more than a prediction of what a company's financial statements will look like at the end of the forecast period. These predictions may be the outgrowth of intensive, detailed operating plans and budgets or nothing more than rough, back-of-the-envelope projections. In either case, the pro forma format displays the information in a logical, internally consistent manner. A major use of pro forma forecasts, as will become apparent below, is to estimate the company's future need for external financing.

Percent-of-Sales Forecasting

One simple yet effective way to project company financial performance is to tie many of the income statement and balance sheet figures to future sales. The rationale for the percent-of-sales approach is the tendency, noted earlier, for all variable costs and most current assets and current liabilities to vary directly with sales. Obviously, this will not be true for all of the entries in a company's financial statements, and certainly some independent forecasts of individual items will be required. Nonetheless, the percent-of-sales method does provide simple, logical estimates of many important variables.

The first step in a percent-of-sales forecast should be an examination of historical data to determine which financial statement items have varied in proportion to sales in the past. This will enable the forecaster to decide which items can safely be estimated as a percent of sales and which must be forecast by using other information. The second step is to forecast sales. Because so many other items will be linked mechanically to the sales forecast, it is critically important to estimate sales as accurately as possible. In addition, once pro forma statements are complete, it is important to test the sensitivity of the results to reasonable variations in the sales forecast. The final step in the percent-of-sales forecast is to estimate individual financial statement items by extrapolating the historical patterns to the newly estimated sales. Thus, if inventories have historically been about 20 percent of sales, and if next year's sales are forecast to be $10 million, we would expect inventories to be $2 million. It's as simple as that.

To illustrate the use of the percent-of-sales method, consider the problem faced by Suburban National Bank. R&E Supplies, Inc., a modest-sized wholesaler of plumbing and electrical supplies, has been a customer of the bank for a number of years. The company has maintained average deposits of approximately $30,000 and has had a $50,000 short-term, renewable loan for five years. The company has prospered over the years, and the loan has been renewed annually with only cursory analysis.

In early 1982, the president of R&E Supplies visited the bank and requested an increase in the short-term loan for 1982 to $500,000. The president explained that despite the company's growth, accounts payable had increased steadily and cash balances had declined. A number of suppliers had recently threatened to put the company on COD for future purchases unless payments were received more promptly. When asked why he was requesting $500,000, the president replied that this amount seemed about right and that it would enable him to pay off his most insistent creditors and to rebuild his cash balances.

Knowing that the bank's credit committee would never approve a loan request of this magnitude without careful financial projections, the lending officer suggested that he and the president prepare pro forma financial statements for 1982. He explained that these statements would provide a more accurate indication of R&E's credit needs.

The first step in preparing the pro forma projections was to examine the company's financial statements for the years 1978 to 1981, shown in Table 4–1 in search of stable patterns. The results of this ratio analysis appear in Table 4–2. The president's concern about declining liquidity and increasing trade payables is well founded; cash and securities as a percent of sales have fallen from 6 to 2 percent, while accounts payable have risen from 9 to 16 percent. In terms of a payables period, defined as accounts payable divided by cost of goods sold per day, the increase has been from 39 days to 66 days. Another worrisome trend is the increase in cost of goods sold and general, selling, and administrative expenses in proportion to sales. Earnings clearly are not keeping pace with sales.

The last column in Table 4–2 contains the projections agreed to by the president and the lending officer. In line with recent experience, sales are predicted to increase 25 percent over 1981. General, selling, and administrative expenses will continue to rise as a result of an unfavorable labor settlement. The president feels that cash and securities should rise to at least 5 percent, or 18 days sales. Since much of this money will sit in his bank, the lending officer concurs. The president also feels that accounts payable should decline to no more than 14 percent, giving the company a payables period of 59 days.[1] The tax rate and the dividends-to-earnings ratio are expected to stay constant.

The resulting pro forma financial statements appear in Table 4–3. Looking first at the income statement, the implication of the above assumptions is that earnings after tax will decline to $234,000. The only entry on this statement requiring further comment is net interest expense. Net interest expense will clearly depend on the size of the loan required by the company. However, because we do not know this yet, net interest expense is initially

---

[1]
$$\frac{\text{Payables}}{\text{period}} = \frac{\text{Accounts payable}}{\text{Cost of goods sold per day}} = \frac{14\% \text{ Sales}}{86\% \text{ Sales} \div 365}$$

Table 4–1
R&E SUPPLIES, INC.
Financial Statements
($000)

	December 31,			
	1978	1979	1980	1981
Income Statement				
Net sales................................	$11,190	$13,764	$16,104	$20,613
Cost of goods sold......................	9,400	11,699	13,688	17,727
Gross profit	1,790	2,065	2,416	2,886
Expenses:				
General, selling, administrative expenses ...	1,019	1,239	1,610	2,267
Net interest expense.....................	100	103	110	90
Income before tax	671	723	696	529
Tax....................................	302	325	313	238
Earnings after tax	$ 369	$ 398	$ 383	$ 291
Balance Sheet				
Assets				
Current assets:				
Cash and securities	$ 671	$ 551	$ 644	$ 412
Accounts receivable.....................	1,343	1,789	2,094	2,886
Inventories	1,119	1,376	1,932	2,267
Prepaid expenses	14	12	15	18
Total current assets..................	3,147	3,728	4,685	5,583
Net fixed assets	128	124	295	287
Total assets............................	$ 3,275	$ 3,852	$ 4,980	$ 5,870
Liabilities and Owners' Equity				
Current liabilities:				
Bank loan	$ 50	$ 50	$ 50	$ 50
Accounts payable......................	1,007	1,443	2,426	3,212
Current portion long-term debt............	60	50	50	100
Accrued wages........................	5	7	10	18
Total current liabilities	1,122	1,550	2,536	3,380
Long-term debt	960	910	860	760
Common stock.........................	150	150	150	150
Retained earnings.......................	1,043	1,242	1,434	1,580
Total liabilities and owners' equity...........	$ 3,275	$ 3,852	$ 4,980	$ 5,870

Table 4–2. Selected Financial Statement Items as a Percent of Sales for R&E Supplies, Inc.

	1978	1979	1980	1981	1982*
Annual increase in sales	—	23%	17%	28%	25%
Percent of sales:					
Cost of goods sold	84	85	85	86	86
General, selling, administrative expenses	9	9	10	11	12
Cash and securities	6	4	4	2	5
Accounts receivable	12	13	13	14	14
Inventories	10	10	12	11	10
Accounts payable	9	10	15	16	14
Tax ÷ Income before tax	.45	.45	.45	.45	.45
Dividends ÷ Earnings after tax	.50	.50	.50	.50	.50

*Forecast.

assumed to equal last year's value with the understanding that this assumption may have to be modified later.

Estimating the Plug. To most operating executives, a company's income statement is more interesting than its balance sheet because the income statement measures profitability. The reverse is true for the financial executive. When the object of the exercise is to estimate future financing requirements, the income statement is interesting only in so far as it affects the balance sheet. To the financial executive, the balance sheet is key.

The first entry on R&E's pro forma balance sheet (Table 4–3) that requires comment is prepaid expenses. Like accrued wages, prepaid expenses is a small item which increases erratically with sales. Since the amounts are small and a high degree of precision in the forecast is not required, rough estimates will suffice. When asked about new fixed assets, the president indicated that a capital budget in the amount of $43,000 had already been approved for 1982. Further, depreciation for the year would be $50,000, so net fixed assets would decline $7,000 to $280,000.

Note that the bank loan is labeled PLUG. This is the unknown in our problem. We will calculate the bank loan which must be plugged into the balance sheet to make total assets equal liabilities and owners' equity. Continuing down the balance sheet, current portion of long-term debt is just the principal repayment due in 1982. It is a contractual commitment specified in the loan agreement. As this required payment becomes a current liability, the accountant shifts it from long-term debt to current portion of long-term debt.

Table 4–3
R&E SUPPLIES, INC.
Pro Forma Financial Statements
($000)

	December 31, 1982	*Comments*
Income Statement		
Net sales..............................	$25,766	25% increase
Cost of goods sold....................	22,159	86% of sales
Gross profit	3,607	
Expenses:		
General, selling, administrative expenses ..	3,090	12% of sales
Net interest expense	90	Initially constant
Income before tax......................	425	
Tax	191	At 45%
Earnings after tax	$ 234	
Balance Sheet		
Assets		
Current assets:		
Cash and securities	$ 1,288	5% of sales
Accounts receivable...................	3,607	14% of sales
Inventories	2,577	10% of sales
Prepaid expenses	20	Rough estimate
Total current assets.................	7,492	
Net fixed assets	280	See text discussion
Total assets...........................	$ 7,772	
Liabilities and Owners' Equity		
Current liabilities:		
Bank loan...........................	PLUG	
Accounts payable.....................	$ 3,607	14% of sales
Current portion long-term debt	100	See text discussion
Accrued wages.......................	22	Rough estimate
Total current liabilities..............	3,279 + PLUG	
Long-term debt	660	
Common stock........................	150	
Retained earnings	1,697	See text discussion
Total liabilities and owners' equity	$ 6,236 + PLUG	

$$\text{Total assets} = \text{Total liabilities} + \text{Owners' equity} + \text{PLUG}$$
$$\$7,772,000 = \$6,236,000 + \text{PLUG}$$
$$\text{PLUG} = \$1,536,000$$

The last entry in need of explanation is retained earnings. Since the company does not plan to sell new equity in 1982, common stock remains constant. Retained earnings are determined as follows:

$$\text{Retained earnings}_{1982} = \text{Retained earnings}_{1981} + \text{Earnings after tax}_{1982} - \text{Dividends}_{1982}$$

$$\$1,697,000 = \$1,580,000 + \$234,000 - \$117,000$$

Sometimes companies will complicate this equation by charging nonrecurring gains or losses directly to retained earnings. But this is not a problem here.

The final step in constructing R&E's pro formas is to determine the size of the plug. We know from the principles of double entry bookkeeping that:

$$\text{Total assets} = \text{Liabilities} + \text{Owners' equity}$$

Using the forecast amounts, this means that:

$$\$7,772,000 = \$6,236,000 + \text{PLUG}$$
$$\text{PLUG} = \$1,536,000$$

According to our forecast, R&E Supplies needs not $500,000 but over $1.5 million to achieve the president's objectives.

The lending officer for Suburban National Bank is apt to be of two minds about this result. On one hand, R&E has a projected 1982 accounts receivable balance in excess of $3.5 million, which would probably provide excellent security for a $1.5 million loan. On the other hand, R&E's cavalier attitude toward financial planning and the president's obvious lack of financial knowledge would be definite negatives.

Pro Forma Statements and Financial Planning

To this point R&E's pro forma statements have just displayed the financial implications of the company's operating plans. This is the forecasting half of the problem. Now R&E management is ready to begin its financial planning. This involves the evaluation of its forecasts and the consideration of possible modifications. The first step in the process is to decide whether the initial pro formas are satisfactory. This involves an assessment of the financial health of the company as revealed in the pro formas. Special attention is devoted to determining whether the estimated plug is too large. If the answer is yes, either because R&E does not want to borrow $1.5 million or because the bank is unwilling to grant such a large loan, management must modify its plans to conform to its financial limitations. This is where operating plans and financial plans merge to create a coherent strategy.

To illustrate, suppose R&E management wants to reduce the size of the plug. It might thus decide to test the following revisions in its operating plans for their impact on the company's external financing needs: (1) moderate the buildup in liquidity so that cash and securities are only 4 percent of sales instead of 5, (2) tighten up collection of accounts receivable so that receivables are 12 percent of sales rather than 14 percent, and (3) settle for a more modest improvement in trade payables so that payables equal 15 percent of sales rather than 14 percent. In combination, these reductions in assets and increases in liabilities would reduce R&E's plug by just under $1 million [(3% reduction in assets + 1% increase in liabilities) × net sales = $1 million].

Although each of these actions reduces R&E's need for external financing, each clearly has some offsetting disadvantages; so we cannot say for certain that the revised operating plan is necessarily better than the original one. It should be evident, however, that the pro forma format is useful for evaluating the financial dimensions of alternative operating strategies.

Sensitivity Analysis

Sensitivity analysis is equivalent to asking a series of "what if" questions. What if R&E's sales grow by 15 percent instead of 25 percent? What if cost of goods sold is 84 percent of sales instead of 86 percent? It involves systematically changing one of the assumptions on which the pro forma statements are based and observing how the forecast responds. The exercise is useful for at least two reasons. First, it provides information about the range of possible outcomes. For example, suppose that sensitivity analysis reveals that depending on the future sales volume attained, a company's need for future external financing could vary between $1 and $2 million. This tells management that it had better provide enough flexibility in its financing plans to add another $1 million dollars in new debt as the future unfolds. A second use of sensitivity analysis involves management by exception. Sensitivity analysis enables managers to determine which assumptions strongly affect the forecast and which are secondary. This enables management to concentrate their data gathering and forecasting efforts on those assumptions which are critical. Subsequently during the implementation of the plan, it enables management to focus their efforts on those factors most critical to the success of the plan.

Simulation

Simulation is an elaborate, computer-assisted, extension of sensitivity analysis. To perform a simulation we begin by assigning a probability distribution to each uncertain parameter in the forecast. The distribution describes the possible values which the parameter could conceivably take on, and it states the probability that each value will occur. The next step is to ask a computer randomly to pick a value for each uncertain parameter consistent with the assigned probability distribution and to generate a set of pro forma statements based on the selected values. This creates one *trial.* Performing the last step many times produces a large number of trials. The output from a simulation is a table summarizing the results of many trials. For example, the output from a simulation study of R&E's loan needs for 1982 involving 1,000 trials might be the following.

Projected Loan Need	Number of Trials Occurring	Percent of Trials Occurring
$ 751,000–$1,000,000	150	15%
1,001,000– 1,250,000	200	20
1,251,000– 1,500,000	300	30
1,501,000– 1,750,000	200	20
1,751,000– 2,000,000	100	10
More than $2,000,000	50	5
Total	1,000	100%

The principal advantage of simulation over sensitivity analysis is that all of the uncertain input values are allowed to vary at once. Another advantage is that interdependencies among the uncertain parameters can be included. For example, if selling price and quantity sold are two uncertain parameters, simulation enables us to specify that the two parameters vary inversely; that is, a high selling price will be associated with a low quantity sold, and vice versa.

The principal disadvantage of simulation, in my experience, is that the results are often hard to interpret. One reason is that few executives are used to thinking about future events in terms of a range of possible outcomes or probabilities of outcomes. In terms of the above chart, should the company be prepared to raise in excess of $2 million, or is the 5 percent chance of this need occurring too remote to warrant concern? What is a reasonable maximum loan need the company should be prepared to meet?

A second reason simulation is less useful than sensitivity analysis in practice recalls President Eisenhower's dictum that "It's not the plans, but the planning." With simulation much of the "planning" occurs inside the computer, and management sees only the resulting plans. Consequently management does not develop the depth of insight into the plans, which occurs when simpler techniques are used.

Interest Expense.   One thing that bothers novices about pro forma forecasting is the circularity involving interest expense and indebtedness. As noted above with regard to R&E Supplies, net interest expense on the income statement cannot be estimated accurately until the plug has been determined. Yet because net earnings after tax affects the addition to retained earnings, the size of the plug depends on net interest expense. So how do you figure out one without knowing the other?

There are two responses to this question. One is that if we really want to, we can define a set of simultaneous equations to solve for interest expense and the plug. The other more pragmatic response is that given the likely forecast errors in predicting sales and other variables, the additional error caused by a failure to accurately determine interest expense is not crucial. To illustrate, R&E Supplies' pro formas assume a net interest expense of $90,000, whereas the balance sheet indicates that total interest-bearing debt will be over $2.2 million. At an assumed interest rate of 10 percent, this volume of debt implies an interest expense of $220,000. If we subtract, say, $20,000 for interest earned on newly purchased securities, net interest expense should be about $200,000. We are off by $110,000 in our estimate. But think what happens as we trace the impact of a $110,000 addition to interest expense through the income statement.

	Original	Revised	Difference
Gross profit.	$3,607	$3,607	
General, selling, administrative expenses.	3,092	3,092	
Net interest expense	90	200	+$110
Income before tax	425	315	− 110
Tax.	191	142	− 49
Earnings after tax.	234	173	− 61
Dividend at 50%	117	87	− 30
Addition to retained earnings	$ 117	$ 86	−$ 31

The increase in net interest expense reduces the addition to retained earnings by $31,000 and increases the plug by the like amount. But this is an increase of less than 1.5 percent in the plug. Increasing interest expense has a noticeable impact on income before tax, but by the time the increase filters through taxes and dividend payments, the impact on the plug is quite modest.

Seasonality. A more serious potential problem with pro forma statements and, indeed, all of the forecasting techniques mentioned in this chapter, is that the results are applicable only on the forecast date. The pro formas in Table 4–3 present an estimate of R&E Supplies' loan requirements on December 31, 1982. They say nothing about the company's need for financing on any other date before or after December 31. If a company has seasonal financing requirements, knowledge of year-end loan needs may be of little use in financial planning, since the year-end may bear no relation whatever to the date of the company's peak financing need. To protect against this, it is necessary to make monthly or quarterly forecasts rather than annual ones. Alternatively, if the date of peak borrowing need is known, you can simply make this date the forecast horizon.

Cash Flow Forecasts

A cash flow forecast is just a listing of all anticipated sources of cash to the company and uses of cash by the company over the forecast period. The difference between forecast sources and forecast uses is the plug, which must be financed externally. Table 4–4 shows a cash flow forecast for R&E Supplies for 1982. The assumptions underlying the forecast are the same as those used to construct R&E's pro forma statements. Note that the sources and uses are grouped in categories. One category, spontaneous sources of cash, deserves mention. In most businesses, some sources of cash arise in the normal course of trade. The company pays no directly measurable fee for these sources, nor must they negotiate for them. Instead the sources arise spontaneously. Examples of such spontaneous sources are accounts payable and accrued wages.

Cash flow forecasts are quite straightforward and easily understood. Their principal weakness compared to pro forma statements is that they are less informative. R&E's pro forma statements not only indicate the size of

Table 4–4
R&E SUPPLIES, INC.
Cash Flow Forecast
($000)

	December 31, 1981 to December 31, 1982
Sources of cash:	
Cash from operations:	
Earnings after tax	$ 234
Depreciation	50
Spontaneous sources of cash:	
Increase in accounts payable	395
Increase in accrued wages	4
Total sources of cash	683
Uses of cash:	
Investments:	
In fixed assets	43
In current assets	1,909
Financial payments:	
Dividends	117
Long-term debt repayment	100
Short-term debt repayment	50
Total uses of cash	$2,219

Determination of PLUG:

$$\text{Total sources} + \text{PLUG} = \text{Total uses}$$
$$\$683,000 + \text{PLUG} = \$2,219,000$$
$$\text{PLUG} = \$1,536,000$$

the loan required, they also provide information which is useful for evaluating the company's creditworthiness. Thus, the loan officer can evaluate the company's future financial position by analyzing the pro forma statements. Because the cash flow forecast presents only *changes* in the quantities represented, a similar analysis using cash flow forecasts would be much more difficult.

Cash Budgets

A cash budget is a list of all anticipated receipts of cash and disbursements of cash over the forecast period. It can be thought of as a detailed cash flow forecast in which all traces of accrual accounting have been eliminated.

Table 4–5 presents a monthly cash budget of TransInternational Manufac-

**Table 4–5. Cash Budget for TransInternational Manufacturing—
3rd Quarter, 1981 ($000)**

Raw Data

	Actual		Forecast		
	May	*June*	*July*	*August*	*September*
Credit sales	$10,000	14,000	16,000	19,000	15,000
Credit purchases	$ 5,000	6,000	5,000	12,000	6,000
Cash Budget					
Cash receipts:					
Sales for cash			$ 1,000	$ 1,000	$ 1,000
Collections from credit sales			10,000	14,000	16,000
(assumes 60-day lag sale to collection)					
Sale of used machinery				19,000	
Total cash receipts			20,000	34,000	17,000
Cash disbursements:					
Purchases for cash			1,000	1,000	2,000
Payment for credit purchases			14,000	16,000	19,000
(assumes 30-day lag purchase to payment)					
Wages and salaries			4,000	4,000	4,000
Interest payments					2,000
Principal repayments					10,000
Dividends					8,000
Tax payments			3,000		
Total cash disbursements			22,000	21,000	45,000
Net cash receipts (disbursements)			$(2,000)	$13,000	$(28,000)
Determination of cash needs:					
Beginning cash			$ 15,000	$13,000	$ 26,000
Net receipts (disbursements)			(2,000)	13,000	(28,000)
Ending cash			13,000	26,000	(2,000)
Minimum cash desired (assumed)			10,000	10,000	10,000
Cash surplus (deficit)			$ 3,000	$16,000	$(12,000)

turing (TIM) for the third quarter of 1981. To purge the accounting data of all accrual effects, it is necessary to remember that a period of time elapses between a credit sale or a credit purchase and the receipt or disbursement of the associated cash. In TIM's case, a 60-day collection period on accounts receivable means that there is an average lag of 60 days between a credit sale and the receipt of cash. Consequently, cash collections in any month equal credit sales two months prior. The analogous lag for credit purchases is one month. Note that depreciation does not appear on a cash budget because it does not involve a disbursement of cash.

The bottom portion of TIM's cash budget illustrates the determination of cash needs. Observe that the ending cash balance for one month becomes the beginning balance for the next month. Comparing the ending cash balance to the desired minimum balance, as determined by management, yields an estimate of TIM's monthly cash surplus or deficit. The deficit corresponds to the plug in a pro forma forecast; it is the amount of money which must be raised on the forecast date to cover the disbursements and to leave ending cash at the desired minimum. A forecast cash surplus means that the company will have excess cash on that date and that ending cash will exceed the desired minimum by the forecast amount.

Because a cash budget focuses so narrowly on the cash account, it is seldom used by nonfinancial executives as a general forecasting tool. Its principal application is by treasury specialists for managing the company's cash balances. TIM's cash budget suggests that surplus cash will be available for investment in July and August but that the investments chosen had better be liquid, because all of the excess cash, plus $12 million from other sources, will be required in September.

The Techniques Compared

Although the presentation of the information differs among the three forecasting techniques considered, it should come as a relief to learn that they all produce the same results. That is, as long as the assumptions are the same and no arithmetic or accounting mistakes occur, all three forecasting techniques will produce the same estimate of a company's need for new financing. Moreover, as long as the assumptions are the same, it is possible to transpose the forecast results from one format to another.

A second reassuring fact is that regardless of which forecasting technique is used, the resulting estimate of new financing needs is not biased by the presence of inflation. Consequently, there is no need to resort to elaborate inflation adjustments when making financial forecasts under inflation. This is not to say that the need for new financing is independent of the inflation rate. In fact, the financing needs of most companies rise with the inflation rate because inflation increases nominal sales and interest expense. Rather, we are saying that for a given set of estimates, including nominal sales, the forecasting techniques previously described correctly determine the need for external financing.

Mechanically, then, the three forecasting techniques are equivalent, and the choice of which to use can depend on the purpose to which the forecast is to be put. For most planning purposes and for credit analysis by lenders, pro forma statements are superior because they present the information in a form which is suitable for additional financial analysis. For short-term forecasting and the management of cash and securities, the cash budget is appropriate. The principal appeal of the cash flow forecast is that it presents a broader picture of company operations but can be understood more easily than pro forma statements by accounting novices.

Planning in a Large Company

In a well-run company, financial forecasts are only the tip of the planning iceberg. Executives throughout the organization devote substantial time and effort toward developing strategic and operating plans which eventually become the basis for the company's financial plans. This formalized planning process is especially important in large, multidivision corporations because planning is a key to coordination and communication within such organizations.

Effective planning in a large company usually involves three formal stages which recur on an annual cycle. In broad perspective, these stages can be viewed as a progressive narrowing of the strategic choices under consideration. In the first stage, headquarters executives and division managers hammer out a corporate strategy. This involves a broad-ranging analysis of the market threats and opportunities facing the company, an assessment of the company's own strengths and weaknesses, and a determination of the performance goals to be sought by each of the company's business units. At this initial stage, the process is creative and largely qualitative. The role of financial forecasts is limited to outlining in general terms the resource constraints faced by the company and to testing the financial feasibility of alternative strategies.

In the second stage, division managers and department personnel translate the qualitative, market-oriented goals established in stage 1 into a set of internal division activities that is deemed necessary to achieve the agreeupon goals. For example, if a stage 1 goal is to increase product X's market share by at least 2 percent in the next 18 months, the stage 2 plans define what division management must do to achieve this objective. At this point, headquarters management will likely have indicated, in general terms, the resources to be devoted to each division, although no specific spending plans will have been authorized. So division management will find it necessary to prepare at least rough financial forecasts to make certain their plans are generally consistent with senior management's resource commitments.

In the third stage of the planning process, department personnel develop a set of quantitative plans and budgets based on the activities defined in stage 2. This essentially involves putting a price tag on the agreed-upon division activities. The price tag appears in two forms: operating budgets and capital budgets. Although each company has its own definition of which expenditures are to appear on which budget, capital budgets customarily include expenditures on costly, long-lived assets, whereas operating budgets include recurring expenditures, such as materials, salaries, and so on.

The integration of these detailed divisional budgets at headquarters produces the corporation's financial forecast. If management has been realistic about available resources throughout the planning process, the forecast will contain few surprises. If not, headquarters executives may discover that in aggregate the spending plans of the divisions exceed available resources and that some revisions in division budgets will be necessary.

In Chapter 6, we will devote considerable attention to the financial analysis of investment opportunities. To put that material in perspective, it is important to realize that corporate investment decisions are not made in a vacuum. Rather, the investment decision is just a part of the planning process described above. This means that even though a capital expenditure proposal may apppear financially attractive, it is likely to be rejected by senior management unless it is consistent with the attainment of the agreed-upon corporate objectives. The proper perspective with regard to investment analysis is that the company's strategic plans create an umbrella under which operating and capital budgeting take place.

Chapter Summary

1. The purpose of this chapter has been to present the principal techniques of financial forecasting and planning.

2. Pro forma statements are the best all-around means of financial forecasting. They are a projection of the company's income statement and balance sheet at the end of the forecast period.

3. Percent-of-sales forecasting is a simple but useful technique in which most income statement and many balance sheet entries are assumed to change in proportion to sales.

4. Most operating managers are concerned chiefly with the income statement. When the goal is forecasting the need for outside financing, the income statement is of interest only insofar as income affects the balance sheet.

5. Financial forecasting involves the extrapolation of past trends and

agreed-upon changes into the future. Financial planning occurs when management evaluates the forecasts and considers possible modifications.

6. A cash budget is a less general way to forecast than pro forma statements. It consists of a list of anticipated cash receipts and disbursements and their net impact on the firm's cash balances. Done correctly and using the same assumptions, cash budgets and pro forma statements generate the same estimated need for outside financing.

7. Planning in most large companies involves three continuing cycles: (*a*) a strategic planning cycle in which senior management is most active, (*b*) an operational cycle in which divisional managers translate qualitative strategic goals into concrete plans, and (*c*) a budgeting cycle which essentially puts a price tag on the operational plans. Financial forecasting and planning are increasingly important in each succeeding stage of the process.

Additional Reading

Vancil, Richard F., ed. *Financial Executive's Handbook.* Homewood, Ill.: Dow Jones-Irwin, 1970. 1,314 pages.
A bit dated, but still a solid, practical set of readings. Part IV, Planning and Budgeting, is especially relevant to the material covered in this chapter.

Vancil, Richard F., and Peter Lorange. "Strategic Planning in Diversified Companies," *Harvard Business Review,* January–February 1975, pp. 81-90.
A more detailed discussion of the three-stage approach to planning discussed in this chapter.

Chapter Problems

1. Below are 1982 financial statements for Parker Pharmaceuticals. For 1983 assume that:

   Sales will increase 30 percent.

   Investment in fixed assets will be $30 million.

   Cost of goods sold, accounts receivable, inventories and accounts payable will rise in proportion to sales.

   General selling expenses, depreciation, the tax rate, dividends, long-term debt and common stock will not change.

   a. If Parker wants to maintain a minimum cash balance of at least $10 million, how large a bank loan will be required in 1983? You may ignore any increases in interest expense.

PARKER PHARMACEUTICALS
Income Statement and Balance Sheet
December 31, 1982
($ million)

Net sales	$100
Cost of goods sold	60
Gross profit..................	40
General selling expenses	10
Depreciation	10
Interest expense	5
Profit before tax	15
Tax at 33%	5
Profit after tax	10
Dividends paid	8
Additions to retained earnings...	$ 2

Assets		*Liabilities and Shareholders' Equity*	
Current assets:		Current liabilities:	
Cash	$ 10	Accounts payable.........	$ 8
Accounts receivable.......	17	Bank loan	22
Inventories	23	Total current	
Total current assets....	50	liabilities	30
Gross fixed assets	130	Long-term debt	50
Accumulated depreciation....	60	Common stock.............	20
Net fixed assets	70	Retained earnings	20
Total assets................	$120	Total liabilities and	
		shareholders' equity	$120

b. How large a bank loan will Parker need if its collection period rises to 75 days? (Assume all sales are on credit.)

2. The financial manager of Dashman Enterprises, a wholesale distributor of novelty toys, was interested in estimating the company's financing needs for the last three months of 1982. The following data were available:

Sales (one-half for cash, one-half on 30-day terms):

September actual	$300,000
October forecast	100,000
November forecast	40,000
December forecast	40,000

Purchases (all on 60-day credit terms):

August actual	100,000
September actual	200,000

October forecast	100,000
November forecast	20,000
December forecast	20,000
Wages, payable each month	30,000
Interest and principal payments, due in December	50,000
Dividends payable in December	60,000
Taxes payable in November	30,000
Cash balance October 1	150,000
Minimum desired cash balance	50,000

Construct a cash budget to estimate Dashman's financing needs for the last three months of 1982.

5 | Managing Growth

Growth and the management of growth present special problems in financial planning, in part because many executives see growth as something to be maximized. Their reasoning is simply that as growth increases, the firm's market share and profits should rise as well. From a financial perspective, however, growth is not always a blessing. Rapid growth can put considerable strain on a company's resources, and unless management is aware of this effect and takes active steps to control it, rapid growth can lead to bankruptcy. Companies literally can grow broke. It is a sad truth that almost as many companies go bankrupt because they grow too fast as do those who grow too slow. It is doubly sad to realize that those companies which grew too fast met the market test by providing a product people wanted and failed only because they lacked the financial acumen to manage their growth properly.

Our purpose in this chapter is to look at the financial dimensions of growth management. We begin by defining a company's *sustainable growth rate*. This is the maximum rate at which company sales can increase without depleting financial resources. Then we will look at the options open to management when a company's target growth rate exceeds its sustainable growth rate. An important conclusion will be that growth is not necessarily something to be maximized. In many companies, it may be necessary to limit growth to conserve financial strength. This is a hard lesson for operating managers used to thinking that more is better; however, it is a critical one because nonfinancial managers bear major responsibility for managing growth.

Sustainable Growth

It is possible to think of companies as passing through a predictable life cycle. The cycle begins with a start-up phase in which the company loses money while developing products and establishing a foothold in the market. This is followed by a rapid growth phase in which the company is profitable but is growing so rapidly it needs regular infusions of outside financing. The third phase is maturity, characterized by a decline in growth and a switch from absorbing outside financing to generating more cash than it can profitably reinvest. The last phase is decline during which the company is perhaps marginally profitable, generates more cash than it can reinvest internally, and has declining sales. Mature and declining companies typically devote considerable time and money to seeking investment opportunities in new products or firms which are still in their growth phases.

Although each phase of a company's life cycle presents its own financial challenges, our discussion will begin by looking at the growth phase when financing needs are most pressing. Later in the chapter we will consider briefly the growth problems of mature and declining firms. Central to our discussion is the notion of sustainable growth. Intuitively, sustainable growth is just a formalization of the old adage, "It takes money to make money." Increased sales require more assets of all types which must be paid for. Retained profits and the accompanying new borrowing generate some cash but only in limited amounts. Unless the company is prepared to sell common stock, this limit puts a ceiling on the growth a company can achieve without straining its resources. This is the firm's sustainable growth rate.

The Sustainable Growth Equation

Let's begin by writing a simple equation to express the dependence of growth on financial resources. For this purpose, assume the following:

The company wants to grow as rapidly as market conditions permit.

Management is unwilling or unable to sell new equity.

The company has a target debt-to-equity ratio and a target dividend payout ratio which it wishes to maintain.

I will say more about these assumptions in a few pages. Presently, it is sufficient to realize that although they are certainly not appropriate for all firms, the assumptions are descriptive of a great many.

The variables used in the equation are:

P = the profit margin on all sales
D = the target dividend payout ratio (Dividends ÷ Earnings)
L = the target total debt to equity ratio
T = the ratio of total assets to sales

S = annual sales

ΔS = the increase in sales during the year

To develop the sustainable growth equation, refer to Figure 5–1 which shows a company's balance sheet as two rectangles, one for assets, the other for liabilities and owners' equity. The two long, unshaded rectangles repre-

Figure 5–1. New Sales Require New Assets Which Must Be Financed

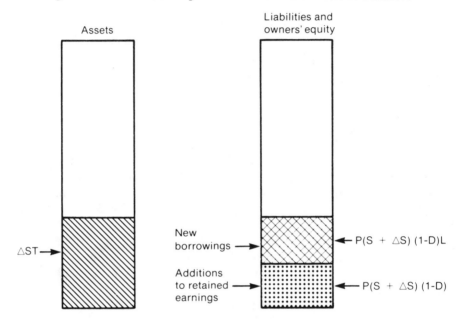

sent the company's balance sheet at the beginning of the year. Now if the company wants to increase sales by $\$\Delta S$ during the year, it must increase its assets. Assuming the assets-to-sales ratio, T, is constant over time, the required increase in assets is just ΔST. This is shown in the figure as the cross-hatched area in the assets column.

Because the company is not raising new equity by assumption, the cash to finance this increase in assets must come from retained profits and new borrowings. The retained profits are just:

Retained profits = Profits − Dividends

            = Profit margin × Total sales − Dividends

            = $P(S + \Delta S)(1 - D)$

Further, because the company wants to maintain a target debt-to-equity ratio equal to L, each dollar added to owners' equity enables it to increase its indebtedness $L. And since owners' equity will rise over the year by an amount equal to retained profits,

$$\text{New borrowings} = \text{Retained profits} \times \text{Target debt-to-equity ratio}$$
$$= P(S + \Delta S)(1 - D)L$$

The final step is to recognize that the use of cash represented by the increase in assets must equal the two sources of cash, retained profits and new borrowings.

$$\text{Uses of cash} = \text{Sources of cash}$$
$$\text{Increased assets} = \text{Retained profits} + \text{New borrowings}$$
$$\Delta ST = P(S + \Delta S)(1 - D) + P(S + \Delta S)(1 - D)L$$

Using a little algebra to rewrite this expression:[1]

$$\frac{\Delta S}{S} = g^* = \frac{P(1 - D)(1 + L)}{T - P(1 - D)(1 + L)}$$

This is the sustainable growth equation. Let's see what it tells us. $\Delta S/S$ is the growth rate in company sales, which we will refer to as g^*. It is the firm's sustainable growth rate. The equation says that given the assumptions noted above, a company's growth rate in sales must equal the indicated combination of four ratios P, D, L, and T. Further, *g* is the only growth rate in sales which is consistent with stable values of the four ratios.* If a company increases sales at any rate other than g^*, one or more of the ratios *must* change. For example, suppose a company grows at a rate in excess of its sustainable growth rate. Then it must either use its assets more efficiently (represented by an increase in the profit margin or a decrease in the assets-to-sales ratio), or it must alter its financial policies (represented by reducing its payout ratio or increasing its leverage).

The Sustainable Growth Problem

This is the crux of the sustainable growth problem: Because increasing operating efficiency is not always possible and altering financial policies is not always wise, we see that it is entirely possible for a company to grow too fast for its own good. This is particularly true among smaller companies which may do too little financial planning. Such companies see sales growth as something to be maximized and think too little of the financial consequences. They do not realize that rapid growth has them on a treadmill; the

---

[1]Write the equation as:

$$\Delta ST = P(S + \Delta S)(1 - D)(1 + L)$$
$$\Delta ST = P(1 - D)(1 + L)S + P(1 - D)(1 + L)\Delta S$$
$$\Delta S[T - P(1 - D)(1 + L)] = P(1 - D)(1 + L)S$$

$$\frac{\Delta S}{S} = \frac{P(1 - D)(1 + L)}{T - P(1 - D)(1 + L)}$$

faster they grow, even if they are profitable, the more cash they need. They can meet this need for a time by increasing leverage, but eventually the company will reach its debt capacity, lenders will refuse additional credit requests, and the company will find itself without the cash to pay its bills. All of this can be prevented if managers understand that growth above the company's sustainable rate creates financial problems which must be anticipated and solved. We will return to strategies for managing growth after looking at some numerical examples.

Tektronix's Sustainable Growth Rate

To illustrate the sustainable growth equation, let us return to the company discussed in Chapters 1 and 2 and calculate Tektronix, Inc.'s sustainable growth rate for the period 1976–1979. Tables 1–1, 1–2, and 2–3 present financial statements and selected ratios for TEK during this period. Table 5–1 presents the company's actual and sustainable growth rates in sales an-

Table 5–1. Tektronix, Inc., Sustainable Growth Calculations (percent)

		1976	1977	1978	1979
Required ratios:					
Profit margin	(P)	8.2%	9.7%	9.5%	9.8%
Assets to sales	(T)	94.1	91.3	82.0	81.4
Dividend payout	(D)	7.0	9.0	18.8	11.2
Debt to equity	(L)	48.7	51.5	50.2	59.6
TEK's sustainable growth rate	(g*)	13.7	15.0	16.5	20.6
TEK's actual growth rate	(g)	8.9	24.1	31.6	31.4

nually for the years in question. For each year, the sustainable growth rate was calculated by plugging the values of the four required ratios for that year into the sustainable growth equation. Two trends are evident in the table. One is that TEK has increased its sustainable growth rate each year. It has done this on the operating side by increasing P and reducing T and on the financial side by increasing L. These changes have outweighed the modest increase in D. The second trend is that despite these increases in g*, actual growth in sales has been well above the sustainable growth rate.

What does this imply? As of 1979, TEK can increase sales at a 20.6 percent annual rate forever without changing the four critical ratios. If TEK's actual growth rate in the future exceeds 20.6 percent, one or more of these ratios must change. Of particular concern to management is the noticeable increase in leverage. TEK is presently a conservatively financed company and would like to stay that way. However, this objective may not be consistent with the type of sales increases experienced over the last three years. TEK management may have to decide exactly how much growth they can afford.

R&E Supplies' Sustainable Growth Rate

R&E Supplies, the wholesale distributor considered in the last chapter, finds itself in an even more dangerous situation. Table 5–2 shows that the gap between R&E's actual growth rate and its sustainable growth rate is steadily widening, due primarily to a falling profit margin. The result has

Table 5–2. R&E Supplies, Inc., Sustainable Growth Calculations (percent)

		1978	1979	1980	1981	Pro Forma 1982
Required ratios:						
Profit margin	(P)	3.3%	2.9%	2.4%	1.4%	0.9%
Assets to sales	(T)	29.3	28.0	30.9	28.5	30.2
Dividend payout	(D)	50.0	50.0	50.0	50.0	50.0
Debt to equity	(L)	175.0	177.0	214.0	239.0	321.0
R&E's sustainable growth rate	(g*)	18.3	16.7	13.9	9.1	6.7
R&E's actual growth rate	(g)	—	23.0	17.0	28.0	25.0

What if?

	Dividend Payout 20%	Profit Margin 1.9%	Assets-to- Sales 29.2%	All of These Occur
R&E's sustainable growth rate in 1982	11.2%	15.3%	6.9%	28.1%

been an increasing reliance on debt financing. Note that the debt-to-equity ratio has increased from 175 percent in 1978 to a pro forma 1982 figure of 321 percent. As noted in the last chapter, the pro forma bank loan required for 1982 may be possible to obtain, but the trend is a very unhealthy one. In the near future, R&E will reach its debt capacity and will be unable to raise added debt without a significant increase in equity. At this point, R&E will be without the money necessary to pay for added growth. If R&E and its creditors realize what is happening in the near future, remedial action is possible; if not, the probable outcome will be bankruptcy.

"What If" Questions

Once management realizes that it has sustainable growth problems, the sustainable growth equation can be useful in searching for solutions. This is done through a series of "what if" questions, as shown in the bottom portion of Table 5–2. We see, for example, that if R&E Supplies will reduce its payout ratio from 50 percent to 20 percent, its sustainable growth rate in 1982 will rise from 6.7 percent to 11.2 percent. Similarly, a one percentage point increase in the profit margin, holding everything else constant, increases sustainable growth to 15.3 percent, while a one percentage point reduction in the assets-to-sales ratio increases sustainable growth only marginally to 6.9 percent. If R&E did all of these things at the same time, sustainable growth would rise to 28.1 percent, thereby solving its sustainable growth problems. As noted in the last chapter, "What If" questions such as these are an example of sensitivity analysis.

What to Do When Actual Growth Exceeds Sustainable Growth

We have now developed the sustainable growth equation and illustrated its use. The remaining question is what should management do when actual growth exceeds sustainable growth. The first step is to determine how long the situation is likely to continue. If the company's growth rate is likely to decline in the near future as the firm reaches maturity, the problem is only a transitory one which probably can be solved by further borrowing. Then in the future when the actual growth rate falls below the sustainable rate, the company will switch from an absorber of cash to a generator of cash, and the loans can be repaid. For longer-term sustainable growth problems some combination of the strategies described below will be necessary.

Sell New Equity

If a company is willing and able to raise new equity capital by selling shares, its sustainable growth problems vanish. The increased equity, plus whatever added borrowing is possible as a result of the increased equity, are sources of cash with which to finance further growth.

The problem with this strategy is that it is not available to many companies and unattractive to many others. In most countries throughout the world, equity markets are poorly developed or nonexistent. To sell equity in these countries, companies must go through the laborious and expensive task of seeking out investors directly to buy the new shares. This is a difficult task because, without active stock market trading of the shares, new investors will become minority owners of illiquid securities. The result is that those investors interested in buying the new shares will be limited largely to friends and acquaintances of existing owners.

Even in countries with well-developed stock markets, such as the United States, many companies find it very difficult to raise new equity. This is particularly true of smaller concerns which, unless they have a glamorous product, find it difficult to secure the services of an investment banker to help them sell the shares. Without such help, the firms might just as well be in a country without developed markets. For a lack of trading in the stock will again restrict potential buyers largely to friends and acquaintances.

Finally, even those companies that, because of their size and location, have the ability to raise new equity seldom do. This is evidenced in Figure 5–2 which is a pie chart showing the sources of capital to U.S. nonfinancial

Figure 5–2. Sources of Corporate Capital to U.S. Nonfinancial Corporations, 1960–1980

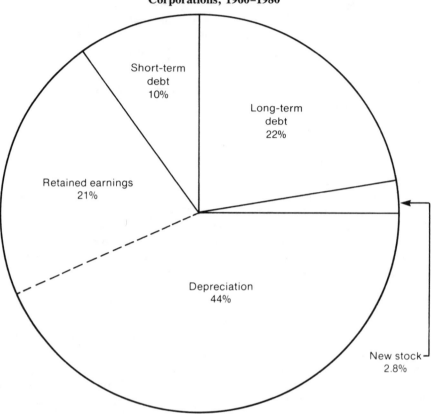

Source: *Survey of Current Business,* U.S. Department of Commerce and *Federal Reserve Bulletin,* Board of Governors of Federal Reserve System, Washington, D.C. Various issues.

corporations over the period 1960–1980. Observe that internal sources, depreciation and increases in retained earnings, were by far the most important sources of corporate capital over this period, accounting for about two thirds of the total. At the other extreme, new equity has averaged only about 3 percent of total sources over the period. This percentage would be even lower if we removed public utilities, which issue about one half of all new equity from the sample. My guess is that with public utilities removed, new equity has provided less than 2 percent of total corporate capital over the past two decades.

Figure 5–3 shows new equity as a percent of total capital to U.S. nonfinancial companies on a year-by-year basis. The highest percentage attained was about 10 percent in 1970, whereas in two years, 1963 and 1968,

Figure 5–3. External Equity as a Percent of Total Corporate Sources of Capital to U.S. Nonfinancial Corporations, 1960–1980

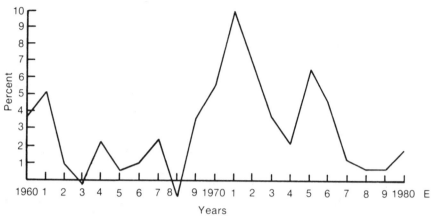

Source: *Survey of Current Business,* U.S. Department of Commerce and *Federal Reserve Bulletin,* Board of Governors of Federal Reserve System, Washington, D.C. Various issues.

new equity was a negative source, or a use, of capital. In these two years companies in aggregate repurchased more shares in terms of value than they issued. Ironically, U.S. companies' reliance on new equity has varied *inversely* with stock prices. In direct opposition to the old buy low–sell high strategy, companies sold very few shares during the late 1960s when stock prices were high but relied more heavily on new equity in the early 1970s as prices fell. This does not speak well of executives' ability to time new equity issues.

Why Don't U.S. Corporations Issue More Equity? There are a number of reasons companies do not sell more equity, none completely convincing. First, new equity is expensive to issue. Issue costs commonly run in the neighborhood of 5 to 10 percent of the amount raised, with the percentage even higher on small issues. This is at least twice as high as the issue costs for a comparable size debt issue. On the other hand, the equity is outstanding forever, so its effective annualized cost is modest. Second, many managers, especially U.S. managers, have a fixation on earnings per share (EPS). They translate a complicated world into the simple notion that whatever increases EPS must be good, and whatever reduces EPS must be bad. In this view, a new equity issue is bad because, at least initially, the number of shares outstanding rises but earnings do not. EPS is said to have been *diluted.* Later, as the company makes productive use of the money it raised, earnings should increase, but in the meantime EPS has suffered. Moreover, as we will see in a later chapter, EPS is almost always higher when debt financing is used in favor of equity.

A third reason companies do not raise more equity is what might be called the "market doesn't appreciate us" syndrome. When a company's stock is selling for $10 a share, management has a tendency to think that the price will be a little higher in the future as soon as the current strategy begins to bear fruit. When the price rises to $15, management tends to think this is just the beginning and that the price will be even higher in the near future. An inherent enthusiasm on the part of managers for their company's prospects produces a feeling that the firm's shares are undervalued at whatever price they currently command, and it creates a bias toward forever postponing new equity issues.

A fourth, and more substantive, reason companies avoid equity financing involves uncertainty. In the United States, the time lag between when a company elects to sell new equity and when it actually gets the cash is usually 60–90 days. During this period, the company has committed itself to raising new equity but does not know the price at which the shares can be sold. And in the stock market 60–90 days can be an eternity. If the stock price falls precipitously during this registration period, the company will be faced with the disagreeable choice of selling the shares on unfavorable terms or of canceling the issue.

In addition to price uncertainty, companies also face the possibility that during some future periods the stock market will not be receptive to new equity issues on any reasonable terms. In finance jargon, the "window" is said to be shut at these times. Naturally, managers are reluctant to develop a growth strategy which is dependent on such an unreliable source of capital. Rather, the philosophy is to formulate growth plans which can be financed from retained profits and accompanying borrowing and to relegate new equity financing to a minor backup role.

Increase Leverage

If selling new equity is not a solution to a company's sustainable growth problems, two other financial remedies are possible. One is to cut the dividend payout ratio, and the other is to increase leverage. A reduction in the payout ratio increases sustainable growth by increasing the proportion of earnings retained in the business, while increasing leverage raises the amount of debt the company can add for each dollar of retained profits.

We will have considerably more to say about leverage in the next two chapters. However, it should be apparent already that there are limits to the use of debt financing. As previously noted, all companies have a creditor-imposed debt capacity which restricts the amount of leverage the firm can employ. Moreover, as leverage increases, the risks borne by owners and creditors rise, as do the costs of securing additional capital.

Reduce the Payout Ratio

Just as there is an upper limit to leverage, there is a lower limit of zero to a company's dividend payout ratio. In general, owners' interest in dividend payments varies inversely with their perceptions of the company's investment opportunities. If owners believe that the retained profits can be put to productive use earning attractive rates of return, they will be willing to forgo current dividends in favor of higher future ones. If the investment opportunities do not promise attractive returns, a reduction in current dividends or in the payout ratio will cause a decline in stock price. An added concern for closely held companies is the impact of changing dividends on the owners' income and tax liabilities.

Profitable Pruning

Beyond modifications in financial policy, there are several operating adjustments a company can make to manage its growth. One is called "profitable pruning." During much of the 1960s and early 1970s, financial experts emphasized the merits of product diversification. The idea was that companies could reduce risk by combining the income streams of businesses in different product markets. As long as these income streams were not affected in exactly the same way by economic events, the thought was that the variability inherent in each stream would "average out" when combined with others. We now recognize two problems with this conglomerate diversification strategy. One is that although it may reduce the risks seen by management, it does nothing for the shareholders. For if shareholders want diversification, they can get it on their own by just purchasing shares of different independent companies. The second problem with conglomerate diversification is that because companies have limited resources, they cannot be important competitors in a large number of product markets at the same time. Instead, they are apt to be followers in many markets, holding small shares and unable to compete effectively with the dominant firms.

Profitable pruning is the opposite of conglomerate merger. It recognizes that when a company spreads its resources across too many products, it may not be able to compete effectively in any. Better to sell off marginal operations and plow the money back into remaining businesses.

Profitable pruning reduces sustainable growth problems in two ways: It generates cash directly through the sale of marginal businesses, and it reduces actual sales growth by eliminating some of the sources of the growth. This strategy was successfully used by Cooper Industries, a large Texas company, in the mid-1970s. Cooper sold several of its divisions during this time, not because they were unprofitable, but rather because Cooper did not believe it had the resources to become a dominant factor in the markets involved.

Profitable pruning is also possible for a single product company. Here, the idea is to prune out slow-paying customers or slow-turning inventory. This lessens sustainable growth problems in three ways. It frees up cash which can be used to support new growth; it reduces the assets to sales ratio, T; and it reduces sales. The strategy will reduce sales because tightening credit terms and reducing inventory selection will drive away some customers.

Sourcing

Sourcing involves the decision of whether to perform an activity in-house or to purchase it from an outside vendor. A company can increase its sustainable growth rate by sourcing more and doing less in-house. When a company sources, it releases assets which would otherwise be tied up in performing the activity, and it reduces its assets to sales ratio. Both diminish growth problems. An extreme example of this strategy is a franchisor who sources out virtually all of the company's capital intensive activities to franchisees and who, as a result, has very little investment.

The key to effective sourcing is determining where the company's distinctive competence lies. If a clear distinctive competence can be identified and if peripheral activities are not critical to the maintenance of this competitive edge, they can be sourced. An example, is Tektronix, Inc. TEK's distinctive competence is clearly in the design and, to a lesser extent, the manufacture of high-technology, electronic equipment. Nonetheless, the company owns a $3 million facility which makes plastic knobs. TEK could easily purchase the same knobs from any one of a number of companies; yet for historical reasons, they make their own. In the future, if financing growth becomes a serious problem at TEK, the knob factory should be considered for possible sale.

Pricing

An obvious inverse relationship exists between price and revenue. When sales growth is too high relative to a company's financing capabilities, it may be necessary to raise prices to reduce the growth. If higher prices increase the profit margin, the price increase will also raise the sustainable growth rate.

Looking again at R&E Supplies' growth problem, it is possible that R&E has been, in effect, buying sales by underpricing competition. This is consistent with the rapid sales growth and the declining profit margin. A price increase might establish a proper balance between sales growth and profitability.

Is Merger the Answer?

When all else fails, it may be necessary to look for a partner. Two types of companies are capable of supplying the needed cash. One is a mature company, known in the trade as a "cash cow," looking for profitable investments for its excess cash flow. The other is a conservatively financed company which would bring liquidity and borrowing capacity to the marriage. Acquiring another company or being acquired by another company is a drastic solution to growth problems. But it is better to merge when a company is still financially strong than to wait until excessive growth forces the issue.

Slow-Growth Firms Have Problems, Too

From the preceding discussion, it may appear that only rapidly expanding companies have growth problems, but this is not the case. Slow-growth firms—those for which the sustainable growth rate exceeds actual growth—have problems, too, but they are of a different kind. Rather than struggling continually for fresh cash to stoke the fires of growth, slow-growth companies face the dilemma of what to do with profits in excess of company needs. This might appear to be an enviable or even trivial problem, but to many companies it is a very real and occasionally frightening one.

Slow-growth companies have three ways to dispose of excess cash. The most direct is to return it to shareholders as dividends or share repurchases. This is certainly done, but there appear to be limits to the practice. The U.S. tax code encourages earnings retention by fully taxing dividends at the corporate and again at the personal level, so that even mediocre investments by corporations can be more attractive to shareholders than increased dividends. More importantly, many managers are psychologically opposed to paying large dividends because the practice hints of failure. Shareholders entrust managers with the task of profitably investing their capital, and for management to return the money suggests an inability to perform a basic managerial function. A cruder way to say the same thing is that dividends reduce the size of management's empire, an act counter to basic human nature.

A second option is to let the cash accumulate as excess liquid assets and unused borrowing capacity. The difficulty here is that corporate capital is suboptimally employed under such a scheme, and, of more immediate concern to management, the firm becomes a likely acquisition target. Underemployed resources produce a depressed stock price and attract raiders intent on redeploying the resources in search of greater profits. And among the first resources to be redeployed in such a raid is incumbent management, who find themselves suddenly reading help wanted ads.

Motivated by pride in their ability as managers and fear of raiders, the usual managerial response to excess cash flow is diversification. Management systematically searches for worthwhile growth opportunities in other more vibrant industries. The principal growth management problem in slow-growth companies, then, is the effective redeployment of resources through mergers and acquisitions. This is a complex and challenging task involving issues, such as the location of growth opportunities, the determination of which opportunities are most consistent with existing managerial skills, the estimation of an appropriate acquisition price and financing package, and the integration of the new acquisition into existing operations.

It is worthwhile to note that important aspects of the growth management problems of mature or declining companies are mirror images of those of rapidly growing firms. It is natural, therefore, that both types of companies will frequently solve their problems by merging, so that the excess cash generated by one organization can finance the rapid growth of the other. From either perspective—slow or rapid growth—knowledge of a company's sustainable growth rate is an important starting point in identifying growth management problems.

Sustainable Growth and Inflation

Growth comes from two sources: increasing volume and increasing prices. Unfortunately, the amount of money a company must invest to support a dollar of inflationary growth is about the same as the investment required to support a dollar of real growth. Imagine a company which has no real growth—it makes and sells the same number of items every year—but which is experiencing 10 percent inflationary growth. Then even though it has the same number of units in inventory, each unit will cost more in nominal terms to build, so the total investment in inventory will be higher. The same is true with accounts receivable. The same volume of customers will purchase the same number of units, but because each unit has a higher nominal selling price, the total investment in accounts receivable will be higher.

A company's investment in fixed assets behaves similarly under inflation but with a delay. When the inflation rate increases, there is no immediate need for more fixed assets. The existing fixed assets can produce the same number of units. However, as the existing assets wear out and are replaced at higher prices, the company's investment in fixed assets rises.

This inflationary increase in assets must be financed just as if it were real growth. It is fair to say then that inflation worsens a company's growth management problems. The degree to which this occurs depends primarily on the degree to which management and creditors understand the impact of inflation on company financial statements.

As noted in Chapter 3, inflation does at least two things to company financial statements. First, it increases the amount of external financing required, and second, in the absence of new equity financing it increases the company's debt-to-equity ratio when *measured on its historical cost financial statements*. This combination can spell trouble. If management or creditors require that the company's historical cost debt-to-equity ratio stay constant over time, inflation will lower the company's real sustainable growth rate. If the sustainable growth rate is 15 percent without inflation, the real sustainable growth rate will fall to about 5 percent when the inflation rate is 10 percent. Intuitively under inflation, cash that would otherwise support real growth must be used to finance inflationary growth.

If managers and creditors understand the effects of inflation, this inverse relation between inflation and the sustainable growth rate need not exist. It is true that the amount of external financing required does rise with the inflation rate. However, because the real value of company liabilities is declining, the *net* increase in external financing may be little affected. Using a *constant dollar* debt-to-equity ratio, the impact of inflation is correctly seen to be much less severe.

In sum, with historical cost financial statements, inflationary growth appears to substitute for real growth on almost a one-for-one basis—each one percentage point increase in inflation appears to reduce the real sustainable growth rate by the same amount. However, using more accurate, inflation-adjusted financial statements, inflation turns out to have relatively little effect on sustainable growth. Let us hope that executives can convince their bankers of this fact.

Sustainable Growth and Pro Forma Statements

It is important to keep the material presented here in perspective. The sustainable growth equation is useful for highlighting the tie between a company's growth rate and its financial resources; however, it is really nothing more than a simplification of pro forma statements. It is possible to learn as much or more about a company's growth management problems with pro forma statements as with the sustainable growth equation. The appeal of the sustainable growth equation is its simplicity and its focus on the company's steady state growth potential.

Chapter Summary

1. The purpose of this chapter has been to study the financial management of growth.

2. Unless a company is willing and able to raise new equity, more growth

is not always a blessing. Without careful financial planning, companies can literally grow broke.

3. A company's sustainable growth rate is the maximum rate it can grow without depleting financial resources. More precisely, it is the growth rate in sales consistent with stable values of four ratios: the profit margin, the assets-to-sales ratio, the dividend payout ratio and the debt-to-equity ratio.

4. If a company's actual growth rate *temporarily* exceeds its sustainable rate, the required capital can likely be provided by increased borrowing.

5. When actual growth exceeds sustainable growth for longer periods, management must formulate a financial strategy from among the following options: sell new equity, permanently increase financial leverage, reduce dividends, liquidate marginal operations, source more activities, increase prices, or find a merger partner.

6. For a variety of not very convincing reasons, most businesses are reluctant to sell new equity.

7. When actual growth is less than the sustainable growth rate, management's principal financial problem is finding productive uses for the excess cash flows. The options are to increase dividends, reduce liabilities, increase liquid assets, or search for attractive growth opportunities in other businesses.

8. If managers and creditors base decisions on historical cost financial statements, inflation reduces a company's sustainable growth rate. If they use inflation adjusted statements, inflation has comparatively little impact on sustainable growth.

Additional Reading

Abell, Derek F., and John S. Hammond. *Strategic Market Planning: Problems and Analytical Approaches.* Englewood Cliffs, N.J.: Prentice-Hall, 1979. 527 pages.
    Part marketing, part strategic planning, part finance, this book reviews recent techniques for growth planning, including experience curves, product portfolios, and PIMS project.

Helfert, Erich A. *Techniques of Financial Analysis,* 5th ed. Homewood, Ill.: Richard D. Irwin, 1982. 304 pages.
    An exceptionally well-written introduction to financial analysis for managers. Chapter 6, Business as a Dynamic System, is particularly good.

Higgins, Robert C. "Sustainable Growth under Inflation." *Financial Management,*
Autumn 1981, pp. 36–40.
A look at the dependence of a company's sustainable growth rate on the
inflation rate. Paper concludes that inflation will reduce sustainable growth
only if an "inflation illusion" exists.

Chapter Problems

1. Below are financial data for H. J. Heinz Company

			($ millions)		
	1981	1980	1979	1978	1977
Income	167	143	110	100	87
Net sales	3,569	2,925	2,471	2,159	1,877
Total assets	2,074	1,954	1,624	1,351	1,289
Dividends	57	51	44	35	27
Equity	987	870	778	711	663
Liabilities	1,087	1,084	846	640	626

   a. Calculate Heinz's sustainable growth rate in each year.
   b. Comparing Heinz's sustainable growth rate to its actual growth rate
in sales, what growth management problems does the company appear to have faced over this period?
   c. How does Heinz appear to have coped with these problems?
   d. If in 1980 Heinz had cut its dividend to $25 million, what impact
would this change have had on the company's sustainable growth
rate in that year?

2. Universal Electronics is a rapidly growing telecommunications company. Plans for 1984 called for a 20 percent increase in sales to $600
million and a corresponding $100 million increase in assets. The profit
margin was forecast to be 10 percent. Management was determined to
keep the total debt-to-equity ratio at 25 percent. Universal did not pay
dividends.
   a. How much new equity must Universal raise to finance the necessary increase in assets?
   b. If Universal presently has 120 million common shares outstanding,
what would earnings per share be in the absence of a new equity
issue?
   c. If Universal's earnings per share last year were $.40 and if it sells
new shares at a price-to-earnings ratio of 12 based on these earnings, what impact will the new equity issue have on earnings per
share calculated in (*b*)? (You may assume that the 10 percent profit
margin is after subtracting all relevant interest expense.)
   d. As a shareholder, how would you react to this change in pro forma
earnings per share?

PART III Financing Operations

6 Financial Instruments and Markets

A major part of the financial executive's job is raising external capital to finance current operations and future growth. In this capacity, the financial manager acts much like a marketing manager. He or she has a product—claims on the company's future income—which must be packaged and sold to yield the highest price to the company. The financial manager's customers are creditors and investors who put money into the business in anticipation of future income. In return these customers receive a *financial security,* such as a stock certificate or a bond, which describes the nature of their claim on the firm's future income.

In packaging his product, the financial executive must select or design a financial security which meets the needs of the company and which is attractive to potential creditors and investors. To do this effectively requires knowledge of financial instruments, of the markets in which they trade, and of the merits of each instrument to the issuing company. This chapter considers the first two topics—financial instruments and markets—and the next chapter looks at the proper choice of a financing instrument from the company's perspective.

Financial Instruments

Fortunately, lawyers and regulators have not yet removed all creativity from raising money. When selecting a financial instrument for sale in securities markets a company is *not* significantly constrained by law or regulation. The company is largely free to select or design any instrument provided only that it appeals to investors and meets the needs of the company. Securities markets in the United States are regulated by the Securities and Exchange Commission (SEC) and, to a lesser extent, by state authorities. SEC regulation creates a lot of red tape and delay; however, the SEC does not pass judgment on the investment merits of a security. It requires only that investors have access to all information relevant to valuing the security and that they have adequate opportunity to evaluate it before purchase. This freedom has given rise to such unusual securities as Litton Industries' prior preference convertible preferred stock and Foote Minerals' $2.20 cumulative, if earned, convertible preferred stock.

But do not let the variety of securities obscure the underlying logic. When designing a financial instrument, the financial executive works with three broad variables: the investor's claim on future income, his right to participate in company decisions, and his claim on company assets in liquidation. Below we will describe the more popular security types in terms of these three variables. In reading the descriptions, bear in mind that the characteristics of a specific financial instrument are determined by the terms of the contract between issuer and buyer, not by law or regulation. So the descriptions below should be thought of as indicative of general security types rather than exact definitions of specific securities.

Bonds

A bond, like any other form of indebtedness, is a *fixed-income* security. The holder receives a specified annual interest income and a specified amount at maturity, no more and no less—unless the company goes bankrupt. The difference between a bond and other forms of indebtedness, such as trade credit, bank loans and private placements, is that bonds are sold to the public in small increments, usually $1,000 per bond. After issue the bonds can be traded by investors on organized security exchanges.

Three variables characterize a bond: *par value, coupon rate,* and *maturity date.* For example, a typical bond might have a $1,000 par value, a 14 percent coupon rate and a maturity date of December 31, 1990. The par value is the amount of money the holder will receive on the bond's maturity date. By custom, the par value of bonds issued in the United States is usually $1,000. The coupon rate is the percentage of par value the holder will receive annually. The above bond will pay $140 per year in interest (14% × $1,000), usually in two semiannual payments of $70 each. On the maturity date, the company will pay the bondholder $1,000 per bond and will cease further interest payments.

On the issue date, companies usually try to set the coupon rate on the new bond equal to the prevailing interest rate on other bonds of similar maturity and quality. This assures that the bond's initial market price will about equal its par value. After issue, the market price of a bond can differ substantially from its par value as market interest rates change. As we will see in a later chapter, when interest rates rise, bond prices fall, and vice versa.

Most forms of long-term indebtedness require periodic repayment of principal. This principal repayment is known as a *sinking fund.* Technically, a sinking fund is a sum of money set aside by the company to meet a future obligation, and this is the way bonds used to work, but no more. Today, a bond sinking fund is a direct payment to creditors which reduces principal. Depending on the indebenture agreement, there are several ways a firm can meet its sinking fund obligation. It can repurchase a certain number of bonds in securities markets, or it can retire a certain number of bonds by paying the holders par value. When a company has a choice, it will naturally repurchase bonds if the market price of the bonds is below par value. This occurs whenever interest rates have risen since the bond's issue date.

Call Provisions.   Virtually all corporate bonds contain a clause giving the issuing company an option to retire the bonds prior to maturity. For example, although a bond might mature on December 31, 1990, the company may have the option to call the bonds for retirement prior to maturity. Frequently, the call price for early retirement will be at a modest premium above par. Many bonds also have a *delayed call,* meaning the company may not call the bond until it has been outstanding for a specified period, usually 5 or 10 years.

Companies want call options on bonds for two reasons. One is that if interest rates fall, the company can pay off its existing bonds and issue new ones at a lower interest cost. The other is that the call option gives a company flexibility. If changing market conditions or changing company strategy requires it, the call option enables management to rearrange its capital structure.

At first glance, it may appear that a call option works entirely to the company's advantage. If interest rates fall, the company can call the bonds and refinance at a lower rate; but if rates rise, investors have no similar option. They must either accept the low interest income or sell their bonds at a loss. It looks like "heads I win, tails you lose," but investors are not so stupid. As a general rule, the more attractive the call provisions are to the company, the higher the coupon rate on the bond.

Covenants.   Under normal circumstances, no creditors, including bondholders, have a direct voice in company decisions. Bondholders and other long-term creditors, exercise control through *protective covenants* specified in the indebenture agreement. Typical covenants include a lower limit on the company's current ratio, an upper limit on its debt-to-equity ratio, and perhaps a requirement that the company may not acquire or sell major assets without prior creditor approval. Creditors have no say in company operations as long as the firm is current in its interest and sinking fund payments and no covenants have been violated. If the company falls behind in its payment or violates a covenant, it is in *default,* and creditors gain considerable power. If they choose, creditors can force the company into bankruptcy, leaving the courts to decide whether the company should be reorganized for the benefit of creditors or simply be liquidated. In liquidation, the courts will sell company assets and use the proceeds to pay off creditors.

Rights in Bankruptcy. The distribution of liquidation proceeds in bankruptcy is determined by the *rights of absolute priority*. At the head of the line are, naturally, the government for past due taxes and the bankruptcy lawyers who wrote the law. Among investors, the first to be repaid are *senior* creditors, then *general* creditors, and finally *subordinated* creditors. Preferred stockholders and common shareholders bring up the rear. Because each class of claimant is paid off in full before the next class receives anything, equity shareholders frequently get nothing in bankruptcy.

Secured Creditors. A secured credit is a form of senior credit in which the loan is collateralized by a specific company asset or group of assets. In liquidation, proceeds from the sale of this asset go only to the secured creditor. If the cash generated from the sale exceeds the debt to the secured creditor, the excess cash goes into the pot for distribution to general creditors. If the cash is too little, the lender becomes a general creditor for the remaining liability.

Bonds as an Investment. For many years, investors thought bonds to be very low risk. Interest income is specified and chances of bankruptcy are remote. However, bonds are a *monetary asset*. Consequently, changes in the rate of inflation have a major impact on real and nominal bond returns. This has led to a growing perception that bonds can be quite risky in an inflationary world.

Table 6–1 presents the rate of return earned by investors in selected securities over the period 1926–1979. Looking at long-term corporate bonds,

Table 6–1. Rate of Return on Selected Securities, 1926–1979 (percent per annum compounded annually)*

Security	Return
Common stocks	9.0%
Long-term corporate bond	3.8
Long-term government bond	3.1
Consumer price index	2.7

*Source: Roger G. Ibbotson and Rex A. Singquefield, *Stocks, Bonds, Bills, and Inflation: Historical Returns (1926–1978),* plus annual update 1979 (Charlottesville, Va.: The Financial Analysts Research Foundation, 1979).

you can see that had an investor purchased a representative portfolio of corporate bonds in 1926 and held them through 1979 (while reinvesting all interest income and principal payments received in similar bonds), his annual return would have been 3.8 percent over the entire 53 years. By comparison, the annual return on an investment in long-term U.S. government bonds would have been 3.1 percent over the same period. We can attribute the 0.7 percent difference to a "default premium." This is the added return an investor in corporate bonds earns over government bonds to compensate for the risk that corporations might default on their liabilities while government securities are presumed to be default free.

These returns are *nominal.* The bottom entry in Table 6–1 contains the annual percentage change in the consumer price index over the period. Subtracting the annual inflation rate from 1926 through 1979 of 2.7 percent from these nominal returns yields real returns of 1.1 percent for corporates and 0.4 percent for governments. Long-term bonds have done little more than keep pace with inflation over this period.

Bond Ratings. Several investment companies in the United States analyze the investment qualities of many publicly traded bonds and publish their findings in the form of bond ratings. A bond rating is a letter grade, like AA, assigned to an issue which reflects the analyst's appraisal of the bond's risk. These ratings are determined using many of the techniques discussed in earlier chapters, including analysis of the company's balance sheet debt ratios and its coverage ratios relative to competitors. Table 6–2 presents the debt rating definitions of Standard & Poor's, a major rating firm. In the next chapter, Table 7–5 illustrates the differences in key performance ratios by rating category.

The rating a company receives on a new bond issue is quite important because it affects the interest rate the firm must offer as well as the pool of potential investors. Many institutional investors, such as pension funds, are prohibited from investing in bonds which are rated less than "investment" grade. Investment grade is usually defined as A rated or above. As a result, there are some periods when companies having less than an A rating find it extremely difficult to raise significant amounts of debt capital in public markets.

Common Stock

Common stock is a *residual income* security. The stockholder has a claim on any income remaining after the payment of all obligations, including interest on debt. *If the firm prospers, stockholders are the chief beneficiaries, whereas if it falters, they are the chief losers.* The amount of money a stockholder receives annually depends on the dividends the company chooses to pay. The board of directors makes this decision quarterly and is under no obligation to pay any dividend at all.

Table 6–2. Standard & Poor's Debt Rating Definitions

A Standard & Poor's corporate or municipal debt rating is a current assessment of the creditworthiness of an obligor with respect to a specific obligation. This assessment may take into consideration obligors such as guarantors, insurers, or lessees.

The debt rating is not a recommendation to purchase, sell, or hold a security, inasmuch as it does not comment as to market price or suitability for a particular investor.

The ratings are based on current information furnished by the issuer or obtained by S&P from other sources it considers reliable. S&P does not perform an audit in connection with any rating and may, on occasion, rely on unaudited financial information. The ratings may be changed, suspended, or withdrawn as a result of changes in or unavailability of such information, or in other circumstances.

The ratings are based, in varying degrees, on the following considerations:

1. Likelihood of default—capacity and willingness of the obligor as to the timely payment of interest and repayment of principal in accordance with the terms of the obligation.
2. Nature of and provisions of the obligation.
3. Protection afforded by, and relative position of, the obligation in the event of bankruptcy, reorganization, or other arrangement under the laws of bankruptcy and other laws affecting creditor's rights.

AAA Debt rated "AAA" has the highest rating assigned by Standard & Poor's. Capacity to pay interest and repay principal is extremely strong.

AA Debt rated "AA" has a very strong capacity to pay interest and repay principal and differs from the highest-rated issues only in small degree.

A Debt rated "A" has a strong capacity to pay interest and repay principal although it is somewhat more susceptible to the adverse effects of changes in circumstances and economic conditions than debt in higher-rated categories.

BBB Debt rated "BBB" is regarded as having an adequate capacity to pay interest and repay principal. Whereas it normally exhibits adequate protection parameters, adverse economic conditions or changing circumstances are more likely to lead to a weakened capacity to pay interest and repay principal for debt in this category than in higher-rated categories.

BB Debt rated "BB," "B," "CCC," or "CC" is regarded, on balance, as pre-
B dominantly speculative with respect to capacity to pay interest and repay
CCC principal in accordance with the terms of the obligation. "B" indicates the
CC lowest degree of speculation and "CC" the highest degree of speculation. While such debt is likely to have some quality and protective characteristics, these are outweighed by large uncertainties or major risk exposures to adverse conditions.

C This rating is reserved for income bonds on which no interest is being paid.

D Debt rated "D" is in default, and payment of interest and/or repayment of principal is in arrears.

Plus (+) or Minus (−): The ratings from "AA" to "B" may be modified by the addition of a plus or minus sign to show relative standing within the major rating categories.

Source: Standard & Poor's Corporation (New York, 1982).

Shareholder Control. Stockholders exercise control over company decisions through their ability to elect the board of directors. In the United States, the wide distribution of share ownership and the laws governing election of the board frequently combine to reduce greatly this authority. In some companies, ownership of as little as 10 percent of the stock is sufficient to control the entire board. In many other firms, there is no dominant shareholder group, and management controls the board, although they may own little or none of the company.

This does not imply that managers in such companies are free to ignore shareholder interests, for they face at least two potential constraints on their actions. One is created by their need to compete in product markets. If management does not make a product or provide a service efficiently and sell it at a competitive price, the company will lose market share to more aggressive competitors and will eventually be forced out of the industry. The actions taken by managers to compete effectively in product markets are consistent with shareholder interests. Securities markets provide a second check on management discretion. If a company wants to raise debt or equity capital in future years, it must maintain its profitability in order to appeal to new investors. Moreover, if managers ignore shareholder interests, stock price will fall, and the firm will run the risk of being acquired by another company in a raid.

Common Stock as an Investment. A common stockholder receives a return on his investment in two forms: dividends and possible share price appreciation. If d_o is the dividends per share during the year and P_o and P_1 are the beginning-of-year and end-of-year stock price, the *annual income* earned by the stockholder is:

$$d_o + P_1 - P_o$$

Dividing by the beginning-of-year stock price, the *annual return* is:

$$\frac{\text{Annual}}{\text{return}} = \frac{\text{Dividend}}{\text{yield}} + \frac{\text{Percentage change}}{\text{in share price}}$$

$$= \frac{d_o}{P_o} + \frac{P_1 - P_o}{P_o}$$

Common stocks are an ownership claim against primarily real assets. If companies can maintain profit margins during inflation, real profits should be relatively unaffected by inflation. For years, this reasoning led to the belief that common stocks are a hedge against inflation. This has not proved to be the case recently. Looking at Table 6–1 again, we see that had an investor purchased a representative portfolio of common stocks in 1926 and

> **Do Dividends Increase Annual Return?**
> It may appear from this equation that annual return rises when current dividends per share rise. But the world is not so simple. An increase in current dividends means one of two things: The company will have less money for investment, or it will have to raise more money from external sources to make the same investments. Either way, an increase in current dividends will reduce the stockholder's claim on future income which will reduce share price appreciation. Depending on which effect dominates, annual returns may or may not increase as dividends rise.

had he reinvested all dividends received in the same portfolio, his annual return in 1979 would have been 9.0 percent. However, since 1967 the return on common stocks has trended downward while the inflation rate has increased.

The common stock return of 9.0 percent from 1926 through 1979 compares with a return of 3.8 percent on corporate bonds and 3.1 percent on government bonds over the same period. The difference between the stock return and the government bond return of 5.9 percent (9.0% − 3.1%) can be thought of as a *risk premium*. It is the extra return earned by common stockholders as compensation for the added risks they bore. Comparing the return on common stocks to the annual percentage change in consumer prices, we see that the *real* return to common stock investors over the years 1926–1979 was 6.3 percent (9.0% − 2.7%).

Figure 6–1 presents much the same information more dramatically. It shows an investor's wealth in 1978 had he invested $1 in various assets in 1926. Common stocks are the clear winners here. By 1978 the original $1 investment would have grown into $89.59. One dollar invested in long-term government bonds by contrast would have been worth only $5.34 in 1978. Common stocks, however, have proved to be a much more volatile investment than bonds, as Figure 6–2 illustrates.

Preferred Stock

Preferred stock is a hybrid security—like debt in some ways, like equity in others. Like debt, preferred stock is a fixed-income security. It promises the investor a fixed dividend annually equal to the security's coupon rate times its par value. Like equity, the board of directors need not distribute this dividend unless it chooses. Also like equity, preferred dividend pay-

Figure 6-1. Wealth Indexes of Investments in the U.S. Capital Markets, 1926–1978 (assumed initial investment of $1 at year-end 1925; includes reinvestment income)

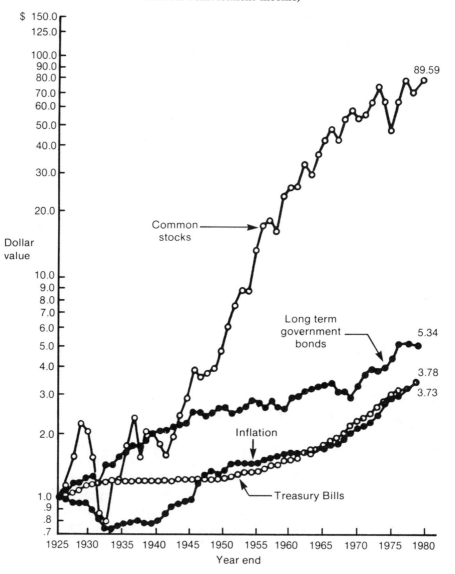

Source: Roger G. Ibbotson and Rex A. Singquefield, *Stocks, Bonds, Bills, and Inflation: Historical Returns (1926–1978)* (Charlottesville, Va.: The Financial Analysts Research Foundation, 1979), p. 4.

Figure 6–2. Volatility of Annual Returns from the U.S. Capital Markets (common stocks versus long-term government bonds)

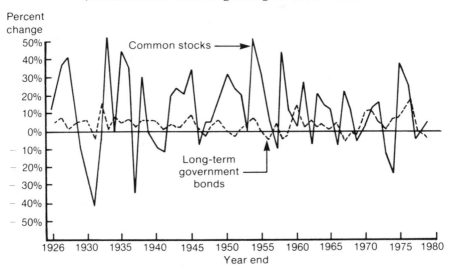

Source: Roger G. Ibbotson and Rex A. Singquefield, *Stocks, Bonds, Bills, and Inflation: Historical Returns (1926–1978)* (Charlottesville, Va.: The Financial Analysts Research Foundation, 1979), p. 5.

ments are *not* a deductible expense for corporate tax purposes. For the same coupon rate, this makes the *aftertax* cost of bonds about one half that of preferred shares. Another similarity with equity is that although preferred stock may have a call option, it frequently has no maturity. The preferred shares are outstanding indefinitely unless the company chooses to call them.

Cumulative Preferred.   Company boards of directors have two strong incentives to pay preferred dividends. One is that preferred shareholders have priority over common shareholders as to dividend payments. Common shareholders receive no dividends unless preferred holders are paid in full. Secondly, virtually all preferred stocks are *cumulative*. If a firm passes a preferred dividend, the arrearage accumulates and must be paid in full before the company can resume common dividend payments.

The control that preferred shareholders have over management decisions varies. In some instances, preferred shareholders approval is routinely required for major decisions; in others, preferred shareholders have no voice in management unless dividend payments are in arrears.

Preferred stock is not a widely used form of financing. Some persons see preferred stock as *cheap equity*. They see that preferred stock gives management much of the flexibility regarding dividend payments and maturity dates that common equity provides. Yet because preferred shareholders have no right to participate in future growth, they see preferred stock as less expensive than equity. The majority, however, sees preferred stock as *debt with a tax disadvantage*. Because few companies would ever omit a preferred dividend payment unless absolutely forced to, the majority places little value on the flexibility of preferred stock. To them the important fact is that interest payments on bonds are tax deductible, whereas dividend payments on preferred stock are not.

Financial Markets

Having reviewed the basic security types, let us turn now to a look at the markets in which these securities are issued and traded. Of particular interest will be the controversial notion of market efficiency.

Private Placement or Public Issue?

Companies raise money in two broad ways: through private negotiations with banks, insurance companies, pension funds, or other financial institutions, or by selling securities to the public. The former is known as a *private placement;* the latter is a *public issue.* Although private placements of equity are rare, private debt placements account for a significant fraction of total corporate debt.

To sell securities to the public, a company must register the issue with the Securities and Exchange Commission. This is an expensive, time-consuming, cumbersome task, but unless registered, securities may not trade on public markets. This is a valuable privilege. It means that the owner of registered securities can sell them by just calling a stockbroker and placing an order. In contrast, when a financial institution wants to liquidate some of its holdings of private placements, it must find another institution willing to purchase a large block of the securities.

A company's choice of whether to raise money via private placement or public issue comes down to this: Private placements are simpler, quicker, and can be tailored more closely to the particular needs of the issuer, but because they are difficult for buyers to resell, private placements carry a higher interest rate than public issues.

Organized Exchanges and Over-the-Counter Markets

Public issues trade on two types of markets: organized exchanges and over-the-counter markets. Organized exchanges, such as the New York Stock Exchange and the American Stock Exchange, are centralized trading locations which maintain active markets in hundreds of securities. Stockbroker members of the exchange transmit client buy-and-sell orders to specialists on the floor of the exchange who attempt to match buyers with sellers. Specialists may buy or sell securities for their own account, but more often they act as agents, pairing buyers with sellers.

Over-the-counter (OTC) markets are much more informal. Any stock brokerage house anywhere in the country can create an OTC market for a security by quoting a bid price at which it will buy the security and a higher-asked price at which it will sell the security. The spread between bid and asked prices is the broker's revenue. In return, the broker must keep an inventory of the security and must frequently trade for his own account to maintain an active market. Most well-known equity securities trade in organized exchanges, whereas the shares of smaller, regional companies and a great many bonds trade in the OTC market.

Investment Banking

Investment bankers are the grease that keeps financial markets running smoothly. They are finance specialists who assist companies in raising money. Other activities performed by investment bankers include stock and bond brokerage, investment counseling, merger and acquisition analysis, and corporate consulting. Some investment banking companies, like Merrill Lynch, employ thousands of brokers and have offices all over the world. Others, like Morgan Stanley and First Boston, specialize in working with companies and are consequently less in the public eye.

The responsibilities of an investment banker are many and varied—not unlike his fees. In a private placement, he or she customarily acts as an agent, bringing issuer and potential buyer together and helping them negotiate an agreement. In a public issue, the investment banker's responsibilities are much broader. When a company begins thinking seriously about selling new securities, management usually calls in an investment banker for advice. In most instances, the company will have worked with the same banker for years, and company executives and the investment banker will have developed a close working rapport.

The banker's first task is to help the company decide what type of security it should sell. Then, if it is to be a public issue, he or she will help the company register the issue with the SEC. This usually takes 30–90 days. A deterrent to registration for many companies, particularly foreign firms, is the extent of the SEC disclosure requirements. Companies must disclose detailed information about their finances, officers, plans, etc.; information some managements would prefer to keep confidential.

During the registration of any significant new issue, the investment banker puts together a *selling* and an *underwriting syndicate*. A syndicate is a team of as many as 100 investment banking houses which join forces for a brief time to place the new securities. Each member of the selling syndicate accepts responsibility for selling a specified portion of the new securities to investors. Members of the underwriting syndicate act, in effect, as wholesalers, purchasing all of the securities from the company at a guaranteed price and attempting to sell them to the public at a higher price.

Given the volatility of security prices and the length of time required to go through registration, it may appear that underwriters bear significant risks when they guarantee the company a fixed price. However, this is not the case. The underwriters do not commit themselves to a firm price until just hours before the sale, and if all goes as planned, the entire issue will be sold to the public on the same day. It is the company, not the underwriters, which bears the risk that the terms on which the securities can be sold will change during registration.

The life of a syndicate is a brief one. Syndicates form several months prior to an issue for the purpose of preselling and disband as soon as the securities are sold. Even on unsuccessful issues, the syndicate breaks up several weeks after the issue date, leaving each underwriter to dispose of his unsold shares on his own.

Cost of New Issues

Financial securities impose two kinds of costs on the issuer: annual costs and issue costs. We will consider the more important annual costs later. Issue costs are the costs incurred by the issuer and its shareholders on initial sale. For a private placement, the only substantive cost is the fee charged by the investment banker in his or her capacity as agent. On a public issue, there are legal, accounting, and printing fees, plus those paid to the invest-ment banker. The investment banker states his fee in the form of a *spread*. To illustrate, suppose ABC Corporation wants to sell 1 million new shares and that its shares are presently trading at $20 on the American Stock Ex-change. A few hours prior to public sale, the lead investment banker might inform ABC management that "Given the present tone of the markets we can sell the new shares at an issue price of $19 and a spread of $1.50, for a net to the company of $17.50." This means that the investment banker in-tends to *underprice* the issue $1 per share ($20 market price less $19 issue price) and that he is charging a fee of $1.50 per share, or $1.5 million for his services. This fee will be split among the managing underwriter, or lead bank, and the syndicate members by prior arrangement according to each bank's importance in the syndicates.

To underprice an issue means to offer the new shares for sale at a price below that prevailing for existing shares. Investment bankers often under-price on the theory that the price of the new shares must be below that of existing shares to induce investors to hold more shares. Underpricing is not an out-of-pocket cost to the company, but it is a cost to shareholders. The greater the underpricing, the more new shares a company must issue to raise a given amount of money. And as the number of shares issued goes up, the percentage ownership of existing shareholders goes down.

Table 6–3 summarizes some of the issue costs of various kinds of securities. Omitted from the table are underpricing costs and payment to investment bankers in the form of warrants and stock options. Two facts are apparent from the data. First, common stock issue costs, which average 12.43 percent of the gross proceeds, are on average over eight times as high as debt issue costs. Second, issue costs fall noticeably as issue size increases. For instance, the total cost of issuing under $500,000 of bonds is 14.15 percent of the gross proceeds, but the same figure for issues in excess of $500 million is only 0.95 percent. Comparable figures for common stock are 23.59 percent for the smallest issues and 3.19 percent for those between $100 and $499.99 million.

Regulatory Changes

Financial market deregulation has ignited a revolution among American financial institutions. In part, deregulation has been the outgrowth of a changing regulatory philosophy, but at least as important has been a wide array of technological and competitive innovations which has made regulation increasingly ineffective.

Prior to the depression, U.S. banks were allowed to engage in commercial and investment banking. In 1933, Congress passed the Glass-Steagall Act to eliminate perceived conflicts of interest between the two activities. Since then, commercial banks have been prohibited from engaging in most securities trading activity, while investment banks have been prohibited from acting as depository institutions. Recently, however, it has become increasingly difficult to draw a clear line of separation between what constitutes commercial banking as opposed to investment banking. As a result, we see today a steady encroachment of each type of bank on what has been thought to be the other's domain. This trend has prompted many observers to predict that the legal barriers separating the two activities cannot be long maintained in the face of heightening competition. In other countries, most banks, including U.S. multinational banks, are free to engage in investment and commercial banking activities.

A second major change in investment banking is what is known as "shelf registration," currently being tested by the SEC on an experimental basis. Until shelf registration, companies wishing to sell new securities had to wait as long as three months before gaining the necessary SEC approval to proceed. This lengthy delay had two effects: (1) it exposed the issuer to considerable uncertainty about the eventual issue price and (2) it gave the investment bankers ample time to put together their syndicates.

Shelf registration eliminates this delay by allowing the issuer to file a general-purpose registration good for up to two years. Once the SEC approves the shelf registration, and provided it is updated periodically, the company can sell new securities whenever it wishes.

The likely impact of shelf registration on the investment banking industry

Table 6–3. Issue Costs as Percentage of Proceeds on SEC-Registered Securities Offered General Public, 1971–72

Size of Issue ($ millions)	Bonds, Notes, and Debentures			Preferred Stock			Common Stock		
	Underwriter's Compensation*	Other Expenses	Total Costs	Underwriter's Compensation*	Other Expenses	Total Costs	Underwriter's Compensation*	Other Expenses	Total Costs
Under .5	11.51%	2.64%	14.15%	—	—	—	13.24%	10.35%	23.59%
.5– .99	5.25	3.70	8.95	—	—	—	12.48	8.26	20.74
1.0– 1.99	12.95	4.00	16.95	8.26%	3.48%	11.74%	10.60	5.87	16.47
2.0– 4.99	4.02	2.21	6.23	1.88	0.66	2.54	8.19	3.71	11.90
5.0– 9.99	2.36	0.78	3.14	1.37	0.42	1.79	6.70	2.03	8.73
10.0– 19.99	1.24	0.65	1.89	1.37	0.29	1.66	5.52	1.11	6.63
20.0– 49.99	1.00	0.43	1.43	1.35	0.20	1.55	4.41	0.62	5.03
50.0– 99.99	0.89	0.28	1.17	2.25	0.18	2.43	3.94	0.31	4.25
100.0–499.99	0.83	0.19	1.02	—	—	—	3.03	0.16	3.19
Over 500.00	0.88	0.07	0.95				—	—	—
Average	1.14%	0.45%	1.59%	1.52%	0.39%	1.91%	8.41%	4.02%	12.43%

*Does not include contingent payments in form of warrants or options paid to underwriter. Such payments are common in small stock issues.

Source: Securities and Exchange Commission, *Cost of Flotation of Registered Securities, 1971–1972* (Washington, D.C.: U.S. Government Printing Office, December 1974).

will be profound. For one thing, it will probably eliminate a large number of smaller regional banks in favor of a few large national ones. With shelf registration, the time an investment banker has to put together his syndicates falls from three months to an impossible 24 hours or less. The likely industry response will be to eliminate syndicates altogether in favor of a comparatively few national investment banks capable of buying the whole issue on the spot. In effect, the smaller investment banks will merge into permanent syndicates. A second effect will be greatly increased price competition. If a company treasurer can sell a new issue by calling one investment banker, he can just as easily call two or three to get the best price.

Although information is still fragmentary, early indications are that shelf registration will significantly reduce debt issue cost but that it will have little impact on equity issues. Displaying their old fear of EPS dilution, very few companies have used shelf registrations for equity issues, arguing that even though shelf registration is only a notice of intent to issue new shares, investors will react as if the new shares were a reality. In effect, they will adjust EPS, ROE, and stock price downward in anticipation of the new equity issue.

Shelf registration is still experimental, and as you might expect, the investment banking industry is lobbying hard against it. So whether sanity will ultimately prevail and whether shelf registration becomes permanent remains to be seen.

Efficient Markets

A recurring issue in raising new capital is that of *timing*. Companies are naturally anxious to sell new securities when prices are high. Toward this end, managers routinely devote considerable time and money to the prediction of future price trends in financial markets.

Concern for proper timing of security issues is natural. However, there is a growing perception among academicians and market professionals that attempts to forecast future prices in financial markets will be successful only in exceptional circumstances, and that unless these circumstances exist, there is nothing to be gained by forecasting.

Such pessimism follows from the notion of *efficient markets,* a much debated and controversial topic in recent years. This is not the place for a detailed discussion of efficient markets; however, because the implications of market efficiency are far reaching and because the concept is beginning to affect the way financial managers think about their jobs, it deserves some attention. The interested reader is referred to the recommended readings at the end of the chapter for more detailed treatments of the topic.

Market efficiency is controversial in large part because many proponents have overstated the evidence supporting efficiency and have misrepresented its implications. To avoid this, let us agree on two things right now. First, market efficiency is not a question of black or white but rather of shades of gray. A market is not efficient or inefficient but rather *more* or *less* efficient. Moreover, the degree of efficiency is an empirical question which can be answered only by studying a particular market. Second, market efficiency depends on one's perspective. The New York Stock Exchange can be efficient to a dentist in Des Moines who doesn't know a stockbroker from a mortgage banker; and at the same time, it can be highly *in*efficient to a specialist on the floor of the exchange who has detailed information about buyers and sellers of each stock and up-to-the-second prices.

What Is an Efficient Market? Market efficiency is a story about how prices in competitive markets respond to new information. The arrival of new information to a competitive market can be likened to the arrival of a lamb chop to a school of flesh-eating piranha, where investors are plausibly enough the piranha. The instant the lamb chop hits the water, there is turmoil as the fish devour the meat. Very soon the meat is gone, leaving only the worthless bone behind, and the water returns to normal. Similarly, when new information reaches a competitive market there is much turmoil as investors buy and sell securities in response to the news, causing prices to change. Once prices adjust, all that is left of the information is the worthless bone. No amount of gnawing on the bone will yield any more meat, and no further study of old information will yield any more valuable intelligence.

An efficient market, then, is one in which current prices fully reflect available information about the assets traded. "Fully reflect" means that investors rapidly pounce on new information, analyze it, revise their expectations and buy or sell securities accordingly. They continue to buy or sell securities until price changes eliminate the incentive for further trades. In such an environment, current prices reflect the cumulative judgment of investors. They *fully reflect* available information.

The degree of efficiency displayed by a particular market depends on the speed with which prices adjust to news and the type of news to which prices respond. It is common to speak of three levels of informational efficiency.

A market is *weak-form* efficient if current prices fully reflect all information about past *prices.*

A market is *semistrong-form* efficient if current prices fully reflect all *publicly available* information.

A market is *strong-form* efficient if current prices fully reflect *all information* public or private.

Extensive tests of many financial markets suggest that with limited exceptions most financial markets are semistrong-form efficient, but not strong-form efficient. This statement needs to be qualified in two respects. First, there is the issue of perspective. The above statement applies to the typical

How Rapidly Do Stock Prices Adjust to New Information?

The following graph, Figure 6–3, gives an indication of the speed with which common stock prices adjust to new information. It is a result of what is known as an "event study." In this instance the researcher is studying the impact of acquisition offers on the stock price of the target firm. It is easiest to think of the graph initially as a plot of the daily price of the target firm's stock from a period beginning 40 days before the announcement of the acquisition offer and ending 40 days after. An acquisition offer is invariably good news to the target firm's shareholders because the offer is at a price well above the prevailing market price of the firm's shares; so we expect to see the target company's stock price rise after the announcement. The question is, How rapidly? The answer evident from the graph is, Very rapidly. We see that the stock price drifts upward prior to the announcement, shoots up dramatically on the announcement day, and then drifts without much direction after the announcement. Clearly, if you read about the announcement in the evening paper and buy the stock the next morning, you will miss out on the major price move. The market will already have responded to the new information.

The upward drift in stock price prior to the announcement is consistent with two possible explanations: Either insiders are buying the stock in anticipation of the announcement, or acquiring firms tend to announce offers after the stock of the target firm has increased for several weeks. I have my own views, but I will leave it to you to decide which explanation is more plausible.

An old Jewish proverb says, "For example is no proof." If the price pattern illustrated by the graph were for just one firm, it would only be a curiosity. To avoid this problem, the researcher has studied the price patterns of 161 target firms involving successful acquisitions which occurred over 15 years ending in 1977. The prices you see are an index composed of the prices of the 161 firms, and the time scale is in "event time" not calendar time. Here the event is the acquisition announcement, defined as day 0, and all other dates are relative to this event date. The pattern observed, therefore, describes general experience, not an isolated event.

In recent years, academicians have performed a number of event studies involving different markets and events, and the preponderance of these studies indicates that financial markets in the United States respond to new, publicly available information within one day or less.

Figure 6–3. Time Series of the Mean Price Index of the Shares of 161 Target Firms Involved in Successful Tender Offers

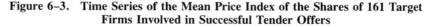
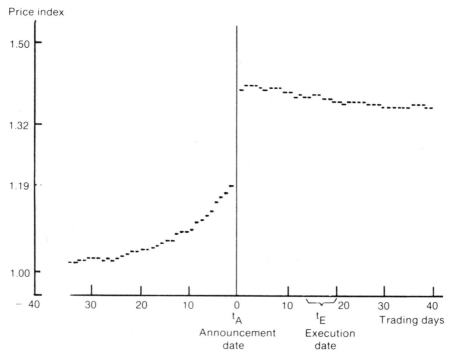

Source: Michael Bradley, "Interfirm Tender Offers and the Market for Corporate Control," *Journal of Business* 53, no. 4 (1980).

investor, subject to brokerage fees and without special information-gathering equipment. It does *not* apply to market makers. Second, it is impossible to test every possible type and combination of public information for efficiency. All we can say is the most plausible types of information tested with the most sophisticated techniques available indicate efficiency. This does not preclude the possibility that a market may be inefficient with respect to some as yet untested information source.

Implications of Efficiency. If the market in which a company sells securities is semistrong-form efficient, the following are true:

Management cannot improve its forecasts of future prices by analyzing publicly available information.

Unless they have access to private information, management's best forecast of future prices is current prices, perhaps adjusted for a long-run trend.

Without private information, a company cannot improve the terms on which it sells securities through timing.

A firm without private information has two choices. It can reconcile itself to efficiency and quit trying to forecast security prices, or it can attempt to make the market inefficient from the company's perspective. The latter involves becoming a market insider by acquiring the best available information-gathering system in hopes of learning about events before others. A variation on this theme—one which is usually illegal—is to seek insider information. Advance knowledge of changes in government monetary policy, for example, would undoubtedly be useful in forecasting interest rates.

As the above comments suggest, market efficiency is a subtle and provocative notion with a number of important implications for investors as well as companies. Our treatment of the topic here has been necessarily brief, but it should be sufficient to suggest that unless executives have inside information or superior information-gathering and analysis systems, there may be little to be gained from trying to forecast prices in financial markets. This conclusion applies to many markets in which companies participate, including those for government and corporate securities, foreign currencies, and commodities.

Appendix

Options and Convertible Securities

An option is a document giving the holder the right to either buy or sell a security at a specified price and for a specified time. For example, a *call option* on Boeing Company stock might give the holder the right to purchase 100 shares of Boeing stock at $69 per share at any time up to August 15, 1981. $69 is the option's *striking price* and August 15, 1981, is its *maturity date.*

The value of this option depends quite obviously on the price of Boeing stock prior to the maturity date. If Boeing stock is trading at prices above $69, the option is clearly valuable. However, even if the stock is trading below $69, investors will still purchase the options, hoping that the price will rise above the striking price prior to maturity. Unexercised options beyond their maturity date are worthless.

There are three basic types of options: *Puts* and *calls* are options written by investors on existing securities and traded on exchanges, *stock options* are granted by companies to managers as part of their compensation, and *warrants* are issued by companies to outside investors. A distinguishing feature of stock options and warrants is their longevity, which can be many years. The longest maturity on puts and calls is only nine months.

Convertible Securities. A convertible security is a fixed-income security with an option attached. To illustrate, convertible bonds of the XYZ Company might be convertible into XYZ common stock and might have the following terms: a par value of $1,000, a coupon rate of 10 percent, a maturity of 20 years, and a *conversion ratio* of 100 to 1. The 100-to-1 conversion ratio means that, at any time, the holder can trade his or her bonds into the company in exchange for common stock in the ratio of 100 common shares for each bond.

Conversion Value and Investment Value. It is appropriate to speak of two values for convertible securities. One is the security's *conversion value,* which is the current value of the common stock a holder would receive upon conversion. In our example, if XYZ common stock were trading at $8 per share, the conversion value of the company's convertible bonds would be $800 per bond ($8 per share × 100 shares). The security's other value is its *investment value.* The investment value of a convertible security is the price at which the convertible would trade if the conversion option were removed. It is the value ignoring the conversion option and viewing the instrument as a conventional fixed-income security.

The market price of a convertible security can never be lower than its conversion value *or* its investment value. Let us see why this is true. If the security's price were below its conversion value, speculators could earn riskless profits by purchasing the convertible, converting to common stock, and immediately selling the stock. For example, if XYZ's convertible was selling for $700 when its common stock was selling $8, a speculator could purchase one convertible bond for $700, exchange it for $800 worth of stock, and sell the stock for a riskless and immediate profit of $100. In the process, the speculator would bid up the price of the convertible and would bid down the price of the stock, until the convertible's price once again equaled or exceeded its conversion value.

If a convertible security's price were less than its investment value, the convertible would offer investors a higher return than similar quality and maturity securities which did not possess the conversion option. Resulting demand for the convertible would raise its price until it once again exceeded the security's investment value.

Forcing Conversion. Virtually all convertible securities give the issuer the right to redeem, or call, the securities for cash at a fixed price. This call price does not put a ceiling on the market price of a convertible security, however, because even after the company has issued its call, investors have a grace period in which to decide whether to accept cash or to convert into common shares. The company can easily predict what investors will do when they issue a call, for if conversion value exceeds the call price, investors will convert; otherwise they will redeem their shares for cash. For example, suppose the XYZ convertible has a call price of $1,050 per bond. If the conversion value is $800 when XYZ calls the securities, holders have the option of receiving $1,050 in cash or $800 worth of common stock, so investors will redeem their bonds for cash. However, if the conversion value is $1,200 on the call date, investors will convert to common stock rather than settle for $1,050 in cash.

Calling a convertible security when its conversion value exceeds its call price is known as *forcing conversion*. In the absence of such a call, few investors will voluntarily convert; first, because the annual income from a convertible usually exceeds the dividend income from the common stock received on conversion, and second, because a convertible security provides *downside protection*. Even if the price of the company's common stock falls to very low levels, the investment value of the convertible will create a floor under the price of the convertible, preventing it from sinking to comparable levels.

Why Issue a Convertible? Historically, a principal use of convertibles has been as *delayed equity financing*. A growing company needs additional equity financing, but feels its stock price will be higher in a few years; so it issues a convertible security, hoping to force conversion in the near future.

The presumed advantage of this strategy is that it enables the firm to secure needed equity on more favorable terms. To illustrate, suppose XYZ Company needs $10 million in new equity. If its current stock price is $8 per share, it would need to sell 1.25 million new shares today to raise the needed funds ($10 million ÷ $8 = 1.25 million). But suppose instead it sells 10,000 convertible bonds with a conversion ratio of 100 to 1 at $1,000 per bond. Then, in a few years, when its stock price is above $10 per share, it can issue a call-and-force conversion. After conversion, only 1 million new common shares will be outstanding, a 20 percent reduction in shares issued (10,000 bonds × 100 shares per bond = 1 million shares).

There are at least two problems with this logic. One is that a company can achieve the same result as delayed equity financing by just issuing debt and then refinancing with equity in a few years. A second problem is that despite the best of expectations, the issuing firm's stock price may not rise. In this case, the company will have a *frozen,* or *hung, convertible;* and more importantly, it will have $10 million in debt when it really needs equity. As discussed in the next chapter, this can prove to be a risky proposition.

Today, there appears to be increased interest in convertible securities and in fixed-income securities with attached warrants. The reason is inflation. Investors have learned that long-term, fixed-income securities are risky investments during times of volatile inflation, and they are increasingly reluctant to hold them. As an enticement, more firms are adding "equity kickers" to such securities in the form of conversion options or warrants.

Chapter Summary

1. This chapter has examined financial instruments and markets. When raising capital, the financial manager acts much like a marketing manager. The product is claims on the firm's assets and income, and the manager's goal is to package and sell these claims in a manner which yields the highest price to the company.

2. Companies are *not* greatly restricted by law or regulation in their ability to select or design a security. The key questions in designing a new security are: What does the investor want, and what meets the company's needs?

3. Fixed-income securities, like bonds and most preferred stock, receive a comparatively safe income stream but do not participate in the growth of the firm. As an investment over the last 50-odd years, corporate bonds have done little more than keep up with inflation.

4. Common stock is a residual income security with claim on all income after payment of prior fixed claims. Common stockholders are the prin-

cipal beneficiaries of company growth. They receive income as dividends and share price appreciation. Since 1926, the average *real* return on common stocks has been about 6.3 percent.

5. Private placement of new securities with a small group of knowledgeable institutions is usually faster and more flexible than a public issue; however, because private placements are illiquid, they customarily carry a higher interest rate.

6. A sizable body of empirical evidence suggests that financial markets in the United States are quite efficient. To earn above-average returns as an investor in these markets, you need access to private information, or you need to be among the first to act upon newly available public information.

Additional Reading

Brealey, Richard, and Stewart Myers. *Principles of Corporate Finance.* New York: McGraw-Hill, 1981. 794 pages.
    A leading graduate-level text. Lively, well-written. Particularly strong on recent developments in the field. Chapter 13, Corporate Financing and the Six Lessons of Market Efficiency, is especially good.

Van Horne, James C. *Financial Market Rates and Flows.* Englewood Cliffs, N.J.: Prentice-Hall, 1978. 241 pages.
    A well-written, informative look at the function of financial markets, the flow of funds through markets, market efficiency, interest rates, and interest rate differentials. Excellent review of empirical studies of financial markets. Intended as a supplement for courses in financial markets and for practitioners interested in issuing or investing in fixed-income securities.

Chapter Problems

1. *a.* Why are the expected returns on most bonds less than the expected returns on most stocks?
   b. Why buy a bond if it has a lower expected return than a stock?
   c. If your answer to (*b*) is "stocks are riskier," can you avoid this risk by purchasing a diversified portfolio of stocks?
   d. How would you respond to the following comment? "Since it is a virtual certainty that stocks will yield a higher return than bonds over the long run, the best investment strategy is to buy stocks and give them time to outperform bonds."
   e. Could the bonds of a company have a higher expected return to investors than the common stock of the same company?
   f. If a company's bonds have a lower expected return to investors than its common stock, does this mean that bonds are less costly

from the company's perspective? If so, why would a company ever sell equity?

2. Gately Manufacturing Company's current stock price is $32 per share. The company wants to raise $100 million by selling newly issued common stock. Gately's investment banker indicates that such a sale would require 5 percent underpricing and a 10 percent spread.
    a. Assuming Gately's stock price does not change, how many shares must the company sell and at what price to the public?
    b. How much does the investment banker stand to earn on the sale?

3. If the stock market in the United States is efficient, how can you explain the fact that some people make very high returns? Would it be more difficult to reconcile very high returns with efficient markets if the same people made extraordinary returns year after year?

7

The Financing Decision

In the last chapter we began our inquiry into the raising of external capital by looking at financial instruments and the markets in which they trade. We continue here by examining the proper choice of a financing instrument by the company.

Selecting the proper financing instrument is a two-step process. The first is to decide how much external capital is required. Frequently, this is the straightforward outcome of the forecasting and budgeting process described in Chapter 4. Management estimates sales growth, the need for new assets, and the money available internally. Any remaining monetary needs must come from outside sources. Increasingly, however, this is only the first stage in the process. Following it is a careful consideration of financial markets and the terms on which the company can raise capital. If management does not believe that it can raise the required sums on agreeable terms, a modification of operating plans to bring them within budgetary constraints is required.

Once the amount of external capital to be raised has been determined, the second step is to select—or, more accurately, design—the instrument to be sold. This is the heart of the financing decision. As indicated in the last chapter, the company can choose from a tremendous variety of financial securities. The proper choice will provide the company with needed cash on attractive terms. An improper one will result in an excessive cost of funds, undue risk, or an inability to sell the securities.

For simplicity in this chapter, we will frequently consider a single financing choice: The XYZ Company needs to raise $20 million this year; should it sell bonds or stock? But do not let this focus obscure the complexity of the topic. First, bonds and stocks are just extreme examples of a whole spectrum of possible security types. Fortunately, the conclusions drawn regarding these extremes will apply in modified degree to other instruments along the spectrum. Second, and more important, financing decisions are never one-time events. Instead, the raising of money at any point in time is just one event in an evolving financial strategy. Yes, XYZ Company needs $20 million today but will likely need $15 million in two years and an undetermined amount in future years. Consequently, a major element of XYZ's present financing decision is the effect today's choice will have on the company's future ability to raise capital. At bottom a company's financing strategy relates closely to its long-run competitive goals and to the way it intends to manage growth.

This chapter begins by considering a central topic in finance known as OPM: other people's money. We will look at the advantages and disadvantages of OPM in financing operations and will examine how the choice of a financing strategy affects company performance. This will involve a close look at *financial leverage* and at techniques for evaluating alternative financing options. The chapter will conclude by considering financing decisions in light of a company's growth objectives and its access to financial markets. We will see that smaller companies and those which are unable or unwilling to sell new equity view financial leverage from a different perspective than other firms. The appendix to the chapter takes up the related topic of operating leverage.

Financial Leverage

In physics, a lever is a device to increase force. In business OPM, or what is commonly called financial leverage, is a technique for increasing owners' returns. It involves the prudent substitution of fixed-cost debt financing for owners' equity in the *hope* of increasing equity returns. The word *hope* is important here because leverage does not always have the intended effect. If company operating profits are below a critical value, financial leverage will reduce, not increase, equity returns. If we think of the increased variability in the return to owners as an increase in risk, we can say that financial leverage is the proverbial two-edged sword: It increases the return to owners in most instances, but it also increases their risk.

To see these effects more clearly, let's look at the impact of financial leverage on ROE. Recall from Chapter 2 that despite some problems ROE is the most widely used single measure of financial performance. It is defined as:

$$ROE = \frac{\text{Profit after tax}}{\text{Equity}}$$

In Chapter 2 we said that an increase in financial leverage usually increases ROE. Here, we want to explore this linkage more closely. To begin, write profit after tax as:

$$\text{Profit after tax} = (\text{EBIT} - \text{ID})(1 - T)$$

where EBIT is *earning before interest and tax*, I is the interest rate, D is debt outstanding, and T is the firm's tax rate. This equation reflects the steps an accountant goes through to calculate profit after tax from EBIT.

Then using some basic algebra, as shown in the footnote below,[1] we can rewrite ROE as:

$$\text{ROE} = r + (r - i)\frac{D}{E}$$

where r is the company's *operating return on assets,* defined as:

$$r = \text{Operating return on assets} = \frac{\text{EBIT}(1 - T)}{\text{Assets}}$$

and i is the aftertax interest rate, defined as:

$$i = \text{Aftertax interest rate} = I(1 - T)$$

E is the firm's equity. r is the return on assets of an all-equity company; you can think of it as the return earned by the company before the effects of financial leverage are considered. i is the aftertax interest rate. Recall that because interest is a tax-deductible expense, a company's tax bill declines whenever its interest expense rises; i takes this relationship into account.

The revised expression for ROE is a revealing one. It shows clearly that the impact of financial leverage on ROE depends on the size of r relative to i. If r exceeds i, financial leverage—as measured by D/E—increases ROE. However, the reverse is also true; if r is less than i, leverage reduces ROE. Leverage improves financial performance when things are going well but worsens it when things are going poorly.

An Example. Table 7–1 presents the same analysis in the form of a numerical example. It shows ROE for a representative company assuming three degrees of financial leverage—zero, moderate, and high—and under three different operating scenarios—boom, expected, and bust. The degrees of leverage correspond to a debt-to-equity ratio of 0, 1.00, and 4.00, re-

---

[1]
$$\text{ROE} = \frac{(\text{EBIT} - \text{ID})(1 - T)}{E} = \frac{\text{EBIT}(1 - T)}{E} \cdot \frac{A}{A} - \frac{\text{ID}(1 - T)}{E}$$
$$= r \cdot \frac{D + E}{E} - i\frac{D}{E} = r + (r - i)\frac{D}{E}$$

Table 7–1. Financial Leverage and ROE at Differing EBITs
(assumptions: assets = $600, interest rate = 16%, tax rate = 50%)

	Case 1: No Leverage D = 0, D/E = 0			Case 2: Moderate Leverage D = $300, D/E = 1.00			Case 3: High Leverage D = $480, D/E = 4.00		
	Boom	Expected	Bust	Boom	Expected	Bust	Boom	Expected	Bust
EBIT ($)	150	100	50	150	100	50	150	100	50
r (%)	12.50	8.33	4.17	12.50	8.33	4.17	12.50	8.33	4.17
ROE (%)	12.50	8.33	4.17	17.00	8.67	0.34	30.50	9.65	−11.15

spectively. The operating scenarios involve a boom EBIT of $150, an expected EBIT of $100, and a bust EBIT of $50.

In case 1, no leverage, we see that ROE ranges from a high of 12 50 percent under boom conditions to a low of 4.17 percent under bust, with an expected ROE of 8.33 percent. In case 2, moderate leverage, the boom and expected ROE rise, but the bust ROE falls to 0.34 percent. This is because r is below i in this instance. Finally, in the third case of high leverage the pattern becomes more exaggerated: Boom and expected ROE are higher still, but bust ROE falls to a miserable −11.15 percent.

Figure 7–1. Leverage Increases Expected Return and Risk

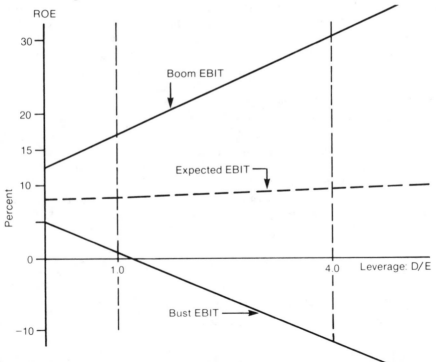

Figure 7-1 shows the same results graphically. It plots ROE versus financial leverage—measured by D/E—at differing EBITs. We see that increasing leverage has two effects: It increases the expected ROE, *and* it increases the range of possible ROEs.

It is customary to think of the range of possible ROEs as a measure of *risk*. There are two reasons for this. One is that a greater range of possible outcomes means more uncertainty about what ROE the company will earn and more variability in ROE over time. The second reason is that a greater range of possible ROEs means a greater chance of bankruptcy. Look at the bust EBIT in the figure. With zero leverage, the worst the company will do is earn a ROE of 4.17 percent, but with a debt-to-equity ratio of 4.00, the same level of operating income results in a *loss* of 11.15 percent on equity. In this situation operating income is not sufficient to cover interest expense, and a loss results. If the loss is large enough or persistent enough, bankruptcy can occur. To summarize, *financial leverage increases expected return to shareholders and risk*. The trick is to balance one against the other.

Techniques for Evaluating Financing Alternatives

If management knew the value of r, the financing decision would be easy: Whenever r exceeds i, pile on the debt; whenever r is less than i, finance with equity. The thing that makes life exciting for financial managers is that future values of r are unknown and frequently subject to considerable uncertainty. The financing decision therefore comes down to a comparison of the possible benefits of leverage against the possible costs.

To demonstrate how this comparison should be made in practice, consider the problem faced by Clark Thompson, vice president finance, of Harbridge Fabrics in early 1981. Harbridge Fabrics, a manufacturer of quality cotton and wool fabrics, was trying to decide how to raise $30 million to finance acquisition of a Spanish manufacturer of cotton materials. After considerable negotiation, a price of $35 million cash had been agreed to. Thompson had determined that $5 million could be financed internally, leaving $30 million to be financed from outside sources. Harbridge's investment bankers indicated that the following two options were possible:

1. Sell 1.5 million new shares of common stock at a net price of $20 per share.
2. Sell $30 million, par value bonds at an interest rate of 14 percent. The maturity would be 20 years, and the bonds would carry an annual sinking fund of $1.5 million.

Looking to the future, Mr. Thompson expected that the addition of the Spanish manufacturer would increase Harbridge's earnings before interest and taxes (EBIT) to $30 million in 1981. Past EBIT levels had been as follows:

	1974	1975	1976	1977	1978	1979	1980
EBIT ($ millions)	$15	$10	$30	$26	$5	$15	$24

Mr. Thompson anticipated that Harbridge's need for outside capital in coming years would be substantial, ranging from $5 to $20 million annually. The company had paid annual dividends of 50 cents per share in recent years, and Mr. Thompson believed it was management's intention to con-

Table 7–2
HARBRIDGE FABRICS
Income Statement
1980
($ millions)

Sales	$192.3
Cost of goods sold	131.2
Gross profit	61.1
General and administrative expenses	40.3
Profit before tax	20.8
Tax at 50 percent	10.4
Profit after tax	10.4
Preferred dividends	.4
Available for common	$ 10.0
Number of shares outstanding	5 million
Earnings per share	$ 2.00

Table 7–3
HARBRIDGE FABRICS
Balance Sheet
1980
($ millions)

Assets		Liabilities and Owners' Equity	
Cash and securities	$ 14.0	Accrued expenses	$ 15.1
Accounts receivable	32.1	Accounts payable	20.9
Inventories	21.8	Short-term debt	2.0
Total current assets	67.9	Current portion long-term debt	4.0
Net fixed assets	68.3	Total current liabilities	42.0
Total assets	$136.2	Long-term debt[1]	34.0
		Preferred stock[2]	4.0
		Common stock	5.0
		Retained earnings	51.2
		Total liabilities and owners' equity	$136.2

[1]Average interest rate on debt in 1980 was 8 percent; annual sinking fund requirements were $4 million. Both of these numbers will stay at this level through 1985.

[2]Dividend rate on preferred stock is 10 percent; there are no principal payment requirements on the preferred.

tinue doing so. Tables 7–2 and 7–3 present Harbridge's recent financial statements.

Range-of-Earnings Chart

Mr. Thompson's first step in analyzing the financing options available to Harbridge should be to measure the impact of the decision on Harbridge's return to shareholders. This could be done by calculating the company's ROE under alternative financing plans. Instead, the common practice is to simplify the procedure somewhat by looking at the decision's impact on earnings per share (EPS) rather than ROE.

The two perspectives are almost identical. Rewriting ROE as:

$$ROE = \frac{\text{Profit after tax}}{\text{Equity}}$$

$$= \frac{1}{\text{Equity per share}} \; EPS$$

we conclude that if the term in brackets is constant as leverage changes, ROE is just a constant times EPS. This means that if EPS increases, say, 20 percent with debt financing, ROE will increase the same percentage. Hence, assuming the bracketed term stays constant, we can concentrate on the impact of leverage on EPS knowing the story will be the same for ROE.[2]

To see the effect of financial leverage on Harbridge's EPS we need to look at the company's income statement under the two financing plans. We can save considerable work in doing this by noting that all of the income statement entries from sales down through EBIT are unaffected by the way a company is financed. Consequently, we can ignore these items and begin with EBIT. The figures below show the bottom portion of a 1981 pro forma income statement for Harbridge under bust and boom conditions. Bust corresponds to a recessionary EBIT of only $10 million, whereas boom represents a very healthy EBIT of $40 million.

The accounting here is straightforward. Interest expense under the stock financing alternative is 8 percent of the debt outstanding in 1981. Debt outstanding in 1981 equals present short- and long-term debt of $40 million, less the $4 million sinking fund due during 1981, or $36 million. Interest expense under the bond alternative is higher by an amount equal to the interest on the new bonds. Preferred dividends are an aftertax expense, so

---

[2]Is it reasonable to assume the term in brackets is constant as leverage changes? Usually, but not always. It is constant for debt financing and for equity financing when the issue price of the new shares equals the book value of equity per share. For equity issues at any other price, the assumption is not correct; however, in the usual case where the new equity issue is small relative to the number of shares already outstanding, it is a reasonable first approximation.

HARBRIDGE FABRICS
Partial Pro Forma Income Statement
1981
($ millions except EPS)

	Bust		Boom	
	Bonds	Stock	Bonds	Stock
EBIT	$10.0	$10.0	$40.0	$40.0
Interest expense......................	7.1	2.9	7.1	2.9
Earnings before tax.....................	2.9	7.1	32.9	37.1
Tax at 50 percent	1.5	3.6	16.5	18.6
Profit after tax........................	1.4	3.5	16.4	18.5
Preferred dividends....................	.4	.4	.4	.4
Available for common	1.0	3.1	16.0	18.1
Number of shares (in millions)	5	6.5	5	6.5
EPS	$ .20	$ .48	$ 3.20	$ 2.78

they are subtracted from profit aftertax. Finally, selling stock increases the number of shares outstanding from 5 to 6.5 million.

Several noteworthy observations emerge from these figures. One involves the tax advantage of debt financing. Regardless of the value of EBIT, Harbridge's tax liability is always $2.1 million lower under bond financing. This figure equals one half of the added interest expense of the debt financing option over stock financing. In effect, the government is paying companies a subsidy, in the form of reduced taxes, which encourages the use of debt financing. A second observation is that stock financing does produce higher profits after tax simply because it involves no interest expense. However, the most important observation is what the financing decision does to EPS. Looking at the boom conditions, we see the expected impact of leverage: EPS with debt financing is a healthy 15 percent higher than EPS with equity financing. Under bust conditions, the reverse is true; stock financing produces a significantly higher EPS. This corresponds to our earlier example when r was less than i.

To display this information more informatively, it is useful to construct a *range-of-earnings chart*. To do so, we need only plot the EBIT–EPS pairs calculated above on a graph and connect the appropriate points with straight lines. Figure 7–2 shows the resulting range-of-earnings chart for Harbridge. This chart presents the EPS Harbridge will report for any level of EBIT under the two financing plans. Note that the bond financing line passes through an EPS of $3.20 at $40 million EBIT and $.20 at $10 million EBIT, whereas the corresponding figures for stock financing are $2.78 and $.48, respectively.

Mr. Thompson will be particularly interested in two aspects of the range-of-earnings chart. One is the increase in EPS Harbridge will report at the

Figure 7–2. Range-of-Earnings Chart for Harbridge Fabrics

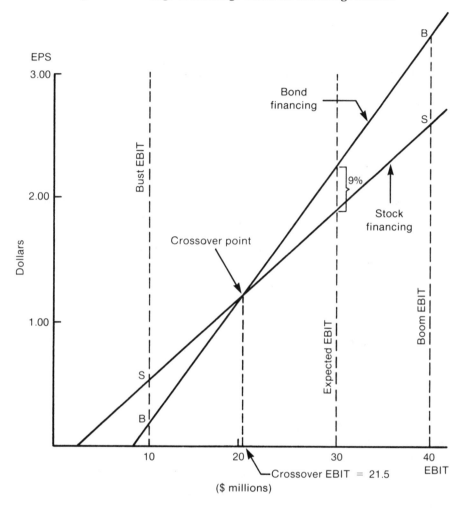

expected EBIT level if the company selects bond financing over stock financing. As shown on the graph, this increase will be 9 percent at an expected EBIT of $30 million. Thompson also will observe that in addition to an immediate increase in EPS, bond financing also puts Harbridge on a faster growth trajectory. This is represented by the steeper slope of the bond financing line. For each dollar Harbridge adds to EBIT, EPS will rise more with bond financing than with equity financing. Unfortunately, the reverse is also true; for each dollar EBIT declines, EPS will fall more with bond financing than with equity financing.

The second aspect of the range-of-earnings chart which will catch Mr.

Thompson's eye is that bond financing does not yield a higher EPS at all EBIT levels. In particular, if Harbridge's EBIT should fall below a critical crossover value of $21.5 million, EPS will actually be higher with stock financing than with bond financing. Harbridge's expected EBIT is well above the crossover value. However, the historical record presented earlier indicates that EBIT has been quite volatile in past years. In fact, it has been below $21.5 million in four of the seven years for which we have data. A higher EPS with bond financing is clearly not assured.

Coverage Ratios

The primary use of a range-of-earnings chart is to examine the return dimension of financial leverage: What EPS or ROE can a company anticipate at expected levels of operating income for the various financing plans under consideration? The risk dimension of leverage is best considered by calculating coverage ratios. Because coverage ratios were treated in Chapter 2, our discussion here will be brief.

The before- and aftertax burdens of Harbridge Fabric's financial obligations appear below.

Financial Obligations ($ millions)

	Bonds		Stock	
	Aftertax	Before-Tax	Aftertax	Before-Tax
Interest expense		$ 7.1		$2.9
Principal payment	$5.5	11.0	$4.0	8.0
Preferred dividends	0.4	0.8	0.4	0.8
Common dividends	5.0	5.0	3.25	6.5

Recall that because we wish to compare these financial obligations to the company's EBIT, it is necessary to calculate the *before-tax* income required to meet the obligation. Hence, our chief interest is in the before-tax numbers. Since Harbridge is in the 50 percent tax bracket, the before-tax burden is double the aftertax burden for all obligations except interest, which is a tax-deductible expense.

Four coverage ratios, corresponding to the progressive addition of each of these financial obligations, appear below for an assumed EBIT of $30 million.

	Bonds		Stock	
	Coverage	Percent EBIT Can Fall	Coverage	Percent EBIT Can Fall
Times interest earned	4.23	76%	10.34	90%
Times burden covered	1.66	40	2.75	64
Times preferred covered	1.59	37	2.56	61
Times common covered	1.26	21	1.65	39

To illustrate calculation of these ratios, "times common covered" equals $30 million EBIT divided by the sum of all four financial burdens in before-tax dollars. [For bonds, $1.26 = 30 \div (7.1 + 11.0 + 0.8 + 5.0)$.]

The column headed "Percent EBIT Can Fall" presents a second way to interpret coverage ratios. It is the percentage amount that EBIT can decline from its expected level before coverage equals 1.0. For example, interest expense with bond financing is $7.1 million; hence, EBIT can fall from $30 million to $7.1 million, or 76 percent, before times interest earned for bond financing equals 1.0. A coverage of 1.0 is critical in the sense that a lower coverage indicates the financial burden under examination cannot be covered out of operating income and another source of cash must be available.

Harbridge's coverage ratios clearly illustrate the added risks implied by debt financing. For each ratio, coverage is significantly worse with bond financing than with stock financing. Given the instability of Harbridge's operating income over past years, debt financing implies a worrisome increase in the possibility of default.

Table 7–4 presents times interest earned ratios for representative industries for the period 1978 through first quarter 1982. Note the steady decline in virtually every industry. Table 7–5 shows the variation in key performance ratios by Standard & Poor's rating category over the years 1979–1981. Observe that the median times interest earned ratio falls steadily from $18.25\times$ for AAA corporations down to $1.76\times$ for B corporations.

Table 7–4. Times Interest Earned Ratios for Representative Industries
(upper quartile, median, lower quartile)

Type and Number of Firms Reporting in 1982	Times Interest Earned Ratio First Quarter Ending:				
	1982	1981	1980	1979	1978
Manufacturing					
Men's and boys' sport clothing (68)	6.6	5.4	5.0	5.6	10.2
	2.3	2.3	2.3	3.0	4.6
	1.2	1.2	1.3	1.7	2.1
Industrial chemicals (62)	10.3	11.4	13.7	15.4	12.5
	3.1	4.1	5.9	4.6	5.4
	1.6	1.6	2.4	2.5	2.7
Electronic components and accessories (282)	9.2	11.2	11.2	12.3	13.5
	3.7	5.2	5.6	5.6	5.7
	1.5	2.0	2.4	2.5	2.4
Farm machinery and equipment (127)	3.6	3.9	6.0	5.5	8.1
	1.8	1.7	2.7	2.5	3.0
	1.0	0.8	1.6	1.3	1.3
Wholesaling					
Electrical supplies and apparatus (416)	7.2	9.5	10.0	11.2	11.3
	3.1	4.0	4.6	4.7	4.9
	1.5	2.0	2.3	2.4	2.3

Table 7–4 *(concluded)*

Type and Number of Firms Reporting in 1982	Times Interest Earned Ratio First Quarter Ending:				
	1982	*1981*	*1980*	*1979*	*1978*
Wholesaling (continued)					
Sporting goods and toys (172)	5.1	4.7	5.8	7.4	7.6
	1.9	2.3	2.6	3.4	3.5
	1.1	1.3	1.5	1.7	1.7
Retailing					
Hardware stores (222)	5.3	6.0	7.7	9.3	10.6
	2.1	2.6	3.5	4.2	4.9
	1.1	1.4	1.5	2.1	2.1
Jewelry (225)	5.9	7.3	10.0	10.5	10.1
	2.4	4.0	4.4	5.0	5.0
	1.3	1.8	2.4	2.6	2.5
Service					
Motels, hotels and tourist courts (195)	3.7	3.5	3.1	3.3	3.6
	1.7	2.0	1.7	1.7	1.7
	1.1	1.2	1.2	1.1	1.1
Management consulting and public relations (212)	11.5	13.1	15.2	19.8	19.4
	3.5	4.5	6.4	8.4	8.1
	1.4	2.0	2.4	2.3	2.8

Source: Copyright Robert Morris Associates, *Annual Statement Studies* (Philadelphia, 1978–1982). Used with permission. See pp. 53–54 of this text.

Table 7–5. Averages of Key Ratios by Rating Category Standard & Poor's Ratings (three-year median figures, 1979–1981)

	AAA	*AA*	*A*	*BBB*	*BB*	*B*
Times interest earned	18.25×	8.57×	6.56×	3.82×	3.27×	1.76×
Times interest and rental expense earned	8.02	4.95	4.05	2.75	2.41	1.52
Cash flow/Total debt	136.23%	80.41%	57.96%	36.58%	26.43%	13.25%
Pretax return on average long-term capital	31.27	26.29	21.75	18.31	18.44	13.19
Operating income/sales	16.25	14.27	12.72	10.90	11.86	9.04
Long-term debt/Capitalization*	11.83	19.02	26.30	34.47	44.09	54.13

Note: These figures are not meant to be minimum standards.
*Capitalization = All long-term sources of capital = Total assets − Short-term liabilities
Source: Standard & Poor's Corporation (New York, 1982).

Financial Flexibility

Up to now, we have looked at the financing decision as if it were a one-time event. Should Harbridge Fabrics raise $30 million today by selling bonds or stock? Realistically, such individual decisions are part of a longer-run financing strategy which is shaped in large part by the firm's access to capital markets over time.

At one extreme, if a company has the luxury of always being able to raise debt or equity capital on acceptable terms, the financing is straightforward. Management can simply select a target capital structure based on long-run risk-return considerations and then base the individual debt-equity decisions on transitory market conditions and on the proximity of the firm's present capital structure to its target.

When access to capital markets is usually possible, but not assured, the decision becomes more complex. In this case, management must worry about how today's decision will affect the company's future access to capital markets. This is the notion of *financial flexibility:* the concern that today's decision not jeopardize future financing options or growth opportunities. Consider Harbridge Fabrics and its need to raise $5 to $20 million annually. Given Harbridge's volatile EBIT in past years and the comparatively low coverage ratios, it is possible that selling bonds now will "close off the top" for the next few years, meaning that Harbridge may be unable to raise meaningful amounts of additional debt without a proportional increase in equity. "Top" refers to the top portion of the liabilities side of the balance sheet. Having thus reached its debt capacity, Harbridge may be dependent on the equity market over the next few years for any additional external capital. This is a precarious position, for if equity cannot be sold on reasonable terms when needed, Harbridge might be forced to forgo attractive investment opportunities for lack of funds. Such an inability to make competitively necessary investments can result in a permanent loss of market share. Consequently, a concern for financing future growth would suggest issuing equity now while it is available, thereby maintaining financing flexibility to meet future contingencies.

At the other extreme, if a company cannot, or will not, sell new equity, the financing decision becomes part of managing growth. As noted in Chapter 5, the main appeal of financial leverage to such companies is not so much its effect on EPS or ROE but the fact that leverage increases sustainable growth. With equity financing impossible, the only feasible way to finance more rapid growth is frequently to increase leverage. Consequently, the financing decision comes down to a trade-off between *growth* and *risk.* Increased leverage raises a firm's sustainable growth rate but also increases the risk of bankruptcy.

Because many companies have a strong aversion to raising external equity, this latter perspective is a common one. Debt's impact on EPS and

ROE are interesting, but the real benefits of increased leverage are seen to be the new assets, and perhaps the enhanced market share, which the borrowing makes possible. Like all companies, however, these firms must monitor their indebtedness closely to keep bankruptcy risk at prudent levels. The coverage ratios described above are appropriate tools for this task.

Selecting a Maturity Structure

When a company elects to raise debt capital, the next question is what maturity should the debt be? Should the company take out a 1-year loan, sell 7-year notes, or sell 30-year bonds? Looking at the firm's entire capital structure, *the minimum risk maturity structure occurs when the maturity of liabilities equals or exceeds that of assets* for, in this configuration, cash generated from operations over coming years should be sufficient to repay

---

Academic Views of the Debt-Equity Choice

Rather than study the impact of financial leverage on company risk and return as we have done, the usual academic perspective has been to examine the impact of leverage on the market value of the firm. Fundamentally, these are not conflicting approaches because a capital structure which effectively balances risk against return in the long-run interests of the company should also increase firm value.

At one extreme, some academicians argue that in properly functioning markets with no taxes and no transactions costs, the increased risk to equity from debt financing just counterbalances the increased expected return, so that the degree of financial leverage a company chooses has no effect on its market value. Others argue that this may be true under idealized conditions, but that under more realistic conditions, financial leverage does affect share values. At low levels of indebtedness, the tax advantage of debt financing predominates; so that increases in leverage produce higher market values. But beyond some prudent range, the increasing probability of bankruptcy begins to outweigh the tax advantage and firm value begins to fall with further increases in leverage.

To date, academic research has greatly clarified our thinking about the financing decision, but it has been of only modest help to financial executives in developing practical financing strategies. The principal difficulty has been that by assuming the continuous availability of debt and equity capital to firms, academicians have assumed away a major part of the problem as it really exists. As a result, academic treatments of the topic tend to involve one-time, debt-equity choices without any consideration for future financing flexibility.

existing liabilities as they mature. In other words, the liabilities will be self-liquidating. If the maturity of liabilities is less than that of assets, the company incurs a refinancing risk because some maturing liabilities will have to be paid off from the proceeds of newly raised capital. And as noted in an earlier chapter, the rollover of maturing debt is not an automatic feature of capital markets. When the maturity of liabilities is greater than that of assets, cash provided by operations should be more than sufficient to repay existing liabilities as they mature. This provides an extra margin of safety, but it also means that the firm may have excess cash in some periods.

If maturity matching is minimum risk, why do anything else? Why allow the maturity of liabilities to be less than that of assets? Companies mismatch either because long-term debt is unavailable on acceptable terms or because management anticipates that mismatching will reduce total borrowing costs. If management believes that interest rates will decline in the future, an obvious strategy is to use short-term debt financing now and hope to roll it over into longer-term debt at lower rates in the future. Efficient markets advocates would criticize this strategy on the grounds that management has no reason to believe it can forecast future interest rates in an efficient market.

Inflation and Financing Strategy

An old saying in finance is that it's good to be a borrower during inflation. As noted in Chapter 3, this saying is incorrect when we are speaking of *expected* inflation. When creditors expect inflation, the interest rate they charge rises to compensate them for the expected decline in the purchasing power of the loan principal. This means that it is not necessarily advantageous to borrow during inflation.

Inflation, Taxes, and Borrowing Costs

A related consideration involves taxes. Although much of the interest rate during inflation is really compensation for the declining principal value of the loan, the tax authorities nonetheless allow the entire payment as a tax-deductible expense. This works to the borrower's benefit. However, because the lender must declare the entire interest receipt as income, it works to the lender's disadvantage. If borrower and lender were in the same tax bracket, we would expect interest rates to increase to the point where the real, aftertax cost of borrowing was unaffected by inflation. However, if a borrower in a high tax bracket can find a lender in a low bracket, this need not happen. And inflation can result in lower real borrowing costs to the company and higher real returns to the lender. In this case, only "we the people" would lose in the form of reduced governmental tax receipts.

Appendix

Operating Leverage

We observed in the chapter that financial leverage involves the substitution of fixed-cost debt financing for owners' equity. A second form of leverage is *operating* leverage. Operating leverage occurs whenever a company has fixed costs which must be met regardless of volume. Companies vary tremendously in their use of operating leverage, depending primarily on available technology. Examples of firms with high operating leverage include airlines, steel mills, and heavy-equipment manufacturers; among those with low operating leverage are residential contractors and wholesale distributors.

The impact of operating leverage on the financial performance of a company is remarkably like that of financial leverage: Increases in operating leverage raise ROE whenever volume exceeds a minimum break-even level but reduce ROE when volume is below break-even.

This is not the place for a detailed treatment of operating leverage. The topic, however, does merit attention, for as we will see, the amount of operating leverage a company employs influences the amount of financial leverage it can use. In other words, the two types of leverage are at least partial substitutes for one another. A second reason for considering operating leverage is that the related technique of break-even analysis can be useful in evaluating investment opportunities, the subject of the following two chapters. Readers interested in a more thorough treatment of the topic are directed to the references at the end of this chapter.

Operating Leverage and ROE. To see the impact of operating leverage on ROE, write ROE as:

$$ROE = \frac{\text{Profit after tax}}{\text{Equity}} = \frac{1 - T}{\text{Equity}} \text{ Profit before tax}$$

where T is the tax rate.

Because operating leverage has no effect on the term in brackets, we can focus our attention on profit before tax, knowing that operating leverage's effect on ROE will be the same except for a constant factor.

Next, write profit before tax as:

$$
\begin{aligned}
\text{Profit before tax} &= \text{Revenue} - \text{Variable cost} - \text{Fixed cost} \\
&= PQ - VQ - F \\
&= Q(P - V) - F
\end{aligned}
$$

where Q is the number of units of the product or service produced and sold, P is the selling price per unit, V is variable cost per unit, and F is the fixed cost over the accounting period. Recall that by definition fixed costs do not vary with the number of units sold, whereas variable costs change in direct proportion to sales. Examples of fixed costs include heat, light, depreciation, and managerial salaries; examples of variable costs are materials and labor.

Figure 7A–1 illustrates the above equation for Star Enterprises, Inc., a manufacturer of rubber stamps. The average selling price of a Star stamp is $1, its variable production costs are 50 cents per stamp, and its annual fixed costs are $2 million. The diagram—known variously as *break-even chart* or a *profit graph*—shows fixed costs (F) constant regardless of the number of stamps produced and sold, but variable costs (VQ) increasing linearly with the number of stamps produced and sold. Total revenue (PQ) also varies in the same way. Total costs (VQ + F) in the figure are the sum of fixed and variable costs. Finally, the difference between revenue and total costs is, of course, profit or loss.

Observe that if the quantity produced and sold exceeds the break-even volume, labeled Q*, Star earns a profit; otherwise, it loses money. Q* is an

Figure 7A–1. Star Enterprises, Inc., Break-Even Chart—Present Production Methods

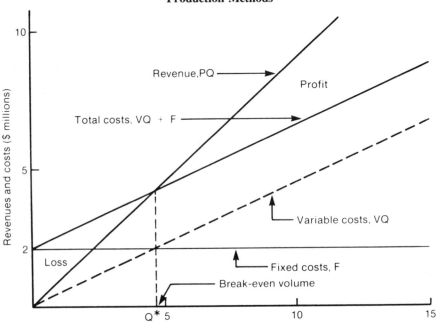

Units produced and sold (millions)

important quantity; to solve for it, just set profit equal to zero in the above equation.

$$0 = Q^*(P - V) - F$$

$$Q^* = \frac{F}{P - V}$$

In words, break-even volume equals fixed costs divided by the difference between price per unit and variable cost per unit. Frequently, this denominator is called the *contribution* per unit. It is the cash generated by each unit sold that is available, after covering variable costs, to pay for fixed costs and contribute to profits. Star's break-even volume is:

$$Q^* = \frac{\$2 \text{ million}}{\$1.00 - \$.50} = 4 \text{ million units}$$

Unless Star sells 4 million stamps annually, it will lose money.

Analysis of Increased Operating Leverage.   To appreciate the tie between operating leverage and ROE and to see how break-even analysis can aid in investment evaluation, suppose the production manager of Star Enterprises believes the variable production cost per stamp can be reduced from 50 cents to 30 cents by substituting automated equipment for hand labor in the assembly process. She estimates the equipment will increase fixed costs to $3 million. Management expects next year's sales will be about $8 million and wonders what impact the automated equipment would have on profits and ROE. One worrisome fact is that a growing number of Star stamps are fad items; so that annual sales are becoming increasingly difficult to predict. For the coming year, management believes that under bust conditions sales could be as low as $4 million but under boom conditions could reach $12 million.

A useful starting point in evaluating the equipment purchase proposal is to calculate Star's break-even sales volume after acquiring the new equipment.

$$Q^* = \frac{\$3 \text{ million}}{\$1 - \$.30} = 4.3 \text{ million units}$$

Star's break-even sales volume rises from 4 to 4.3 million stamps with the new equipment.

For some investment proposals calculation of break-even sales is sufficient to eliminate the proposal from further consideration. Certainly, if Q* with the new equipment had equaled 9 million stamps, acquisition would be ill advised. In the present case sales are expected to exceed break-even except under extreme circumstances, so further study is warranted.

Table 7A–1 shows Star's profit before tax under present and proposed

Table 7A–1. Star Enterprise's Profits with Differing Sales Levels and Levels of Operating Leverage ($ millions)*

	Present Production Methods: Fixed Costs = $2 Million, Variable Cost = 50¢/Stamp			Proposed Production Methods: Fixed Costs = $3 Million, Variable Cost = 30¢/Stamp		
	Boom	*Expected*	*Bust*	*Boom*	*Expected*	*Bust*
Sales (Q)	12	8	4	12	8	4
Profits	$4.0	$2.0	$0.0	$5.4	$2.6	−$0.2

*Selling price per stamp is $1.

production methods and at three sales levels: boom, expected, and bust. Note that the automated equipment increases profits at boom and expected sales but reduces them when sales are a bust. At sales of 4 million stamps, profits are zero under present conditions but fall to a loss of $200,000 with the new equipment.

Figure 7A–2 shows the break-even chart for the proposed production method. Comparing the two break-even charts, we see that increased operating leverage rotates the total costs line in a clockwise direction, rais-

Figure 7A–2. Star Enterprises, Inc., Break-Even Chart—Proposed Production Methods

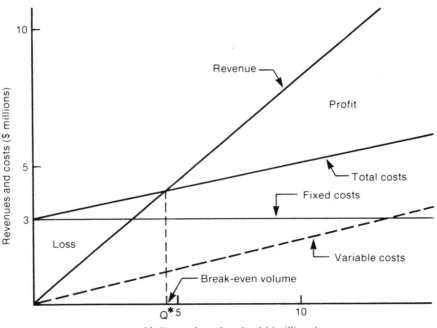

ing fixed costs and contribution per unit. This rotation widens the "profit wedge" but also raises break-even volume. The net effect of increased operating leverage on ROE depends on volume. If Q is comfortably above the new Q*, added operating leverage raises profits and ROE; otherwise, the reverse is true.[3]

This is demonstrated in Figure 7A–3 which shows how Star's profits and ROE vary with fixed costs under the three sales scenarios. Just as with financial leverage, increased operating leverage raises expected profits and expected ROE, but increases risk as well. Comparison of Figures 7–1 and 7A–3 should convince you that operating and financial leverage have similar effects on financial performance.

Figure 7A–3.   Operating Leverage Increases Expected Profits and Risk

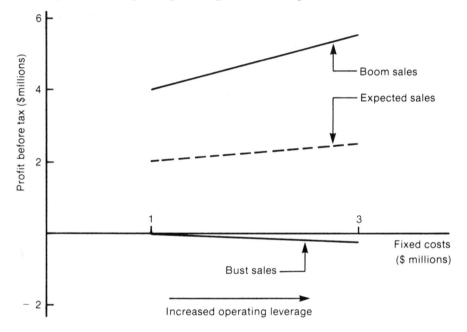

---

[3]Technically, Star's volume must exceed 5 million units before the automated equipment will increase profits. To see this, let VC_1 and F_1 be variable cost per unit and fixed cost with present production methods, and let VC_2 and F_2 be the same quantities for proposed production methods. Write profits for the two alternatives, set the profits equal to one another, and solve for Q.

$$Q(P - VC_1) - F_1 = Q(P - VC_2) - F_2$$

$$Q = \frac{F_1 - F_2}{VC_2 - VC_1} = 5 \text{ million units}$$

Profits with the proposed production techniques will exceed profit with present techniques at all sales volumes above 5 million units.

What should Star management do? Read Chapters 8 and 9. The automated equipment is a major investment for Star, and break-even analysis indicates it is neither a clear accept nor a clear reject. Further study is therefore required before management can make a reasoned decision. The next two chapters present techniques for conducting such a study.

Lessons from Break-Even Analysis. The break-even charts appearing above are limited by a number of well-known, artificial assumptions. Many costs are neither purely fixed nor purely variable. Instead, they are "semivariable," increasing with volume but at a less than proportional rate. Moreover, total costs and revenues may not bear a straight-line relation with volume. This is particularly true when a company approaches full capacity. Price concessions may be necessary to increase sales further, and costs may rise at an accelerating rate as production bottlenecks occur. Finally, the distinction between fixed and variable costs depends implicitly on the observation period. In the very short run of, say, the next hour, virtually all costs are fixed, but as the time period lengthens, costs become increasingly variable, until in the very long run all costs are variable. Break-even analysis is thus appropriate only for a specific time period.

Despite these limitations, break-even analysis has proved to be a useful technique. In the early stages of investment evaluation, break-even analysis offers a quick, back-of-the-envelope tool for deciding if the proposal merits careful study. The technique also explains why some industries respond differently to recessions than others. In industries with low operating leverage—like construction—the standard response to recession is to reduce volume but maintain prices. Reduced volume is not a major concern to construction companies because most costs are variable and break-even volume is low. In industries with high operating leverage—like airlines or steel—declining volume can be disastrous. Costs are predominantly fixed and break-even quantities are high; so that losses mount rapidly as volume falls. The natural response to declining demand in these industries is to cut prices in an effort to maintain volume.

The most important lesson of break-even analysis for the financial manager is that the amount of operating leverage a company employs is an important determinant of the amount of financial leverage it can prudently sustain. Because both types of leverage increase risk, management must adapt its financing policies to the company's operating characteristics. If it fails to do so, bankruptcy risks can become excessive, and the company's growth plans can be jeopardized. This is yet another example of the fact that sound financial policy must reflect and support the company's operating plans.

Chapter Summary

1. The intent of this chapter has been to study the corporate financing decision and, in particular, to look at the advantages and disadvantages of financial leverage.

2. For businesses that are unable or unwilling to raise new equity, debt financing increases growth. It enables the business to acquire assets that are otherwise unattainable, and it increases the firm's sustainable growth rate. For businesses with access to new equity, debt financing increases the expected return on equity.

3. The principal disadvantages of debt financing are increased variability of income and of return on equity and increased bankruptcy risk.

4. Coverage ratios are useful for evaluating the added risk of debt financing, whereas a range-of-earnings chart is useful for looking at the return dimensions of the decision.

5. Because money from external sources is not always available on agreeable terms, a major concern in most financing decisions is the impact of today's choice on tomorrow's options. Decisions that constrain a company's future ability to raise capital reduce financial flexibility.

Additional Reading

Donaldson, Gordon. "New Framework for Corporate Debt Capacity." *Harvard Business Review,* March–April 1962, pp. 117–131.
  Old, but still one of the best practical discussions of the financing decision.

Piper, Thomas R., and Wolf A. Weinhold, "How Much Debt Is Right for Your Company?" *Harvard Business Review,* July–August 1982, pp. 106–114.
  A practical, well-balanced look at the financing decision with particular emphasis on flexibility.

Van Horne, James C. *Financial Management and Policy.* 5th ed. Englewood Cliffs, N.J.: Prentice-Hall, 1980. 808 pages.
  A leading graduate-level financial management text. Chapter 27, Operating and Financial Leverage, and the references present a thorough treatment of subjects.

Chapter Problems

1. This chapter considered the financing decision of Harbridge Fabrics. Looking at Harbridge's coverage ratios and range-of-earnings chart presented in the chapter, explain how each of the following changes would affect these ratios and the range-of-earnings chart. Which changes would make equity more attractive? Which would make debt more attractive?

   a. An increase in the interest rate on the new debt.
   b. An increase in Harbridge's stock price.
   c. Increased uncertainty about Harbridge's future earnings.
   d. Increased common stock dividends.

2. City Computer wants to raise $300 million in new capital. The company can sell equity at $20 per share, or it can sell bonds at par with a 14 percent coupon rate. City currently has an interest expense of $100 million and pays $2 million in preferred dividends. The company has 40 million common shares outstanding and is in the 40 percent tax bracket.

   a. Draw a range-of-earnings chart for the company.
   b. Can you calculate the value of EBIT at the crossover point?

3. Texas Mining has the opportunity to invest $100 million in a project promising an annual EBIT of $30 million. The firm's investment bankers indicate that the markets would not be receptive to an equity issue at this time, and recommend instead a debt issue at 20 percent interest. Without the investment, the company's EBIT next year is expected to be $150 million; its interest expense will be $90 million. The tax rate is 50 percent, and there are 30 million common shares outstanding.

   a. Calculate expected EPS with and without the new investment.
   b. Calculate the company's times interest earned ratios with and without the investment.
   c. Based on these calculations, what conclusions can you draw, if any, about the merit of financing the investment with new debt?

PART IV

Evaluating Investment Opportunities

8 Discounted Cash Flow Techniques

The chief determinant of what a company will become is the investments it undertakes today. The generation and evaluation of creative investment proposals is too important a task to be left to finance specialists; instead it is the ongoing responsibility of all managers throughout the organization. In well-managed companies the process starts at a strategic level with senior management specifying the businesses in which the company will compete and determining the means of competition. Operating managers then translate these strategic goals into concrete action plans involving specific investment proposals. A key aspect in this translation of strategic goals into action plans is the financial evaluation of investment proposals, or what is frequently called *capital budgeting*. The achievement of some strategic objective requires the outlay of money today in the expectation of increased future income. It is necessary to decide, first, whether the anticipated future income is large enough, given the risks, to justify the current expenditure, and second, whether the proposed investment is the most cost-effective way to achieve the objective. The remainder of the book addresses these questions.

Figures of Merit

The financial evaluation of any investment opportunity can be broken down into three discrete steps:

1. Estimate the relevant cash flows.
2. Calculate a figure of merit for the investment.
3. Compare the figure of merit to an acceptance criterion.

A figure of merit is a number that summarizes an investment's economic worth. A common figure of merit is the rate of return. Like the other figures of merit to be discussed, the rate of return translates the complicated cash inflows and outflows associated with the investment into a single number summarizing its economic worth. An acceptance criterion is a standard of comparison that helps the analyst decide if an investment's figure of merit is attractive enough to warrant acceptance. It's like a fisherman who must throw back all fish shorter than 10 inches. To the fisherman, the length of the fish is the relevant figure of merit, and 10 inches is the acceptance criterion.

Although figures of merit and acceptance criteria may appear difficult on first exposure, the first step, estimating the relevant cash flows, is the most challenging in practice. Difficulties include the proper treatment of depreciation, financing costs, and working capital investments, as well as sunk costs and excess capacity. Another pervasive problem is that significant costs and benefits frequently cannot be stated in monetary terms and must be treated qualitatively.

The plan in this chapter is initially to set aside questions of relevant cash flows and acceptance criteria in order to concentrate on figures of merit. Later in the chapter, we will return to the estimation of relevant cash flows. Acceptance criteria will be addressed in the following chapter under the general heading, "Risk Analysis in Investment Decisions."

To begin our discussion of figures of merit, let's consider a simple numerical example. Pacific Rim Resources, Inc., is contemplating construction of a container loading pier in Seattle. The company's best estimate of the cash flows associated with constructing and operating the pier for a 10-year period appear in Table 8–1. Figure 8–1 presents the same information

Table 8–1. Cash Flows for Container Loading Pier ($ millions)

Year	0	1	2	3	4	5	6	7	8	9	10
Cash flow	$(40)	$7.5	$7.5	$7.5	$7.5	$7.5	$7.5	$7.5	$7.5	$7.5	$17

Figure 8–1. Cash Flow Diagram for Container Loading Pier

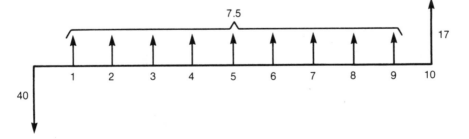

in the form of a cash flow diagram. The pier will cost $40 million to construct and is expected to generate cash inflows of $7.5 million annually for 10 years. In addition, the company expects to salvage the pier for $9.5 million at the end of its useful life, bringing the 10th year cash flow to $17 million.

The Payback Period and the Accounting Rate of Return

The problem facing Pacific management is deciding whether the anticipated benefits from the pier justify the $40 million cost. As we will see shortly, a proper answer to this problem must reflect the time value of money. But before addressing this topic, it will be useful to consider two commonly used, back-of-the-envelope type figures of merit. One, known as the payback period, is defined as the time the company must wait before recouping its original investment. For an investment with a single cash outflow followed by uniform annual inflows:

$$\text{Payback period} = \frac{\text{Investment}}{\text{Annual cash inflow}}$$

For the pier, the payback period is $5\frac{1}{3}$ years (40/7.5).

The second widely used figure of merit is the accounting rate of return, defined as:

$$\text{Accounting rate of return} = \frac{\text{Average annual cash inflow}}{\text{Total cash outflow}}$$

The accounting rate of return for the proposed pier is 21.1 percent [(7.5 × 9 + 17)/10) ÷ 40].

Regrettably, the payback period and the accounting rate of return are both inadequate figures of investment merit. The problem with the accounting rate of return is its insensitivity to the timing of cash flows. For example, a postponement of all of the cash inflows from Pacific's container loading pier to year 10 obviously reduces the value of the investment but does not affect the accounting rate of return. In addition to ignoring the timing of cash flows, the payback period is also insensitive to all cash flows occurring beyond the payback date. Thus an increase in the salvage value of the pier from $9.5 million to $90.5 million clearly makes the investment more attractive. Yet, it has no effect on the payback period; nor does any change in cash flows in years 6 through 10.

In fairness to the payback period, I should add that although it is clearly an inadequate figure of investment merit, it has proved to be useful as a rough measure of investment risk. For in most settings, the longer it takes to recoup an original investment, the greater the risk. This is especially true in high-technology environments where management can only forecast a few years into the future. Under these circumstances an investment which does not promise to pay back within the forecasting horizon is the equivalent of a night in Las Vegas without the floor show.

The Time Value of Money

An accurate figure of merit must reflect the fact that a dollar today is worth more than a dollar in the future. This is the time value of money, and it exists for at least three reasons. One is that inflation reduces the purchasing power of future dollars relative to current ones; another is that in most instances the uncertainty surrounding the receipt of a dollar increases as the date of receipt recedes into the future. Thus the promise of $1 in 30 days is usually worth more than the promise of $1 in 30 months, simply because it is likely to be more certain.

A third reason money has a time value involves the notion of *opportunity costs.* By definition, the opportunity cost of any investment is the return one could earn on the next best investment. A dollar today is worth more than a dollar in one year because the dollar today can be productively invested and will grow into more than a dollar in a year. Waiting to receive the dollar until next year carries an opportunity cost equal to the return on the foregone investment.

Compounding and Discounting. Because money has a time value, we cannot simply combine cash flows occurring at different dates as is done in calculating the payback period and the accounting rate of return. To adjust investment cash flows for their differing time value, we use the notions of compounding and discounting. Everyone who has ever had a bank account knows about compounding intuitively. Suppose you have a bank account paying 10 percent annual interest, and you deposit $1 at the start of the year, what will it be worth at the end of the year? Obviously, $1.10. Now, suppose you leave the dollar in the account for two years, what will it be worth then? This is a little harder, but most of us realize that, because you earn interest on your interest, the answer is $1.21. Compounding is the process of determining the future value of a present sum. The simple cash flow diagrams below summarize the exercise.

Discounting is just compounding turned on its head: It is the process of finding the present value of a future sum. Yet despite the obvious similarities, many persons find discounting somehow mysterious. Suppose you can invest money to earn a 10 percent annual return and that you are promised $1 in one year; what is the value of this promise today? Clearly, it is worth less than $1, but the exact figure is probably not something that pops immediately to mind. The answer is $0.909. This is the *present value* of $1 to be received in one year because if you had $0.909 today, you could invest it at 10 percent interest, and it would grow into $1 in one year [$1.00 = 0.909 (1 + .10)].

Now, if we complicate matters further and assume the dollar is to be received in two years, intuition fails most of us completely. We know the

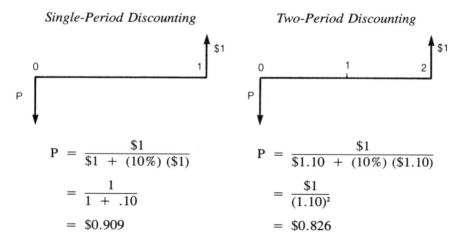

Interest Rate = 10%

Single-Period Compounding

$$F_1 = \$1 + (10\%)(\$1)$$
$$= \$1(1 + .10)$$
$$= \$1.10$$

Two-Period Compounding

$$F_2 = 1.10 + (10\%)(\$1.10)$$
$$= \$1(1 + .10)^2$$
$$= \$1.21$$

answer must be less than $0.909, but beyond that things are a fog. In fact, the answer is $0.826. This sum, invested for two years at 10 percent interest will grow, or compound, into $1 in two years. The following cash flow diagrams illustrate these discounting problems. Note the formal similarity to compounding. The only difference is that in compounding we know the present amount and we seek the future sum; whereas in discounting we know the future sum and seek the present amount.

Interest Rate = 10%

Single-Period Discounting

$$P = \frac{\$1}{\$1 + (10\%)(\$1)}$$
$$= \frac{1}{1 + .10}$$
$$= \$0.909$$

Two-Period Discounting

$$P = \frac{\$1}{\$1.10 + (10\%)(\$1.10)}$$
$$= \frac{\$1}{(1.10)^2}$$
$$= \$0.826$$

Present Value Tables. How did I know the answers to the discounting problems? I could have used the formulas appearing below the cash flow diagrams, or I could have used one of several brands of pocket calculators, but I did neither. I looked up the answers in Appendix A at the end of the book. Appendix A, known as a present value table, shows the present value of $1 to be received at the end of anywhere from 1 to 50 periods hence, and at interest rates ranging from 1 to 50 percent per period. The present values appearing in the table are generated from repeated application of the above formulas for differing time periods and interest rates. It might be useful to consult Appendix A for a moment to confirm the present values mentioned above.

As a matter of semantics, the interest rate in present value calculations is frequently called the *discount rate*. The discount rate can be interpreted two ways. If the company already has the money in hand, the discount rate is the rate of return which could be earned on alternative investments. In other words, it is the company's opportunity cost of the capital. If the firm must raise the money by selling securities, the discount rate is the rate of return expected by holders of the securities. In other words, it is the investors' opportunity cost of capital. As we will see in the next chapter, the discount rate is frequently used to adjust the investment cash flows for risk and is hence known as a risk-adjusted discount rate.

Appendix B at the end of the book is a close cousin to Appendix A. It shows the present value of $1 to be received at the end of *each period* for anywhere from 1 to 50 periods, and at discount rates ranging from 1 to 50 percent per period. To illustrate both appendixes, suppose a professional baseball player signs a contract to receive $500,000 per year for four years. What is this contract worth today if the ballplayer has investment opportunities yielding 15 percent per year?

The cash flow diagram is as follows.

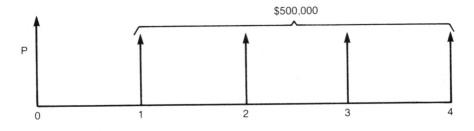

To find the present value, P, using Appendix A, we must find the present value at 15 percent of each individual payment. The arithmetic is:

$$\text{Present value of contract} = .870 \times \$500 + .756 \times \$500$$
$$+ .658 \times \$500 + .572 \times \$500$$

$$= \$1,428,000$$

A much simpler approach is to recognize that since the dollar amount is the same each year, Appendix B can be used. Consulting Appendix B, we learn that the present value of $1 per period for four periods at a 15 percent discount rate is $2.855. Thus, the present value of $500,000 is:

$$\frac{\text{Present value}}{\text{of contract}} = 2.855 \times \$500,000 = \$1,428,000$$

Although the baseball player will receive a total of $2 million over the next four years, the present value of these payments is only just over $1.4 million. Such is the power of compound interest.

Equivalence

The important fact about the present value of future cash flows is that the present value is *equivalent* in worth to the future cash flows. It is equivalent because if the analyst had the present value today, he or she could transform it into the future cash flows simply by investing it at the discount rate. To confirm this important fact, the table below shows the cash flows involved

Year	Beginning-of-Period Principal	Interest at 15 percent	End-of-Period Principal	Withdrawals
1	$1,428,000	$214,200	$1,642,200	$500,000
2	1,142,200	171,330	1,313,530	500,000
3	813,530	122,030	935,560	500,000
4	435,560	65,334	500,894	500,000

in transforming $1,428,000 today into the baseball player's contracted salary. We begin by investing the present value at 15 percent interest. At the end of the first year, the investment has grown to over $1.6 million, but the first $500,000 salary payment reduces the principal to just over $1.1 million. And so it goes until at the end of four years the $500,000 salary payments just exhaust the account. Hence, from the baseball player's perspective, $1,428,000 today is equivalent in worth to $500,000 per year for four years.

The Net Present Value

Let's use the notion of equivalence to analyze Pacific's container pier investment. More specifically, let us use Appendixes A and B to convert the future cash flows appearing in Figure 8–1 into a single cash flow of equivalent worth occurring today. Because all cash flows will then be in current dollars, we will have eliminated the time dimension from the problem and can proceed to a direct comparison of present value cash inflows against present value outflows.

Assuming Pacific has other investment opportunities yielding 10 percent, the present value of the cash inflows for the pier investment is as follows:

Present value cash inflows = 5.759 × $7.5 + .386 × $17
                                      = $49.755 million

In this calculation, 5.759 is the present value of $1 per year for nine years at a discount rate of 10 percent, and .386 is the present value of $1 in year 10 at the same discount rate. The cash flow diagrams below show the effect of this calculation. The present value calculation transforms the messy original cash flows into two cash flows of equivalent worth, each occurring at time zero.

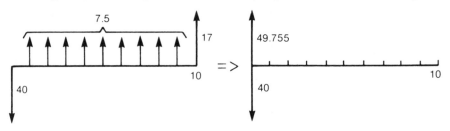

Our decision is now elementary. Should Pacific invest $40 million today for a stream of future cash flows with a value today of $49.755 million? Yes, obviously. Paying $40 million for something worth $49.755 million makes sense.

What we have just done is calculate an important figure of investment merit known as the net present value (NPV).

$$\text{NPV} = \frac{\text{Present value of}}{\text{cash inflows}} - \frac{\text{Present value of}}{\text{cash outflows}}$$

The NPV for the container pier is $9.755 million.

Formally, the NPV equals the change in wealth the investor will experience by undertaking the investment. Thus Pacific's wealth rises $9.755 million when it builds the pier because it pays $40 million for an asset worth $49.755 million. We conclude that all investments with a positive NPV are acceptable because they add to wealth; all investments with a negative NPV are unacceptable because they reduce wealth; and all investments with a zero NPV are marginal because they leave wealth unchanged.

In symbols,
when

NPV > 0, accept investment
NPV < 0, reject investment
NPV = 0, investment is marginal

The Profitability Index

A second time-adjusted figure of investment merit is the profitability index (PI), or what is sometimes called the benefit-cost ratio, defined as:

$$PI = \frac{\text{Present value of cash inflows}}{\text{Present value of cash outflows}}$$

The container pier's PI is 1.24 ($49.755/$40). Obviously, an investment is acceptable when its PI exceeds 1.0 and is unacceptable when its PI is less than 1.0. It will become clear in the appendix to this chapter why it is useful to learn about more than one figure of merit.

The Internal Rate of Return

The NPV is a valid, widely used figure of merit. An even more popular relative of the NPV is the internal rate of return (IRR), or as it is sometimes called, the discounted cash flow rate of return. To illustrate the IRR and to show its relation to the NPV, let's follow the fanciful exploits of the Seattle area manager of Pacific Rim Resources as he tries to win approval for the container pier investment. After determining that the pier's NPV is positive at a 10 percent discount rate the manager forwards his analysis to the company treasurer with a request for approval. The treasurer responds that he is favorably impressed with the manager's methodology, but that in today's high interest rate environment, he feels a discount rate of 12 percent is more appropriate. So the Seattle manager calculates a second NPV at a 12 percent discount rate and finds it to be $5.434 million, still positive but considerably lower than the original $9.7 million ($5.434 million = 5.328 × $7.5 million + 0.322 × $17 million − $40 million). Confronted with this information, the treasurer reluctantly agrees that the project is acceptable and forwards the proposal to the vice president, finance.

The vice president, finance, being even more conservative than the treasurer, also praises the methodology but argues that with all the risks involved and the difficulty raising money, an 18 percent discount rate is called for. Redoing his calculations a third time, the dejected Seattle manager now finds that at an 18 percent discount rate the NPV is −$4.481 million. Because the NPV is now negative, the vice president, finance, betraying his former career as a bank loan officer, gleefully rejects the proposal. The manager's efforts prove unproductive, but he has helped us to understand the IRR.

Table 8–2 summarizes the manager's calculations. From these figures, it is apparent that something critical happens to the investment merit of the container pier as the discount rate increases from 12 to 18 percent. Somewhere within this range the NPV changes from positive to negative, and the investment changes from acceptable to unacceptable. The critical discount rate at which this change occurs is the investment's IRR.

Formally, an investment's IRR is defined as:

**Table 8–2. NPV of Container Pier at
Differing Discount Rates**

Discount Rate	NPV
10%	$ 9.755 million
12	5.434
	◄————————— IRR = 15%
18	−4.481

IRR = Discount rate at which the investment's NPV equals zero

The IRR is a figure of merit. The corresponding acceptance criterion against which to compare the IRR is the opportunity cost of capital to the firm. If the IRR of the investment exceeds the opportunity cost of capital, the investment is acceptable, and vice versa. If it equals the cost of capital, the investment is marginal.

In symbols, letting K be the percentage cost of capital: when

IRR > K, accept investment
IRR < K, reject investment
IRR = K, investment is marginal

Figure 8–2 illustrates the relation between the container pier's NPV and its IRR by plotting the information in Table 8–2. Note that the pier's NPV = 0 at a discount rate of about 15 percent; this is the project's IRR. At capital costs below 15 percent, the NPV is positive and the IRR exceeds the cost of capital; so the investment is acceptable on both counts. When the cost of capital exceeds 15 percent, the reverse is true, and the investment is unacceptable according to both criteria.

Figure 8–2 suggests several informative ways to interpret an investment's IRR. One is that the IRR is a type of break-even return because at capital costs below the IRR the investment is attractive, but at capital costs greater than the IRR it is unattractive. A second, more important interpretation is that the IRR is the rate at which money remaining in an investment grows or compounds. As such, an IRR is comparable in all respects to the interest rate on a bank loan or a savings deposit. This means we can compare the IRR of an investment directly to the cost of the capital to be invested. We cannot say the same thing about other simpler measures of return such as the accounting rate of return because they do not properly incorporate the time value of money.

Calculating an Investment's IRR. The IRR has considerably more intuitive appeal to most executives than the NPV or the PI. The statement that an

Figure 8–2. NPV of Container Pier at Differing Discount Rates

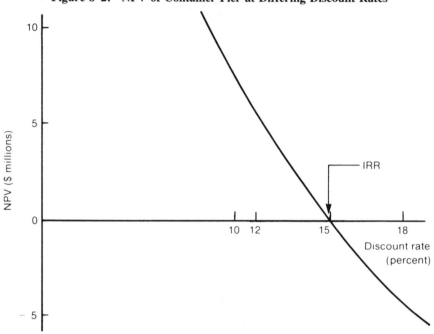

investment's IRR is 25 percent is easier to interpret than one indicating the investment's NPV is $12 million, or that its PI is 1.41. The IRR is, however, usually harder to calculate; for it is frequently necessary to search for the IRR by trial and error or, as the computer people would say, iteratively.

The first step in finding an investment's IRR is to pick a likely IRR, selected in any fashion, and to test it by calculating the investment's NPV using the chosen IRR as the discount rate. If the resulting NPV is zero, you're through. If it is positive, this is usually a signal that you need to try a higher discount rate. Conversely, if the NPV is negative you need to try a lower discount rate. This trial and error process continues until you find a discount rate for which the NPV equals zero.

To illustrate, let us calculate the IRR of the container pier. From Table 8–2 and Figure 8–2 we know that the IRR must be somewhere between 12 and 18 percent because 12 percent yields a positive NPV and 18 percent a negative one. This suggests trying 15 percent. Using Appendixes A and B:

$$\text{NPV} = 4.772 \times \$7.5 + .247 \times \$17 - \$40 \overset{?}{=} 0$$

$$- 0.01 \overset{?}{=} 0$$

For practical purposes, the NPV is zero at a discount rate of 15 percent, so this is the project's IRR. If the opportunity cost of capital to Pacific is less than 15 percent, the pier is acceptable, otherwise, it is not. The need to solve for an investment's IRR iteratively was a problem before the advent of computers and pocket calculators, but this is no longer a significant barrier to its use.

Bond Valuation

Investors regularly use discounted cash flow techniques to value bond investments. To illustrate the pricing of a bond, suppose ABC Corporation bonds have an 8 percent coupon rate paid annually, a par value of $1,000 and nine years to maturity. Let's use discounted cash flow techniques to determine the most an investor should pay for an ABC bond if he wants a return of at least 14 percent on his investment. The cash flow diagram is as follows.

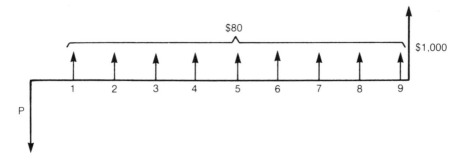

P should be equivalent in value to the future cash receipts at a 14 percent discount rate. Taking the present value of the future receipts:

$$P = \$80 \, (4.946) + \$1,000 \, (.308)$$
$$= \$703.68$$

If the investor pays $703.68 for the bond, his return over nine years will be 14 percent. If he pays more, his return will fall below 14 percent.

In the jargon of the trade, the *yield to maturity* on a bond is the IRR an investor will earn if he purchases the bond at the current price and holds it to maturity. To illustrate the calculation of a bond's yield to maturity, suppose a $1,000 par value bond pays a 10 percent annual coupon, matures in seven years, and is selling presently for $639.54. Let's begin by trying a discount rate of 12 percent.

$$NPV = 4.564 \times \$100 + .452 \times \$1,000 - \$639.54 \stackrel{?}{=} 0$$
$$268.85 \neq 0$$

Clearly, 12 percent is too low a discount rate. Suppose we try 25 percent.

$$NPV = 3.161 \times \$100 + .210 \times \$1,000 - \$639.54 \overset{?}{=} 0$$
$$- 113.44 \neq 0$$

The NPV is now negative, so 25 percent is too high. Let's try 20 percent.

$$NPV = 3.605 \times \$100 + .279 \times \$1,000 - \$639.54 \overset{?}{=} 0$$
$$- 0.04 = 0$$

So the yield to maturity, or IRR, on this bond is approximately 20 percent.

The IRR of a Perpetuity

A perpetuity is an annuity which lasts forever. Many preferred stocks are annuities, as are some British and French government bonds. They have no maturity date and promise the holder a constant annual dividend or interest payment forever. Let us use Appendix B to calculate the approximate present value of a perpetuity yielding $1 per year forever. At a discount rate of say 15 percent, the present value of $1 per year for 50 years is $6.661. Although the holder will receive a total of $50, the present value of this stream is less than $7. Why? Because if the investor put $6.661 in a bank account today yielding 15 percent per year, he could withdraw approximately $1 in interest each year *forever* without touching the principal. (15% × $6.661 = $.999.) Consequently, $6.661 today is equivalent in value to $1 per year forever.

This suggests the following formula for the present value of a perpetuity. Letting A equal the annual receipt, r the discount rate, and P the present value:

$$P = \frac{A}{r}$$

and

$$r = \frac{A}{P}$$

As an example, suppose a share of preferred stock sells for $480 and promises an annual dividend of $82 forever. Then its IRR is 17.1 percent (82/480).

Mutually Exclusive Alternatives and Capital Rationing

Frequently there is more than one way to accomplish an objective, and the investment problem is to select the best alternative. In this case, the investments are said to be mutually exclusive. An example of mutually exclusive alternatives is the choice of whether to build a concrete structure or a wooden one. Even though both options may be attractive individually, the task is to determine which is beter. Mutually exclusive investments are in contrast to independent investments where the capital budgeting problem is simply to accept or reject a single investment. When investments are independent, all three of the figures of merit introduced above will yield the same investment decision, but this is no longer true when the investments are mutually exclusive. All of the examples considered above have been independent investments.

A second complicating factor in many investment appraisals is known as capital rationing. In the preceding discussion we have implicitly assumed that sufficient money is available to enable the analyst to undertake all investments promising an IRR greater than the opportunity cost of capital. Contrastingly, under capital rationing the analyst has a fixed investment budget which he may not exceed. The presence of a limit on investment capital may be externally imposed by investors' unwillingness to supply more money, or it may be internally imposed as part of a management control system. In either case, the investment decision under capital rationing requires the analyst to rank the opportunities according to their investment merit and to accept only the best.

Both mutually exclusive alternatives and capital rationing require a ranking of investments, but here the similarity ends. With mutually exclusive investments, money is available but for technological reasons only certain investments can be accepted, whereas under capital rationing, a lack of money is the complicating factor. Moreover, even the criteria used to rank the investments differ in the two cases; so that the best investment among mutually exclusive alternatives need not be best under conditions of capital rationing. The appendix to this chapter discusses the technicalities of investment appraisal for mutually exclusive alternatives and under capital rationing, and it indicates which figures of merit are appropriate under differing conditions.

Determining the Relevant Cash Flows

Calculating a figure of merit requires an understanding of the time value of money and equivalence, and it necessitates a modicum of algebra. But these difficulties pale to insignificance compared to those arising in the estimation of an investment's relevant cash flows. Two principles govern the determination of relevant cash flows. Both are obvious when stated in the abstract but can be very difficult to apply in practice. They are—

The cash flow principle: Because money has a time value, record investment cash flows when they actually occur, not when the accountant using accrual concepts says they occur.

The with-without principle: Imagine two worlds, one in which the investment is made and one in which it is rejected. All cash flows which are different in these two worlds are relevant to the decision, and all those which are the same are irrelevant.

The following examples illustrate the practical application of these principles to commonly recurring cash flow estimation problems.

Depreciation

Depreciation is a noncash charge and, according to the cash flow principle, is therefore not a relevant cash flow. However, depreciation does influence the determination of income taxes, and taxes are a relevant cash flow. So we need to use the following two-step procedure: (1) Use standard accrual accounting techniques, including the treatment of depreciation as a cost, to calculate taxes due, then (2) add depreciation back to income after tax to calculate the investment's aftertax cash flow (ATCF). ATCF is the correct measure of an investment's operating cash flow. To illustrate, assume that the container loading pier considered earlier in the chapter will generate an annual income before depreciation and taxes of $12 million, that annual depreciation will be $3 million, and that Pacific Rim Resources is in the 50 percent tax bracket. Then, aftertax cash flow is $7.5 million, as shown in the table below.

Operating income	$12	million
Less: Depreciation	3	
Profit before tax	9	
Less: Tax at 50%	4.5	
Earnings after tax	4.5	
Plus: Depreciation	3	
Aftertax cash flow	$ 7.5	million

Another way to say the same thing is:

$$\text{Aftertax cash flow} = \text{Operating income} - \text{Taxes}$$
$$\$7.5 = \$12 - \$4.5$$

Note that this treatment of depreciation is not equivalent to saying that depreciation is irrelevant. The physical deterioration of assets over time is an economic fact of life which is relevant in investment evaluation. However, we include depreciation in our analysis whenever an asset's salvage value is estimated to be below its original cost. To also subtract an annual amount from operating income would be double-counting.

Working Capital

Many investments, especially new product investments, involve an increase in working capital items, such as inventories and receivables, in addition to increases in fixed assets. According to the with-without principle, changes in working capital which are the result of an investment decision are relevant to the decision. In some instances they are the largest cash flows involved.

There are two unique features of working capital investments. One is that such investments are reversible because at the end of the project's life, the liquidation of working capital generates cash inflows. The second unique feature is that many investments requiring working capital increases also generate *spontaneous sources* of cash in the form of increased trade credit and the like, which partially offset the working capital investment. The proper treatment of these spontaneous sources is to subtract them from the increases in current assets when calculating the project's working capital investment.

To illustrate, suppose XYZ Corporation is considering a new product investment which, in addition to an increase in plant and equipment, will require a $3 million investment in inventories and accounts receivable. Partially offsetting this buildup in current assets, management also anticipates that accounts payable, accrued wages, and accrued taxes will rise by $1 million as a result of the new product. So the net increase in working capital is $2 million. Management has agreed to analyze the proposed investment over a 10-year horizon and feels that all of the working capital investment will be recovered at the end of 10 years as the company sells off inventory, collects receivables, and pays off trade creditors. The cash flow associated only with the working capital portion of this investment is shown in the following diagram.

If money had no time value, these offsetting cash flows would cancel one another out, but because money has a time value, we need to include them in our analysis.

Allocated Costs

According to the with-without principle, those cash flows which do not change as a result of an investment are irrelevant for the decision. For example, many companies allocate overhead costs to departments or divisions in proportion to the amount of direct labor expense incurred by the department. Suppose a department manager in such an environment has the opportunity to invest in a laborsaving asset. From the department's narrow perspective, there are two benefits to such an asset: (1) a reduction in direct labor expense and (2) a reduction in the overhead costs allocated to the department. Yet from the total company perspective and from the correct economic perspective, only the reduction in direct labor is a benefit because the overhead costs are unaffected by the decision. They are just reallocated from one cost center to another.

Let us consider a subtler example involving a new product investment. Suppose a company is considering a new product investment which if undertaken will increase sales by 5 percent over the next 10 years. The point at issue is whether allocated costs that are not directly associated with the new product, such as the president's salary, legal department expenses, and accounting department expenses, are relevant to the decision. A narrow interpretation of the with-without principle suggests that if the president's salary does not change as a result of the investment, it is not relevant. Yet we observe that over time as companies grow, presidents' salaries tend to increase; and we observe that presidents of large companies tend to have higher salaries than those of small companies. This suggests that although we are unable to see a direct cause-effect tie between such costs and increasing sales, there is a longer-run relation between the two. Consequently, such costs may well be relevant to the decision.

Sunk Costs

A sunk cost is one which has already been incurred and which according to the with-without principle is not relevant for present decisions. This seems easy enough, but consider some examples. Suppose you purchased some common stock a year ago at $100 per share and that it is presently trading for $70 per share. Even though you believe the stock is fairly priced at $70, would you be prepared to admit your mistake and sell it now, or would you be tempted to hold it in hopes of recouping your original investment? The with-without principle says the $100 price is sunk and hence irrelevant—except for possible tax effects.

Suppose the R&D department of a company has devoted 10 years and $10 million to perfecting a new, long-lasting light bulb. Their original estimate was a development time of two years at a cost of $1 million, and every year since they have progressively extended the development time and increased the cost. Now they are estimating only one more year and an added expenditure of only $1 million. Since the present value of the benefits from such a light bulb is only $4 million, there is considerable feeling in the company that the project should be killed and whoever had been approving the budget increases throughout the years should be fired.

In retrospect, it is clear the company should never have begun work on the light bulb. Even if successful, the cost will be well in excess of the benefits. Yet at any point along the development process, including the current decision, it may have been perfectly rational to continue work. Past expenditures are sunk, so that the only question at issue is whether the anticipated benefits exceed the *remaining* costs required to complete development. Past expenditures are relevant only to the extent that they influence one's assessment of whether the remaining costs are properly estimated.

Excess Capacity

For technological reasons, it is frequently necessary to acquire more capacity than required to accomplish an objective, and a question arises of how to handle the excess. For example, suppose a company is considering the acquisition of a hydrofoil boat to provide passenger service across a lake, but that effective use of the hydrofoil will require construction of two very expensive special purpose piers. Each pier will be capable of handling 10 hydrofoils, and for technical reasons it is impractical to construct smaller piers. If the full cost of the two piers must be borne by the one boat presently under consideration, the boat's NPV will be large and negative; yet if only one tenth of the pier costs is assigned to the boat, its NPV will be positive. How should the pier costs be treated?

The proper treatment of the pier costs depends on the company's future plans. If the company does not anticipate acquiring any additional hydrofoils in the future, the full cost of the piers is relevant for the present decision. However, if this boat is but the first of a contemplated fleet of hydrofoils, then it is appropriate to consider only a fraction of the pier's costs. More generally, the problem faced by the company is that of defining the investment. The relevant question is not should the company acquire a boat, but should it enter the hydrofoil transportation business. The broader question forces the company to look at the investment over a longer time span.

The reverse situation also arises. A company has excess capacity of some sort and is considering an investment which will utilize the unused resources. In this case, the question is what cost, if any, to assign to the excess capacity. As an example, a prominent producer of canned foods was considering the addition of a new product line which would utilize some presently underemployed canning facilities. Some company executives argued that since the facilities had already been paid for, their cost was sunk and consequently irrelevant. Others argued that the canning capacity was a scarce resource and should be assigned a cost. What cost should be assigned to the excess capacity?

The answer again depends upon future plans. If there are no alternative uses for the canning facilities now or in the future, no costs are involved in its use. On the other hand, if the company is likely to have need for the facilities in the future, there is an opportunity cost associated with their use by the new product line.

Financing Costs

Financing costs are relevant in investment evaluation. Care must be taken, however, not to double-count them. As the next chapter will clarify, the most common discount rate used in calculating any of the recommended figures of merit equals the annual percentage cost of capital to the company. It would obviously be double-counting to expect an investment to offer a return greater than the cost of the capital invested *and* to subtract financing costs from the annual cash flows. The standard procedure, therefore, is to reflect the cost of money in the discount rate and to delete all financing costs from the cash flows.

Appendix

Mutually Exclusive Alternatives and Capital Rationing

Two investments are mutually exclusive if accepting one precludes further consideration of the other. The choices between building a steel or a concrete bridge, of laying a 12-inch pipeline instead of an 8-inch one, or of driving to Boston instead of flying are all mutually exclusive alternatives. In each case, there is more than one way to accomplish a task, and the objective is to choose the best. Mutually exclusive investments are in contrast to independent investments where each opportunity can be analyzed on its own without regard to other investments.

When investments are independent and the decision is simply to accept or reject, the NPV, the PI, and the IRR are equally satisfactory figures of merit. You will reach the same investment decision regardless of the figure of merit used. When investments are mutually exclusive, the world is not so simple. Let's consider an example. Suppose Petro Oil and Gas company is considering two alternative designs for new service stations and wants to evaluate them using a 10 percent discount rate. As shown in the cash flow diagrams in Figure 8A-1, the inexpensive option involves a present invest-

Figure 8A-1. Cash Flow Diagrams for Alternative Service Station Designs

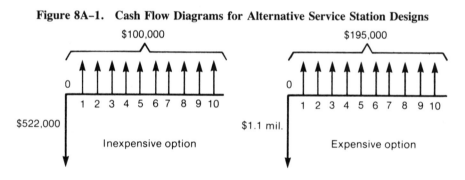

ment of $522,000 in return for an anticipated $100,000 per year for 10 years; while the expensive option costs $1.1 million, but because of its greater customer appeal, is expected to return $195,000 per year for 10 years.

Table 8A-1 presents the three figures of merit for each investment. All of the figures of merit signal that both options are attractive, the NPVs are positive, the PIs are greater than 1.0, and the IRRs exceed Petro's opportunity cost of capital. If it were possible, Petro should make both investments,

Table 8A–1. Figures of Merit for Service Station Designs

	NPV at 10 Percent	PI at 10 Percent	IRR
Inexpensive option	$92,500	1.18	14%
Expensive option	98,275	1.09	12%

but because they are mutually exclusive, this does not make sense technologically. So rather than just accepting or rejecting the investments, Petro must rank them and select the best. However, when it comes to ranking the alternatives, the three figures of merit no longer give the same signal, for although the inexpensive option has a higher PI and a higher IRR, it has a lower NPV than the expensive one.

To decide which figure of merit is appropriate for mutually exclusive alternatives, we need only remember that the NPV is a direct measure of the anticipated increase in wealth created by the investment. Since the expensive option will increase wealth by $98,275, as opposed to only $92,500 for the inexpensive option, the expensive option is clearly superior.

The problem with the PI and the IRR for mutually exclusive alternatives is basically that they are insensitive to the scale of the investment. As an extreme example, would you rather have an 80 percent return on a $1 investment or a 50 percent return on a $1 million investment? Clearly, when investments are mutually exclusive, scale is relevant, and this leads to the use of the NPV as the appropriate figure of merit.

What Happened to the Other $578,000? Some persons feel the above reasoning is incomplete because we have said nothing about what Petro can do with the $578,000 it would save by choosing the inexpensive option. It would seem that if this saving could be invested at a sufficiently attractive return, the inexpensive option might prove to be superior after all. We will address this concern in the section titled Capital Rationing. For now, it is sufficient to say that the problem arises only when there are fixed limits on the amount of money Petro has available for investment. When the company can raise sufficient money to make all investments promising IRRs greater than its opportunity cost of capital, this concern is not an important one.

Unequal Lines. The Petro Oil and Gas example conveniently assumed that both service station options had the same 10-year life. Frequently, mutually exclusive alternatives have different service lives. When this occurs, a simple comparison of NPVs is usually inappropriate. Consider the following example of a company trying to decide whether to build a wooden bridge or a steel bridge.

The wooden bridge has an initial cost of $100,000, requires annual maintenance expenditures of $10,000, and will last 10 years.

The steel bridge costs $200,000, requires $5,000 annual maintenance and will last 40 years.

At, say, a 15 percent discount rate, the present value cost of the wooden bridge is $150,190 ($100,000 + 5.019 × $10,000) versus $233,210 for the steel bridge ($200,000 + 6.642 × $5,000). So if the objective is to minimize the cost of the bridge, a simple comparison of present values would suggest that the wooden structure is a clear winner. However, this obviously overlooks the difference in the life expectancy of the two bridges.

When comparing mutually exclusive alternatives having differing service lives, it is necessary to examine each over the same common investment horizon. For example, suppose the company in the above example believes it will need a bridge for 20 years, that due to inflation, the wooden bridge will cost $200,000 to reconstruct at the end of 10 years, and that the salvage value of the steel bridge in 20 years will be $90,000. The cash flow diagrams for the two options are as follows.

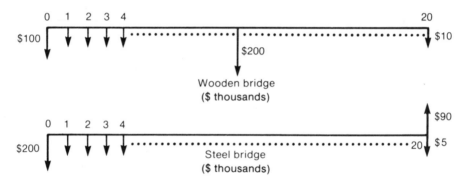

Now the present value cost of the wooden bridge is $211,990 ($100,000 + 6.259 × $10,000 + .247 × $200,000), and that of the steel bridge is $209,065 ($200,000 + 6.259 × $5,000 − .247 × $90,000). Compared over a common 20-year horizon, the steel bridge has the lower present value cost.

Capital Rationing. Implicit in our discussion to this point has been the assumption that investment capital is readily available to companies at a cost equal to the discount rate. At the other extreme is *capital rationing*. Under capital rationing, the company has a fixed investment budget which it may not exceed. As was true with mutually exclusive alternatives, capital rationing requires us to rank investments rather than simply to accept or reject them. Despite this similarity, however, you should understand that the two

Table 8A–2. Four Independent Investment Opportunities under Capital Rationing—Capital Budget = $200,000

Investment	Initial Cost	NPV at 12 Percent	PI at 12 Percent	IRR
A	$200,000	$10,000	1.05	14.4%
B	120,000	8,000	1.07	15.1
C	50,000	6,000	1.12	17.6
D	80,000	6,000	1.08	15.5

conditions are fundamentally different. With mutually exclusive alternatives, the money is available, but for technological reasons, the firm cannot make all investments. Under capital rationing, it may be technologically possible to make all investments, but there is not enough money. This difference is more than semantic, for as the following example illustrates, the nature of the ranking process differs fundamentally in the two cases.

Suppose Sullivan Electronics Company has a limited investment budget of $200,000 and that management has identified the four independent investment opportunities appearing in Table 8A–2. According to the three figures of merit, all investments should be undertaken, but this is impossible because the total cost of the four investments exceeds Sullivan's budget. Looking at the investment rankings, the NPV criterion ranks A as the best investment, followed by B, C, and D in that order, while the PI and IRR rank C best, followed by D, B, and A. So we know that A is either the best investment or the worst.

To make sense of these rankings, we need to remember that the underlying economic objective in evaluating investment opportunities is to increase wealth. Under capital rationing, this means the company should undertake that bundle of investments which generates the highest *total* NPV. How is this to be done? One way is to look at every possible bundle of investments which has a total cost less than the budget constraint and select the bundle with the highest *total* NPV. A short cut is to rank the investments by their PI and work down the list, accepting investments until either the money runs out or the PI drops below 1.0. This suggests that Sullivan should accept projects C, D and $7/12$ of B, for a total NPV of $16,670 [6,000 + 6,000 + $7/12$ × 8,000]. Only $7/12$ of B should be undertaken because the company only has $70,000 remaining after accepting C and D.

Why is it incorrect to rank investments by their NPV under capital rationing? Because under capital rationing, we are interested in the payoff per dollar invested, not simply in the payoff itself. The Sullivan example illustrates the point. Investment A has the largest NPV, equal to $10,000, but it has the smallest NPV per dollar invested. Since investment dollars are limited under capital rationing, we must look at the benefit per dollar invested when ranking investments. This is what the PI does.

Two other details warrant mention. In the above example, the IRR provides the same ranking as the PI, and although this is usually the case, it is not always so. It turns out that when the two rankings differ, the PI ranking is the correct one. However, the explanation of why the rankings differ and why PI is superior are not worth explaining here. It is sufficient to remember that if you rank by IRR rather than PI, you might occasionally be in error, but that in the grand sweep of life, it probably doesn't matter much. A second detail is that when fractional investments are not possible—when it does not make sense for Sullivan Electronics to invest in $7/12$ of project B— then rankings according to any figure of merit are unreliable, and one must resort to the tedious method of looking at each possible bundle of investments in search of the highest total NPV.

The Problem of Future Opportunities.   Implicit in the above discussion is the assumption that as long as an investment has a positive NPV, it is better to make the investment than to let the money sit idle. However, under capital rationing this may not be true. To illustrate, suppose that the financial executive of Sullivan Electronics believes that within six months company scientists will develop a new product costing $200,000 and having an NPV of $60,000. In this event, the company's best strategy is to forgo all of the investments presently under consideration and to save its money for the new product.

As illustrated, investment evaluation under capital rationing involves more than a simple appraisal of current opportunities; it also involves a comparison between current opportunities and future prospects. The difficulty with this comparison at a practical level, is that it is unreasonable to expect a manager to have anything more than a vague impression of what investments are likely to arise in the future. Consequently, it is impossible to decide with any assurance whether it is better to invest in current projects or to wait for brighter future opportunities. This means that practical investment evaluation under capital rationing necessarily involves a large degree of subjective judgment.

A Decision Tree.   Mutually exclusive investment alternatives and capital rationing complicate an already confusing topic. To provide a summary and overview, Figure 8A–2 presents a capital budgeting decision tree. It indicates the figure or figures of merit which are appropriate under the various conditions discussed in the chapter. For example, following the lowest branch in the tree, we see that when evaluating investments under capital rationing which are independent and which can be acquired fractionally,

Figure 8A–2. Capital Budgeting Decision Tree

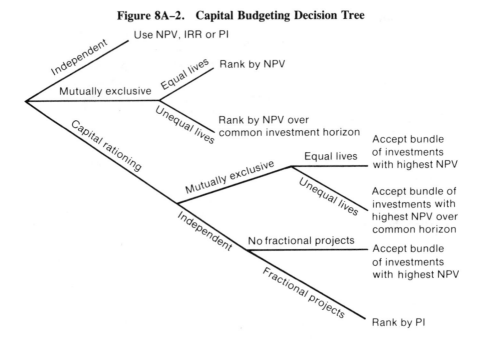

ranking by the PI is the appropriate technique. To review your understanding of the material, see if you can explain why the recommended figures of merit are appropriate under the various conditions indicated whereas the others are not.

Chapter Summary

1. This chapter has examined the use of discounted cash flow techniques in investment appraisal.

2. The three steps in financial evaluation of investment opportunities are: (*a*) estimate the relevant cash flows, (*b*) calculate a figure of merit, and (*c*) compare it with an acceptance criterion. The first step is the hardest in practice.

3. Money has a time value for three reasons: (*a*) risk customarily increases with the futurity of an event, (*b*) inflation reduces the purchasing power of future cash flows, and (*c*) waiting for future cash flows involves a lost opportunity to make interim investments.

4. The payback period and the accounting rate of return ignore the time value of money and, hence, are inferior figures of merit. However, the payback period is a useful indicator of investment risk.

5. Cash flows at two dates are equivalent if it is possible to transform the near-term cash flow into the later cash flow by investing it at the prevailing interest rate. Discounting uses equivalence to convert a messy stream of future receipts and disbursements into equal value cash flows occurring today.

6. A valid figure of merit is the net present value, defined as the difference between the present value of cash inflows and of outflows. Projects with a positive net present value are acceptable.

7. A second popular, valid figure of merit is the internal rate of return, defined as the discount rate at which a project's net present value is zero. It is also the rate at which money left in a project is compounding and is therefore comparable to the interest rate on a bank loan. Investments with an internal rate of return greater than the cost of capital are acceptable.

8. The guiding principles in deciding what cash flows are relevant for an investment decision are the with-without principle and the cash flow principle.

9. Recurring problems in determining relevant cash flows involve depreciation, working capital changes, allocated costs, sunk costs, temporarily excess capacity, and financing costs.

Additional Reading

Bierman, Harold, Jr., and Seymour Smidt. *The Capital Budgeting Decision.* 4th ed. New York: MacMillan, 1975. 463 pages.
    This textbook is more of a finance orientation than *Principles of Engineering Economy* and somewhat harder to follow.

Grant, Eugene L.; W. Grant Ireson; and Richard S. Leavenworth. *Principles of Engineering Economy.* 6th ed. New York: Ronald Press, 1976. 624 pages.
    Everything you ever wanted to know about discounted cash flow techniques and more. A very solid, understandable treatment containing many practical examples.

Chapter Problems

1. Answer the following questions when the interest rate is 15 percent.
    a. What is the present value of $100 in 8 years?
    b. What is the present value of $50 per year for 10 years?

c. What would you pay for a 10-year bond with a par value of $1,000 and a 10 percent coupon rate? Assume interest is paid annually.

d. What would you pay for a share of preferred stock paying $80 per year forever?

e. What will be the value in 5 years of $10 invested today? [Hint: Present value = PVF × Future Value, where PVF is the present value factor from the tables for the appropriate interest rate and time period. So, Future value = 1/PVF × Present value.]

f. About how long will it take for a $100 investment today to double?

g. What will be the value in 5 years of $10 invested at the end of each year for 5 years?

h. A family wishes to save $50,000 over the next 6 years for their child's college education. What uniform annual amount must they deposit at the end of each year to accomplish their objective?

(Answers to alternate problems: a. $32.70, c. $748.90, e. $20.12, g. $67.44).

2. An investment costing $100,000 promises an aftertax cash flow of $35,000 per year for 7 years.

a. Find the investment's accounting rate of return and its payback period.

b. Find the investment's net present value at a 12 percent discount rate.

c. Find the investment's profitability index at a 12 percent discount rate.

d. Find the investment's internal rate of return.

3. A $1,000 par value, 8 percent coupon bond matures in 10 years. If the price of the bond is $613.64, what is the yield to maturity on the bond? Assume interest is paid annually.

4. Consider the following investment opportunity:

Initial cost	$220,000
Annual revenues	$100,000
Annual operating costs, exclusive of depreciation	$ 50,000
Life	15 years
Salvage value after taxes	$ 10,000
Depreciation for tax purposes	$ 15,000/year
Tax rate	40%

What is the rate of return on this investment? Assuming the investor wants to earn at least 10 percent, is this investment an attractive one?

9 Risk Analysis in Investment Decisions

All interesting financial decisions involve considerations of risk as well as return. By their nature, business investments require the expenditure of a known sum of money today in anticipation of uncertain future benefits. Consequently, if the discounted cash flow techniques discussed in the last chapter are to be useful in evaluating such investments, we must incorporate risk effects into the analysis. Two such effects are important: At the practical level, risk increases the difficulty of estimating relevant cash flows, and at the conceptual level, risk itself enters as an important determinant of investment value. A simple example will illustrate the latter point. If two investments promise the same return but have differing risks, risk-averse individuals will place a higher value on the lower risk alternative.

Risk aversion among individuals and corporations creates the recognizable pattern of investment risk and return shown in Figure 9–1. For low-risk investments, such as government securities, the figure shows that the anticipated return is modest, but as risk increases, so too must the anticipated return. I say "must" here because the risk-return pattern shown is more than wishful thinking. Unless higher-risk investments promise higher returns, risk-averse investors will never hold them.

This risk-return trade-off is fundamental to much of finance. Over the past decade, researchers have demonstrated that under idealized conditions, and with risk defined in a specific way, the risk-return trade-off is a straight-line one as depicted in the figure. The line is known as the *Market Line* and represents the combinations of risk and return one can expect in a properly functioning economy.

The details of the Market Line need not detain us here. What is important

197

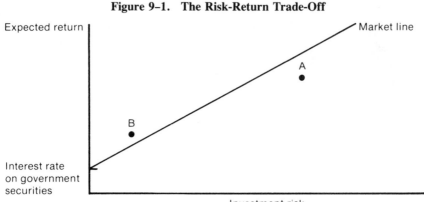

Figure 9–1. The Risk-Return Trade-Off

is the realization that knowledge of an investment's anticipated return is not enough to determine its worth. Instead, investment evaluation is a two-dimensional task involving a balancing of risk against return. The appropriate question when evaluating investment opportunities is not, "what's the rate of return," but rather "is the return sufficient to justify the risk?" The investments represented by points A and B in Figure 9–1 illustrate the point. Investment A has a higher expected return than B; nonetheless, B is the better investment. Despite its modest return, B lies above the Market Line, meaning that it promises a higher return for its risk than available alternatives. Investment A, on the other hand, lies below the Market Line, meaning that alternative investments are available which promise a higher return for the same risk.

This chapter examines the incorporation of risk into investment evaluation with particular emphasis on risk-adjusted discount rates and the cost of capital. After defining terms, we will estimate the cost of capital to Tektronix, Inc., the high-technology company discussed in earlier chapters, and we will examine the limitations of the cost of capital as a risk-adjustment mechanism. The chapter concludes with a look at investment evaluation under inflation. An appendix considers diversification and what is known as β-risk as they affect investment appraisal.

You should know at the outset that the topics in this chapter are not simple, for the addition of a whole second dimension to investment analysis in the form of risk introduces a number of complexities and ambiguities. The result of the chapter, therefore, will be a general road map for how to proceed and an appreciation of available techniques rather than a detailed set of answers. But look on the bright side. If investment decisions under uncertainty were simple, there would be less demand for well-educated managers and aspiring financial writers.

Risk Defined

Intuitively, investment risk is concerned with the range of possible cash flows resulting from an investment; the greater this range, the greater the risk. Figure 9–2 extends this intuitive notion. It shows the possible rates of return which might be earned on two investments in the form of bell-shaped curves. According to the figure, the expected return on investment A is about 12 percent, and the corresponding figure for investment B is about 22 percent.

Figure 9–2.   Illustration of Investment Risk: Investment A Has a Lower Expected Return and a Lower Risk than B

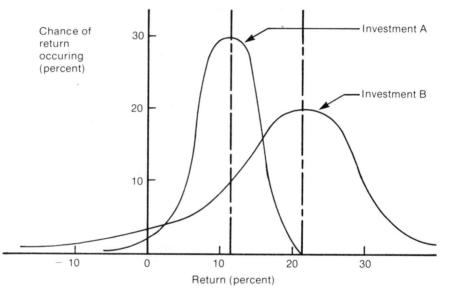

A statistician would define "expected return" as the probability-weighted average of possible returns. To take a simple example, if three returns are possible—8, 12, and 18 percent—and if the chance of each occurring is 40, 30 and 30 percent, respectively, the investment's expected return is:

Expected return = $.40 \times 8\% + .30 \times 12\% + .30 \times 18\% = 12.2\%$

Risk refers to the bunching of possible returns about an investment's expected return. If there is considerable bunching, as with investment A, the dispersion in possible returns is modest, and the investment is low risk. With investment B there is considerably less clustering of possible returns about the expected return, so it has higher risk. Borrowing again from statistics, one way to measure this clustering tendency is to calculate a probability-weighted average of the deviations of possible returns from the expected return. One such average is the standard deviation of returns. The details of calculating an investment's standard deviation of returns need not concern us here.[1] It is sufficient to know that risk corresponds to the dispersion in possible outcomes, and that there exist techniques to measure this dispersion.

Estimating Investment Risk

There are two aspects to risk analysis for investment decisions. One is estimating the magnitude of the risk, and the other is properly reflecting the risk in investment appraisal. Our purpose here is to review techniques for estimating risk magnitude, leaving the incorporation of risk into decision making to later sections.

In some business situations the risk of an investment can be calculated objectively from scientific or historical evidence. This is true of oil and gas development wells. Once an exploration company has found a field and mapped out its general configuration, the probability that a development well drilled within the boundaries of the field will be commercially successful can be determined with reasonable accuracy.

Sometimes history is a guide. A company which has opened 500 fast food restaurants across the country should have a good idea about the expected return and risk of opening the 501st. Similarly, if you are thinking about buying IBM stock, the historical record of annual returns to IBM shareholders and the variability of these returns is an important starting point when estimating future risk and return on IBM shares.

These are the easy situations. More often, business ventures are one-of-a-kind investments for which the estimation of risk must be largely subjective. When a company is contemplating a new product investment, for example,

---

[1]To illustrate calculation of the standard deviation of returns, the differences between the possible returns and the expected return in the above example are (8% − 12.2%), (12% − 12.2%) and (18% − 12.2%). Because some of these differences are positive and others negative, they would tend to cancel one another out if we added them directly. So we square them to assure the same sign, calculate the probability-weighted average of the squared deviations, and then find the square root.

$$\text{Standard deviation} = [.4(8\% - 12.2\%)^2 + .3(12\% - 12.2\%)^2 + .3(18\% - 12.2\%)^2]^{1/2}$$

$$\sigma = 4.1\%$$

The probability-weighted average difference between the investment's possible returns and its expected return is 4.1 percentage points. In symbols:

$$\sigma = [P_i(r_i - \bar{r})^2]^{1/2}$$

Where σ is the investment's standard deviation of returns, P_i is the probability the ith return will occur, r_i is the ith return, and $\bar{r}$ is the expected return.

it has little technical or historical experience on which to base its estimate of investment risk. In this situation, risk appraisal depends on the perceptions of the managers participating in the decision, on their knowledge of the economics of the industry, and their understanding of the investment's ramifications.

Sensitivity Analysis and Simulation

Two previously mentioned techniques, sensitivity analysis and simulation, are useful when investment risk must be estimated subjectively. Although neither technique provides an objective measure of investment risk, both help the executive to think systematically about the sources of risk and their impact on project return. Reviewing briefly, an investment's IRR or NPV depends upon a number of economic factors, such as selling price, quantity sold, useful life, and so on, many of which are not known with certainty. Sensitivity analysis involves a determination of how the investment's figure of merit varies with changes in one of these uncertain factors. A common technique is to calculate three returns corresponding to an optimistic, a pessimistic, and a most likely forecast of the uncertain factor. This provides some indication of the range of possible outcomes.

Simulation is an extension of sensitivity analysis in which the analyst assigns a probability distribution to each uncertain factor, specifies any interdependence among the factors, and asks a computer repeatedly to select values for the factors according to their probability of occurring. For each set of values chosen, the computer calculates the investment's return. The result is a graph, much like Figure 9–2, plotting project return against frequency of occurrence. The chief benefit of sensitivity analysis and simulation are that they force the analyst to think systematically about the individual economic determinants of investment risk, they indicate the sensitivity of the investment's return to each of these determinants, and they provide information about the range of possible returns.

Including Risk in Investment Evaluation

Once a manager has an idea of the magnitude of the risk inherent in an investment, the next step is to incorporate properly this information in the investment's evaluation. Broadly speaking, there are two ways to do this: by fiddling with the cash flows, or by fiddling with the discount rate. The former approach involves what are known as *certainty equivalents.*

A certainty equivalent is a risk-free, or certain, sum of money which has the same value to the analyst as a risky cash flow. For example, suppose a risky cash flow from an investment promises a 50–50 chance at +$2 million or −$1 million. The expected value of this cash flow is $500,000 (.5 × 2 million − .5 × 1 million). But assuming risk aversion, the value of the cash flow to the analyst will be less because the expected value offers no compensation for risk. If the analyst would trade the risky cash flow for a certain one of $400,000, then $400,000 is the risky cash flow's certainty equivalent.

To evaluate risky investments using certainty equivalents, the first step is to replace each risky cash flow with its certainty equivalent. Having thus accounted for risk, the second step is to evaluate the investment as if it were risk free. This means using a risk-free discount rate, such as the government borrowing rate, to calculate the investment's NPV or PI. Or if the IRR is used, it means comparing the certainty equivalent IRR to a risk-free interest rate to determine the investment's acceptability.

Certainty equivalents seldom are used in industry, primarily because there is no practical, objective way to estimate them. When the analyst is making investment decisions on his own behalf, it might be possible to estimate certainty equivalents based on the analyst's own subjective feelings about risk. But when an executive analyzes an investment on behalf of his company, there is no practical way to determine what certainty equivalents are appropriate. This makes risk assessment almost entirely a matter of personal opinion.

Risk-Adjusted Discount Rates

The more common method of incorporating risk into investment appraisal employs risk-adjusted discount rates. With this technique the analyst works with the expected values of the investment's cash flows and adds a premium to the discount rate to compensate for risk. The size of the premium increases with the perceived risk of the investment. If the IRR is used as the figure of investment merit, the analyst calculates the investment's IRR based on the expected values of the cash flows and compares the IRR to a required rate of return which includes the same risk premium.

To illustrate, suppose a $10 million investment promises risky cash flows having an expected value of $2 million annually for 10 years. The problem is to find the investment's NPV if the risk-free interest rate is 8 percent and management has decided to use a 6 percent risk premium as compensation for the uncertainty of the cash flows. The cash flow diagram is as shown on the next page.

The NPV is:

$$NPV = -\$10 \text{ million} + \$2 \text{ million} (5.216)$$
$$= \$432,000$$

where 5.216 is the present value of $1 per year for 10 years at a 14 percent discount rate. Alternatively, the investment's IRR, using expected cash flows, is 15.1 percent—above the 14 percent risk-adjusted discount rate.

If the investment's cash flows were riskless, its NPV at an 8 percent discount rate would be $3.4 million. So use of a 14 percent risk-adjusted dis-

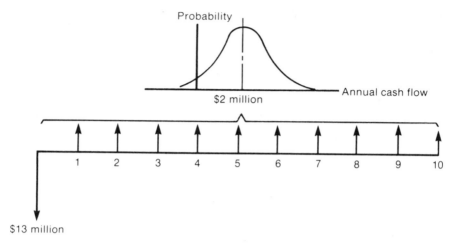

count rate reduces the project's NPV by just under $3 million ($3.4 million − $432 thousand).

Two things make risk-adjusted discount rates superior to certainty equivalents in practical application. One is that most financial executives have at least a rough idea of how an investment's required rate of return should vary with its risk. Stated differently, they have a basic idea of the position of the Market Line in Figure 9–1. As an example, they know from the historical data in Table 6–1 that over many years common stocks have yielded an average annual return which is about 5.9 percent higher than the return on government bonds. If the present return on government bonds is 12 percent, then it is reasonable to expect an investment which is about as risky as common stocks to yield a return of about 18 percent. Similarly, executives know if an investment promises a return of 40 percent, that unless the risk is extremely high, the investment is likely to be acceptable. Granted, such reasoning is imprecise; nonetheless, it does lend some objectivity to risk assessment.

The Cost of Capital

The second attraction of risk-adjusted discount rates involves the cost of capital. When creditors and owners invest money in a company, they incur an opportunity cost equal to the return they could have earned on alternative investments. This opportunity cost is the firm's cost of capital; it is the minimum rate of return the company can earn on existing assets and still meet the expectations of its capital providers. The cost of capital is a risk-adjusted discount rate, and because we can at least estimate the cost of capital for individual companies, it introduces a welcome degree of objectivity into the risk-adjustment process. In following paragraphs we will define the cost of capital more precisely, estimate Tektronix, Inc.'s cost of capital and discuss its use as a risk-adjustment factor.

The Cost of Capital Defined

Suppose we want to estimate the cost of capital to the XYZ Corporation, and we have the following information:

	XYZ Liabilities and Owners' Equity	Opportunity Costs of Capital
Debt	$100	10%
Equity	200	20

Tax rate = 50%

We will discuss the origins of the opportunity costs of capital in a few pages. For now just assume we know that given alternative investment opportunities, creditors expect to earn at least 10 percent on their loans and shareholders expect to earn at least 20 percent on their ownership of XYZ shares. With this information, we need answer only two simple questions to calculate XYZ's cost of capital:

1. *How much money must XYZ earn annually on existing assets to meet the expectations of creditors and owners?* The creditors expect a 10 percent return on their $100 loan, or $10. However, because interest payments are tax deductible, the effective aftertax cost to the company is only $5. The owners expect 20 percent on their $200 investment, or $40. So in total, XYZ must earn $45 [$45 = (1 − .5)(10%) $100 + (20%) $200].

2. *What rate of return must the company earn on existing assets to meet the expectations of creditors and owners?* There is a total of $300 invested in XYZ on which the company must earn $45, so the required rate of return is 15 percent ($45/$300). This is XYZ's cost of capital.

Let's repeat the above reasoning using symbols.

Let

D = debt
E = equity
K_D = expected return on debt, or cost of debt
K_E = expected return on equity, or cost of equity
T = company tax rate
K_w = cost of capital

Then

$$K_w = \frac{(1 - T) K_D D + K_E E}{D + E} \qquad (9\text{-}1)$$

From the above example:

$$15\% = \frac{(1 - 50\%) \times 10\% \times \$100 + 20\% \times \$200}{\$100 + \$200}$$

In words, a company's cost of capital is the cost of the individual sources of capital, weighted according to their importance in the firm's capital structure. The subscript w appears in the cost of capital expression to denote that the cost of capital is a weighted-average cost. To demonstrate, one third of XYZ's capital is debt and two thirds is equity, so its cost of capital is one third the cost of debt and two thirds the cost of equity.

$$15\% = \frac{1}{3} \times 5\% + \frac{2}{3} \times 20\%$$

The Cost of Capital and Stock Price.   An important tie exists between a company's stock price and its cost of capital. If XYZ Corporation earns more than its cost of capital on existing assets, the excess belongs entirely to the owners because the creditors receive a fixed return. The ability of XYZ to provide a return above the owners' opportunity cost of capital will lead to an increase in the company's stock price. Conversely, if XYZ earns less than its cost of capital, the owners will not receive their expected return, and stock prices will fall. Therefore, another definition of the cost of capital is the return the firm must earn on existing assets to keep stock price constant.

TEK's Cost of Capital

To use the cost of capital as a risk-adjusted discount rate in investment evaluation, we must be able to measure it. This involves assigning values to the quantities on the right-hand side of Equation 9–1. To illustrate the process, let's estimate Tektronix, Inc.'s cost of capital at fiscal year-end 1979.

The Weights.   We begin by measuring the weights, D and E. This can be done in two ways: Use the *book values* of debt and equity appearing on the company's balance sheet, or use the *market values*. By "market value," I mean the price of the company's bonds and common shares in securities markets multiplied by the number of each security type outstanding. As shown in Table 9–1, the book values of TEK's debt and equity at the end of

Table 9–1.   **Book and Market Values of Tektronix's Debt and Equity**

Source	Book Value		Market Value	
	Amount ($ millions)	*Percent of Total*	*Amount ($ millions)*	*Percent of Total*
Debt	$ 91	18.4%	$ 76	7.9%
Equity	403	81.6	882	92.1
Total	$494	100.0%	$958	100.0%

fiscal year 1979 were $91 million and $403 million, respectively. The figure for debt includes only interest-bearing debt because other liabilities are spontaneous sources which are treated as part of working capital in the investment's cash flows. The table also indicates that the market values of TEK's debt and equity on the same date were $76 million and $882 million, respectively.

The market value of TEK's debt is below its book value because interest rates rose after the debt was issued; and we know that as interest rates rise, the market value of debt falls. TEK's debt is not publicly traded, so $76 million is my estimate of the price at which it would have traded given its quality, coupon rate, and maturity. The market value of TEK's equity is its price per share at fiscal year-end of $49 times 18 million common shares outstanding. The market value of equity exceeds the book value by more than 2 to 1 because investors believe TEK has unusually good growth prospects.

To decide whether book weights or market weights are appropriate for measuring the cost of capital, consider the following analogy. Suppose that 10 years ago you invested $20,000 in a portfolio of common stocks which, through no fault of your own, is now worth $50,000. After talking to stockbrokers and investment bankers, you feel that a reasonable return on the portfolio, given present market conditions, is 18 percent. Would you be satisfied with an 18 percent return on the original $20,000 cost of the portfolio, or would you expect to earn 18 percent on the current $50,000 market value? Obviously, the current market value is relevant for decision making; the original cost is sunk and therefore irrelevant. Similarly, TEK owners have an investment worth $882 million in the company on which they expect to earn a competitive return. We conclude that the market values of debt and equity are appropriate for measuring the cost of capital.

The Cost of Debt. This is an easy one. High-quality bonds of a maturity similar to TEK's were yielding a return of approximately 9.6 percent in May 1979, and the company's tax rate is about 39 percent. Consequently, the aftertax cost of debt to TEK was 5.9 percent [(1 − 39%) × 9.6%]. Some persons are tempted to use the coupon rate on the debt rather than the prevailing market rate in this calculation. But again the coupon rate is a sunk cost. Moreover, because we want to use the cost of capital to evaluate new investments, we want the cost of new debt.

The Cost of Equity. Estimating the cost of equity is as hard as debt was easy. With debt, or preferred stocks, the company promises the holder a specified stream of future payments. Knowing these promised payments and the current price of the security, it is a simple matter to calculate the expected return. This is what we did in the last chapter when we calculated the yield to maturity on a bond. With common stock, the situation is more complex. Because the company makes no promises about future payments to shareholders, there is no simple way to calculate the return expected.

The following cash flow diagrams illustrate the problem, looking first at the cash flows to a bond investor and then to a stock investor. Finding K_D is a simple discounted cash flow problem. Finding K_E would be just as simple except we do not know the future cash receipts expected by shareholders. This calls for some ingenuity.

Investor's Cash Flow Diagram for Bonds

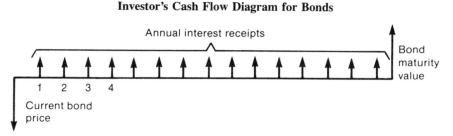

K_D = Discount rate which makes present value of cash inflows equal to current price.

Investor's Cash Flow Diagram for Common Stock

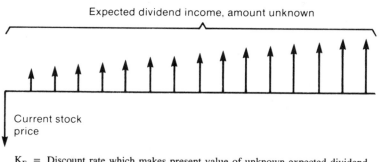

K_E = Discount rate which makes present value of unknown expected dividend income equal current price.

Perpetual Growth. One way out of the dilemma is to make an assumption about the future payments shareholders expect and calculate the return consistent with this assumption. To illustrate, assume shareholders expect a per share dividend next year of $d, and that they expect this dividend to grow at the rate of g percent per annum *forever*. Now, we know the current price, P, and we have assumed a future payment stream, represented by d and g, so all that remains is to find the discount rate which makes the present value of the payment stream equal to the current price. Fortunately, it turns out that this discounted cash flow problem has an unusually simple solution.

Without boring you with the arithmetic details, the present value of the assumed payment stream, at a discount rate of K_E, is:

$$P = \frac{d}{K_E - g}$$

or rearranging terms:

$$K_E = \frac{d}{P} + g$$

This equation says that if the growth assumption is correct, the cost-of-equity capital equals the company's dividend yield (d/P), plus the growth rate in dividends. This is known as the perpetual growth equation for K_E.

The problem with the perpetual growth estimate of K_E is that it is only as good as the assumption on which it is based. For *mature* companies, like railroads, electric utilities, and steel mills, it may be reasonable to assume that observed growth rates will continue indefinitely. And in these cases the perpetual growth equation yields a satisfactory estimate of the cost-of-equity capital. Moreover, we can meaningfully apply the equation to the economy as a whole and say that with an average dividend yield of about 5 percent, and an average nominal dividend growth rate of 10 percent, the cost-of-equity capital to the typical firm is about 15 percent. However, the equation is clearly not applicable to TEK because TEK pays almost no dividends, and because the company is growing at a rate which clearly cannot be maintained indefinitely.

Let History Be Your Guide. A second, and generally more fruitful, approach to estimating the cost-of-equity capital looks at the structure of expected returns on risky investments. In general, the expected return on any risky asset is composed of three factors:

$$\text{Expected return on risky asset} = \text{Risk-free interest rate} + \text{Inflation premium} + \text{Risk premium}$$

The equation says the owner of a risky asset should expect to earn a return from three sources. The first is compensation for the opportunity cost incurred in holding the asset. This is the risk-free interest rate. The second is compensation for the declining purchasing power of his investment over time. This is the inflation premium. The third is compensation for bearing risk. This is the risk premium. Fortunately, we do not need to treat the first two terms as separate factors because together they equal the expected return on a default-free bond such as a government bond. In other words, owners of government bonds expect a return from the first two sources but not the third. Consequently:

$$\text{Expected return on risky asset} = \text{Interest rate on government bond} + \text{Risk premium}$$

Since we can readily determine the government bond interest rate, the only challenge is to estimate the risk premium. When the risky asset is a common stock, it is useful to let history be our guide and recall from Table 6–1 that on average over the period 1926 to 1979 the annual return on common stocks exceeded that on government bonds by 5.9 percent. As a reward for bearing the added risk, common stockholders earned a 5.9 percent higher annual return than government bondholders. Treating this as a risk premium, and adding it to a 1979, government bond rate of 9 percent, yields an estimate of 14.9 percent as the cost-of-equity capital for the typical company.

This is an estimate of the cost of equity to an average-risk company. In the appendix to this chapter, we discuss a technique for modifying this estimate to reflect the risk of a specific company. For now, let us do this more informally. Because of the dynamic nature of its industry, TEK has considerably more business risk than most companies. However, its modest use of debt financing means that TEK imposes very little additional financial risk on its shareholders. Although the above-average business risk and below-average financial risk tend to offset one another, I believe that TEK is somewhat riskier than the average share of stock. Let us, therefore, use 16 percent as an estimate of TEK's cost-of-equity capital.

Calculation of TEK's Cost of Capital. Table 9–2 presents our estimate of TEK's cost of capital in tabular form and in equation form. TEK's weighted-average cost of capital is 15.2 percent. This means that in 1979 TEK had to earn an aftertax return of at least 15.2 percent on the market value of existing assets to meet the expectations of creditors and shareholders and maintain share price. TEK's weighted-average cost of capital is quite close to its cost-of-equity capital because TEK has very little debt.

The Cost of Capital in Investment Appraisal

The cost of capital is the return a company must earn on *existing assets* to meet creditor and shareholder expectations. This is an interesting detail, but

Table 9–2. Calculation of Tektronix, Inc.'s Cost of Capital

Source	Amount ($ millions)	Percent of Total	Cost After Tax	Weighted Cost
Debt	$ 76	7.9%	5.9%	00.5%
Equity	882	92.1	16.0	14.7
Cost of capital				15.2%

In equation form:

$$K_w = \frac{(1 - .39)\,(9.6\%)\,(\$76 \text{ million}) + (16\%)\,(\$882 \text{ million})}{76 \text{ million} + 882 \text{ million}}$$

$$= 15.2\%$$

we are after bigger game here: We want to use the cost of capital as an acceptance criterion for *new investments*.

Are there any problems in applying a concept derived for existing assets to new investments? Not if one critical assumption holds; namely, the new investment must have the same risk as existing assets. If it does, the new investment is essentially a "carbon copy" of existing assets, and the cost of capital is the appropriate risk-adjusted discount rate. If it does not, we must proceed more carefully.

The Market Line appearing in Figure 9–3 clearly illustrates the importance of the constant risk assumption. It emphasizes that the rate of return

Figure 9–3. An Investment's Risk-Adjusted Discount Rate Increases with Risk

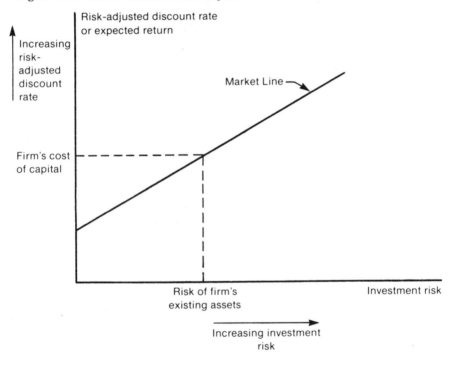

anticipated by risk-averse companies and individuals rises with risk. This means, for example, that management should demand a higher expected return when introducing a new product than when replacing aged equipment because the new product is presumably riskier and, therefore, warrants a higher return. The figure also shows that a company's cost of capital is but one of many possible risk-adjusted discount rates, the one corresponding to the risk of the firm's existing assets. We conclude that the cost of capital is an appropriate acceptance criterion only when the risk of the new investment equals that of existing assets. For other investments, the cost of capital is inappropriate. However, even when inappropriate itself, the cost of capital frequently serves as an important, practical touchstone about which further adjustments are made.

Multiple Hurdle Rates

Many companies adjust for differing levels of investment risk by using multiple hurdle rates, each rate applying to a different level of risk. For example, TEK might use the following array:

Type of Investment	Discount Rate
Replacement or repair	10.0%
Cost reduction	12.0
Expansion	15.2
New product	20.0

Investments to expand capacity in existing products are essentially carbon copy investments, so their hurdle rate equals TEK's cost of capital. Other types of investments have a higher or lower hurdle rate depending on their risk relative to expansion investments. Replacement or repair investments are the safest because virtually all of the cash flows are well known from past experience. Cost reduction investments are somewhat riskier because the magnitude of potential savings is uncertain. New product investments are the riskiest type because both revenues and costs are uncertain.

Multiple hurdle rates are consistent with risk aversion and with the Market Line; however, the amount by which the hurdle rate should be adjusted for each level of risk is largely arbitrary. Whether the hurdle rate for cost reduction investments should be three percentage points or five percentage points below TEK's cost of capital cannot be determined objectively.

The Fallacy of the Marginal Cost of Capital

Some persons look at Equation 9-1 and naively conclude that it is possible to reduce a company's weighted-average cost of capital by using more of the cheap source of financing, debt, and less of the expensive source, equity. In other words, they conclude that increasing leverage will reduce the cost of capital. However, this reasoning evidences an incomplete understanding of leverage. As observed in the last chapter, increasing leverage increases the risk borne by shareholders. And because they are risk averse, shareholders react by demanding a higher return on their investment. Thus, K_E, and to a lesser extent K_D, rise as leverage increases. This means that increasing leverage affects a company's cost of capital in two opposing ways: Increasing use of cheap debt reduces K_W, but the rise in K_E and K_D which accompanies added leverage increases it.

Some economists argue that under restrictive conditions these opposing forces exactly counterbalance one another and that K_W is the same regardless of the company's capital structure. The more widely accepted view is that K_W is U-shaped with respect to leverage. At low levels of indebtedness, the tax deductibility of interest predominates, and K_W falls with increasing leverage; but at higher levels of debt, the increasing likelihood of bankruptcy and its impact on K_D and K_E cause K_W to rise with further increases in leverage.

To review this reasoning, ask yourself how you would respond to a subordinate who made the following argument in favor of an investment. "I know the company's cost of capital is 20 percent and the IRR of this carbon copy investment is only 15 percent. But at the last directors' meeting we decided to finance this year's investments with new debt. Since new debt has a cost of only about 6 percent after tax, it is clearly in our shareholders' interest to invest 6 percent money to earn a 15 percent return."

The subordinate's reasoning is incorrect. Financing with debt means increasing leverage and increasing K_E. Adding the change in K_E to the 6 percent interest cost means the true marginal cost of the debt is well above the interest cost. The minority view is that the true marginal cost of debt equals K_W. The more popular view is that the cost may be slightly more or less than K_W, but that as long as we are not talking about major changes in leverage, we are safe in using K_W as the appropriate acceptance criterion regardless of how an investment is to be financed.

Rather than assign a different discount rate to each type of investment, some multidivision companies assign a different discount rate to each division. A potential advantage of this approach is that if a division competes against one or several single-product firms, the cost of capital of these competitors can be used as the division's hurdle rate for new investment. An offsetting disadvantage of divisional hurdle rates is the implicit assumption that all investments made by the division have the same business risk.

Inflation and Investment Evaluation

The key to capital budgeting under inflation is always to compare "like to like." When cash flows are in nominal dollars, use a nominal acceptance criterion. When cash flows are in real, or constant, dollars, use a real acceptance criterion. Table 9–3 illustrates the point. Suppose TEK is considering a $10,000 carbon copy investment in 1980 which is expected to generate nominal aftertax cash flows of $3,900 annually for four years. The IRR on the investment is 20.5 percent, and because this exceeds TEK's cost of capital as calculated above, the investment is acceptable. The cost of capital calculated earlier is a nominal one because it is the weighted average of the nominal costs of debt and equity. So in the upper half of the table, we have compared a nominal IRR to a nominal cost of capital.

Table 9–3. When Evaluating Investments under Inflation, Always Compare Nominal to Real and Real to Real

Investment evaluation using nominal amounts

	1980	1981	1982	1983	1984
Aftertax cash flow	$(10,000)	$3,900	$3,900	$3,900	$3,900
Nominal IRR	20.5%				
Nominal cost of capital	15.2%				

Investment evaluation using real, 1980 dollars

Assume annual inflation rate = 8%

	1980	1981	1982	1983	1984
Nominal aftertax cash flow	$(10,000)	$3,900	$3,900	$3,900	$3,900
Price index	1.00	1.08	1.17	1.26	1.36
Price deflator	1.00	0.93	0.86	0.79	0.74
Aftertax cash flow (in 1980 dollars)	(10,000)	3,627	3,354	3,081	2,886
Real IRR	11.6%				
Real cost of capital	6.7%				

The lower half of Table 9–3 compares real to real. Assuming an 8 percent inflation rate over the next four years, the first step is to deflate the nominal cash flows to cash flows of constant 1980 purchasing power. We do this by going through the following mental exercise. Suppose a loaf of bread costs $1 in 1980, $1.08 in 1981, $1.17 in 1982, etc. Then, in terms of loaves of bread, $1 in 1980 will buy 1 loaf, $1 in 1981 will buy 0.93 loaves ($1/$1.08), $1 in 1982 will buy 0.86 loaves ($1/$1.17), etc. Using these price deflators, which are just one divided by the price index, we translate the future cash flows into cash flows of constant purchasing power. The IRR using these real cash flows is 11.6 percent.

From the Fisher equation discussed in Chapter 3, we know that a nominal interest rate, i_n, and a real interest rate, i_r, are related according to the following equation, where $\bar{p}$ is the expected inflation rate.:

$$(1 + i_n) = (1 + i_r)(1 + \bar{p})$$

Applying the Fisher equation to TEK's cost of capital:

$$(1 + 15.2\%) = (1 + K_r)(1 + 8\%)$$

where K_r is TEK's real cost of capital. Solving for K_r, we find that it equals 6.7 percent. Comparing the investment's real IRR of 11.6 percent to K_r, we see again that the investment is acceptable.

The two approaches are mathematically equivalent. However, there are several practical reasons for comparing nominal to nominal. One is simply that it is usually more work to calculate real cash flows. Another is that it avoids an error frequently made when calculating real cash flows. Rather than calculating an investment's nominal aftertax cash flows and then deflating to get real cash flows, some analysts attempt to forecast real revenues and costs directly. However, this approach is doomed to failure because income taxes cannot be determined without knowledge of nominal revenues and costs.

A Cautionary Note

An always-present danger when using analytic or numerical techniques in business decision making is that the "hard facts" will assume exaggerated importance compared to more qualitative issues and that the manipulation of these facts will become a substitute for creative effort. It is important to bear in mind that numbers and theories don't get things done, people do. And the best of investments will fail unless capable workers are committed to their success. As Barbara Tuchman put it in another context, "In military as in other human affairs will is what makes things happen. There are circumstances that can modify or nullify it, but for offense or defense its presence is essential and its absence fatal."[2]

---

[2]Barbara W. Tuchman, *Stilwell and the American Experience in China 1911–1945* (New York: Bantam Books, 1971), pp. 561–62.

Appendix

Diversification and β-Risk

In the chapter, we observed that the expected rate of return on a risky asset can be written as:

$$\frac{\text{Expected return}}{\text{on risky asset}} = \frac{\text{Interest rate on}}{\text{government bonds}} + \text{Risk premium}$$

where the interest rate on government bonds is itself the sum of a risk-free interest rate and an inflation premium. We noted too that when the risky asset in question is a typical company's common stock, one measure of the risk premium is the *excess* return earned by common shareholders relative to government bondholders over a long period.

Letting i equal the prevailing interest rate on government bonds, R_m, the annual return on a well-diversified portfolio of common stocks over a long period, and i_b, the annual return on government bonds over the same period, we can say the same thing in symbols:

Expected return on typical company's common stock $= i + (R_m - i_b)$

In mid-1979, the interest rate on government bonds was about 9 percent. Using the figures in Table 6–1 the average annual return earned by investors in the 500 stocks comprising the Standard & Poor's 500 stock index over the period 1926–1979 was 9.0 percent, whereas the average annual return on government bonds over the same period was 3.1 percent. This suggests a risk premium, $(R_m - i_b)$, of 5.9 percent, and an expected return on a typical company's stock, given prevailing interest rates of 14.9 percent (14.9% $=$ 9% $+$ 5.9%).

The above equation provides an estimate of a typical company's cost of equity capital, where by "typical," I mean a company having average risk. However, if we want to use this equation to estimate the cost of capital of an *atypical* company, or if we want to estimate the expected return on any other kind of risky asset, we must modify the equation to reflect the particular risk of the company or asset in question. Letting R_j equal the expected rate of return on risky asset j, the following equation includes the necessary modification:

$$\frac{\text{Expected}}{\text{return on}} = \frac{\text{Interest rate}}{\text{on government}} + \frac{\beta\text{-risk of}}{\text{asset j}} \times \frac{\text{Risk}}{\text{premium}}$$
$$\text{risky asset j} \qquad \text{bonds}$$

$$R_j = i + \beta_j (R_m - i_b) \qquad \qquad (9A\text{–}1)$$

β_j is known as the asset's β-risk, or its volatility. We will talk more about the calculation of β_j in a few paragraphs. For now, think of it as simply the risk of asset j relative to that of the common stock portfolio, m. Specifically:

$$\beta_j = \frac{\text{Risk of asset j}}{\text{Risk of portfolio m}}$$

If the risk of asset j is equal to that of a typical company's common stock, β_j = 1.0, and the equation is just as before. If the asset is of above-average risk, β_j exceeds 1.0, and if it is of below-average risk, β_j is less than 1.0.

In recent years, β-risk has become an important factor in security analysis, so much so that several stock brokerage companies and investment advisors regularly publish the βs of a great many common stocks. Table 9A–1 presents βs for a representative sample of firms, as well as industry average βs. Recalling that a β of 1.0 is typical, or average, note that the range for company βs in the table is from a high of 1.70 for Computervision Corp. to a low of .55 for Detroit Edison Co. Also note that Tektronix's β is 1.20, indicating that TEK's common stock is of slightly above-average risk.

With knowledge of a company's β it becomes easy to use equation 9A–1 above to estimate a company's cost of equity capital. For example TEK's cost of equity in 1979 according to this equation was:

$$R_j = i + \beta_j (R_m - i_b)$$
$$= 9\% + 1.20 \times (9.0\% - 3.1\%)$$
$$= 16.1\%$$

In contrast, Computervision's cost of equity is:

$$9\% + 1.70 \times (9.0\% - 3.1\%) = 19.0\%$$

and that of Detroit Edison is:

$$9\% + .55 \times (9.0\% - 3.1\%) = 12.2\%$$

At a conceptual level, Equation 9A–1 is quite important, for it tells us the rate of return we should expect on any risky asset and how that return varies with the asset's β-risk. Looking at Figure 9–1, another way to say the same thing is that Equation 9A–1 is the equation of the Market Line. To determine the appropriate risk-adjusted discount rate for any risky asset, all we need to do is calculate the asset's β, plug this value into Equation 9A–1, and calculate the expected return on the asset. This expected return, denoted by R_j, is the correct risk-adjusted discount rate for investment evaluation.

Diversification. To understand β-risk more fully, we need to take a slight detour and talk about risk in general. Below is information about two very simple risky investments. For concreteness, suppose investment A is the purchase of an ice cream stand and investment B is the purchase of an um-

Table 9A–1. Industry and Representative Company Beta's

Average Industry Beta		*Representative Company Beta*	
Industry	*Beta*	*Company*	*Beta*
Nonferrous metals	.99	Amdahl Corporation	1.60
Energy raw materials	1.22	American Airlines, Inc.	1.20
Construction	1.27	American Brands, Inc.	.75
Agriculture, food	.99	American Electric Power Co.	.60
Liquor	.89	AT&T	.65
Tobacco	.80	BankAmerica Corporation	1.00
Apparel	1.27	Boeing Company	1.25
Forest products, paper	1.16	Caterpillar Tractor Co.	1.00
Containers	1.01	Citicorp	1.10
Media	1.39	Coca-Cola Company	.90
Chemicals	1.22	Computervision Corporation	1.70
Drugs, medicine	1.14	Control Data Corporation	1.60
Soaps, cosmetics	1.09	Detroit Edison Co.	.55
Domestic oil	1.12	General Electric Co.	1.00
International oil	.85	General Foods Corporation	.80
Tires, rubber goods	1.21	General Motors Corporation	.85
Steel	1.02	Hilton Hotels Corporation	1.30
Producer goods	1.30	Honda Motor	.60
Business machines	1.43	IBM	.95
Consumer durables	1.44	McDonnell Douglas	1.25
Motor vehicles	1.27	National Semiconductor	1.50
Aerospace	1.30	RCA Corporation	1.25
Electronics	1.60	Shell Oil Company	1.10
Photographic, optical	1.24	Sony Corporation	.75
Nondurables, entertainment	1.47	Tektronix, Inc.	1.20
Trucking, freight	1.31	U. S. Steel	1.00
Railroads, shipping	1.19	Westinghouse Electric	1.20
Air transport	1.80	Xerox Corporation	1.20
Telephone	.75		
Energy, utilities	.60		
Retail, general	1.43		
Banks	.81		
Miscellaneous finance	1.60		
Insurance	1.34		
Real property	1.70		
Business services	1.28		
Travel, outdoor recreation	1.66		
Gold	.36		
Miscellaneous, conglomerate	1.14		

Sources: Industry beta's—Barr Rosenberg and James Guy, "Prediction of Beta from Investment Fundamentals," *Financial Analysts Journal,* July–August 1976, p. 66. Company betas—*The Value Line Investment Survey, Part I Summary and Index* (New York: Arnold Bernhard and Co., May 15, 1981). Reprinted by permission of the publisher. Copyright 1981 by Arnold Bernhard and Co., Inc.

brella stand. Further, suppose the states of nature refer to tomorrow's weather: State 1 represents sun; and state 2, rain. Investment A is clearly a risky undertaking since the investor stands to make $600 if it is sunny tomorrow but will lose $200 if it rains. Investment B is also risky since the investor will lose $300 if tomorrow is sunny but will make $500 if it rains.

Investment A

State of Nature	Probability	Outcome	Weighted Outcome
1	.40	$600	$240
2	.60	− 200	− 120
		Expected outcome	$120

Investment B

State of Nature	Probability	Outcome	Weighted Outcome
1	.40	−$300	−$120
2	.60	500	300
		Expected outcome	$180

Yet despite the fact that these two investments are risky when viewed in isolation, they are not risky when viewed as members of a portfolio containing both investments.

Portfolio of A and B

State of Nature	Probability	Outcome	Weighted Outcome
1	.40	300	$120
2	.60	300	180
		Expected outcome	$300

In a portfolio, the losses and gains from the two investments counterbalance one another in each state of nature, so that regardless of tomorrow's weather, the outcome is a riskless $300. The expected outcome from the portfolio is just the sum of the expected outcomes from each investment in the portfolio, but the risk of the portfolio is zero.

This is an extreme example, but it does illustrate an important fact. When a decision maker owns a portfolio of assets, the relevant measure of risk is not the asset's risk in isolation but rather its risk as part of the portfolio. And as the example demonstrates, the difference between these two perspectives can be substantial.

An asset's risk in isolation is greater than its portfolio risk whenever the asset's cash flows and the portfolio's cash flows are less than perfectly correlated. In this commonplace situation, some of the asset's cash flow variability is offset by variability in the portfolio's cash flows, and the effective risk borne by the investor is reduced. Look again at the above example. The ice cream stand cash flows are highly variable, but because they are inversely correlated with those from the umbrella stand, cash flow variability for the two investments disappears. An "averaging out" process occurs when assets are added to a portfolio which reduces risk.

Because most business investments are dependent to some extent on the same underlying business cycle, it is unusual to find investment opportunities with perfectly inversely correlated cash flows as in the ice cream–umbrella example. However, the described diversification effect still exists. Whenever investment cash flows are less than perfectly positively correlated—whenever individual investments are unique in some respects—an investment's risk in a portfolio context is less than its risk in isolation.

Let us refer to an asset's risk in isolation as its *total risk* and to its risk as part of a portfolio as its *nondiversifiable risk*. This is the risk remaining after the rest has been diversified away in the portfolio. The part which is diversified away is known as the asset's *diversifiable risk*. Then, for any risky asset j:

$$\begin{array}{c} \text{Total risk} \\ \text{of asset j} \end{array} = \begin{array}{c} \text{Nondiversifiable} \\ \text{risk of asset j} \end{array} + \begin{array}{c} \text{Diversifiable} \\ \text{risk of asset j} \end{array}$$

From the above discussion, we know that the portion of an asset's total risk which is nondiversifiable depends on the correlation of the returns on the asset and on the portfolio. When the correlation is high, nondiversifiable risk is a large fraction of total risk, and vice versa. To say the same thing in symbols, let σ_j equal asset j's total risk and ϱ_{jm} equal a scale factor reflecting the degree to which asset j's returns correlate with those of portfolio m. Then:

$$\text{Nondiversifiable risk of asset j} = \varrho_{jm}\sigma_j$$

(ϱ and σ are lowercase Greek symbols for rho and sigma, respectively. They have become standard notation in the literature.)

Studying this expression, the scale factor ϱ_{jm} can have any value between $+1.00$ and -1.00. At one extreme, when the returns on asset j and portfolio m are perfectly positively correlated, $\varrho_{jm} = 1.00$, and nondiversifiable risk equals total risk. In this case, there are no benefits from diversification. At the other extreme, when the returns on asset j and portfolio m are perfectly negatively correlated, as in the ice cream–umbrella stand example, $\varrho_{jm} = -1.00$, and nondiversifiable risk is negative. This means that addition of an appropriate amount of asset j to the portfolio will eliminate risk entirely. For most business investments, ϱ_{jm} is in the range .5 to .8, meaning that 20 to 50 percent of an investment's total risk can be diversified away.

Measuring β. We are now ready to reconsider β-risk. Recall that β_j was described as a factor of proportionality defined as:

$$\beta_j = \frac{\text{Risk of asset j}}{\text{Risk of portfolio m}}$$

When diversification is possible, we now know that the relevant measure of asset j's risk is its nondiversifiable risk. Consequently:

$$\beta_j = \frac{\varrho_{jm} \, \sigma_j}{\varrho_{mm} \, \sigma_m}$$

This expression says that the β-risk of asset j is the ratio of asset j's non-diversifiable risk to the nondiversifiable risk of the analyst's portfolio. However, a moment's reflection should convince you that ϱ_{mm} equals one because any asset's or portfolio's return must be perfectly positively correlated with itself. Thus:

$$\beta_j = \frac{\varrho_{jm} \, \sigma_j}{\sigma_m} \tag{9A-2}$$

If you have studied a little statistics, it will come as no surprise to learn that σ_j and σ_m are commonly defined to be the *standard deviation* of returns for asset j and portfolio m, respectively, whereas ϱ_{jm} is the *correlation coefficient* between these returns.

Using these definitions and the above equation, the βs appearing in Table 9A-1 were calculated as follows. First, for each stock calculate the monthly return to investors, including price appreciation and dividends, over the past five years. Then calculate the average monthly return and the standard deviation of returns about this average. The latter is σ_j. Second, go through the same exercise for a broad portfolio of common stocks such as the Standard & Poor's 500 stock averages. This generates σ_m. Third, calculate the correlation coefficient, ϱ_{jm}, between the monthly returns for stock j and the portfolio. Forth, plug these numbers into Equation 9A-2 to calculate the stock's β.

Using β in Investment Evaluation. β can be used two ways in investment evaluation. As already suggested, one way is to use the β of the company's common stock to calculate the firm's cost of equity and its weighted average cost of capital.

A more direct approach is to calculate the β of an individual investment and plug it into Equation 9A-1 to calculate the investment's risk-adjusted discount rate. This reduces risk adjustment to a totally mechanical, objective exercise. The approach has obvious conceptual appeal, but a number of problems must be solved before it can be applied in practice. The most serious is that there is usually no objective way to estimate an investment's β. Some researchers have experimented with using the βs of publicly traded, single-product companies engaged in the same business as the proposed investment as surrogates for the investment's β. But this has proved to be a complicated, imprecise exercise. One difficulty is that company β depends on leverage as well as business risk. So before using a company β as a surrogate for an investment's β, it is necessary to eliminate the effect of leverage. This can be done, but the process is complex and of unknown accuracy. A second difficulty pervading all β applications is that the real object of interest is the β which will prevail in future years. But because this is unknown, we must calculate an historical β and assume it will hold in the future. Empirical studies of β over time suggest this is a reasonable, but not infallible, assumption.

The bottom line in practice is that β is useful for estimating a company's cost of equity capital. However, the calculation of project βs is still only a distant hope.

β-Risk and Conglomerate Diversification.   Some executives have seized on the idea that diversification reduces risk as a justification for conglomerate diversification. Even when merger promises no increase in profitability, it is said to be beneficial because the resulting diversification reduces the risk of company cash flows. Because shareholders are risk averse, this reduction in risk is said to increase the value of the firm.

Such reasoning is at best incomplete. If shareholders wanted the risk-reduction benefits of such a conglomerate merger, they could have achieved them much more simply by just owning shares of the two independent companies in their own portfolios. Shareholders are not dependent on company managements for such benefits. Executives intent on acquiring other firms must look elsewhere for a rationale for their actions.

Chapter Summary

1. The purpose of this chapter has been to incorporate risk into investment evaluation with particular emphasis on risk-adjusted discount rates and the cost of capital.

2. Investments involve a trade-off between risk and return. The appropriate question when evaluating investment opportunities is not, What's the rate of return? but rather Is the return sufficient to justify the risk?

3. Risk refers to the range of possible outcomes for an investment. Some-

times risk can be calculated objectively, but usually risk estimation must be subjective.

4. The most popular, practical technique for incorporating risk into investment decisions uses a risk-adjusted discount rate in which the analyst adds a premium to the discount rate reflecting the perceived risk of the project.

5. The cost of capital is a risk-adjusted discount rate suitable for a firm's average risk, or carbon copy, investments. It is the average cost of individual capital sources, weighted by their relative importance in the firm's capital structure. Average risk investments yielding above the cost of capital increase stock price.

6. Estimating the cost of equity is the most difficult step in measuring the cost of capital. For most businesses the best estimate is the currrent cost of government borrowing plus a risk premium based on historical experience of about 6 percent. If the equity is above or below average risk, it is necessary to adjust the risk premium accordingly.

7. It is also necessary to raise or lower the discount rate relative to the cost of capital depending on whether a specific project is above or below average risk for the business.

8. Under inflation one must always use nominal cash flows and a nominal discount rate, or real cash flows and a real discount rate. Never mix the two.

9. Proper technique is never a substitute for thought or leadership. People, not analysis, get things done.

Additional Reading

Brealey, Richard, and Stewart Myers. *Principles of Corporate Finance.* New York: McGraw-Hill, 1981. 794 pages.
    A leading graduate text. Part 3, Risk, is especially good.

Mullins, David W., Jr. "Does the Capital Asset Pricing Model Work?" *Harvard Business Review,* January–February 1982, pp. 105–114.
    A practical look at the concepts discussed in the appendix to this chapter, including β-risk, the Market Line, and diversification.

Chapter Problems

1. A risky investment costs $1 million and has an expected, nominal, aftertax cash flow of $350,000 each year for seven years. The risk-free rate of interest is 8 percent including a 6 percent inflation premium.

  a. What is the net present value of the investment assuming a risk premium of 7 percent?

  b. By how much does the fact that the investment is risky reduce its net present value?

  c. If the certainty-equivalent of the cash flows in years 1 through 4 is $275,000, and the certainty-equivalent of each of the remaining cash flows is $225,000, what is the net present value of the investment?

2. Calculate Travis Inc.'s weighted average cost of capital given the following information:

    The company's tax rate is 46 percent. The opportunity cost of capital to Travis's shareholders is 20 percent. Travis has 10 million shares outstanding; the current price per share is $40. Using book values, the company's debt-to-equity ratio is 120 percent. Using market values, the ratio is 80 percent. Travis's debt has a coupon rate of 7 percent and an annual principal repayment of $10 million. The yield to maturity is 12 percent.

3. For Travis Inc. discussed in question 2, show that if Travis invests in a perpetuity with an internal rate of return equal to its weighted average cost of capital, and if Travis finances the investment such that the debt-to-equity ratio equals 80 percent, then the company can just pay creditors and provide a return of 20 percent to its shareholders. Assuming a "carbon copy" investment, what will be the impact of such an investment on Travis's stock price?

4. If the interest rate is 15 percent, what is the present value of a stream of cash receipts starting at $10 next year and growing 5 percent per year forever?

5. If the expected dividend of a mature company next year is $1.50 per share and if the dividend is expected to grow 6 percent per year forever, use the perpetual growth equation to estimate the company's cost-of-equity capital when the firm's current stock price is $12.50.

Appendixes

Appendix A.   Present Value of $1 Discounted at Discount Rate k, for n Years

Percent

Period	1%	2%	3%	4%	5%	6%	7%	8%	9%	10%	11%	12%
1	0.990	0.980	0.971	0.962	0.952	0.943	0.935	0.926	0.917	0.909	0.901	0.893
2	0.980	0.961	0.943	0.925	0.907	0.890	0.873	0.857	0.842	0.826	0.812	0.797
3	0.971	0.942	0.915	0.889	0.864	0.840	0.816	0.794	0.772	0.751	0.731	0.712
4	0.961	0.924	0.885	0.855	0.823	0.792	0.763	0.735	0.708	0.683	0.659	0.636
5	0.951	0.906	0.863	0.822	0.784	0.747	0.713	0.681	0.650	0.621	0.593	0.567
6	0.942	0.888	0.837	0.790	0.746	0.705	0.666	0.630	0.596	0.564	0.535	0.507
7	0.933	0.871	0.813	0.760	0.711	0.665	0.623	0.583	0.547	0.513	0.482	0.452
8	0.923	0.853	0.789	0.731	0.677	0.627	0.582	0.540	0.502	0.467	0.434	0.404
9	0.914	0.837	0.766	0.703	0.645	0.592	0.544	0.500	0.460	0.424	0.391	0.361
10	0.905	0.820	0.744	0.676	0.614	0.558	0.508	0.463	0.422	0.386	0.352	0.322
11	0.896	0.804	0.722	0.650	0.585	0.527	0.475	0.429	0.388	0.350	0.317	0.287
12	0.887	0.788	0.701	0.625	0.557	0.497	0.444	0.397	0.356	0.319	0.286	0.257
13	0.879	0.773	0.681	0.601	0.530	0.469	0.415	0.368	0.326	0.290	0.258	0.229
14	0.870	0.758	0.661	0.577	0.505	0.442	0.388	0.340	0.299	0.263	0.232	0.205
15	0.861	0.743	0.642	0.555	0.481	0.417	0.362	0.315	0.275	0.239	0.209	0.183
16	0.853	0.728	0.623	0.534	0.458	0.394	0.339	0.292	0.252	0.218	0.188	0.163
17	0.844	0.714	0.605	0.513	0.436	0.371	0.317	0.270	0.231	0.198	0.170	0.146
18	0.836	0.700	0.587	0.494	0.416	0.350	0.296	0.250	0.212	0.180	0.153	0.130
19	0.828	0.686	0.570	0.475	0.396	0.331	0.277	0.232	0.194	0.164	0.138	0.116
20	0.820	0.673	0.554	0.456	0.377	0.312	0.258	0.215	0.178	0.149	0.124	0.104
25	0.780	0.610	0.478	0.375	0.295	0.233	0.184	0.146	0.116	0.092	0.074	0.059
30	0.742	0.552	0.412	0.308	0.231	0.174	0.131	0.099	0.075	0.057	0.044	0.033
40	0.672	0.453	0.307	0.208	0.142	0.097	0.067	0.046	0.032	0.022	0.015	0.011
50	0.608	0.372	0.228	0.141	0.087	0.054	0.034	0.021	0.013	0.009	0.005	0.003

Percent

Period	13%	14%	15%	16%	17%	18%	19%	20%	25%	30%	35%	40%	50%
1	0.885	0.877	0.870	0.862	0.855	0.847	0.840	0.833	0.800	0.769	0.741	0.714	0.667
2	0.783	0.769	0.756	0.743	0.731	0.718	0.706	0.694	0.640	0.592	0.549	0.510	0.444
3	0.693	0.675	0.658	0.641	0.624	0.609	0.593	0.579	0.512	0.455	0.406	0.364	0.296
4	0.613	0.592	0.572	0.552	0.534	0.515	0.499	0.482	0.410	0.350	0.301	0.260	0.198
5	0.543	0.519	0.497	0.476	0.456	0.437	0.419	0.402	0.320	0.269	0.223	0.186	0.132
6	0.480	0.456	0.432	0.410	0.390	0.370	0.352	0.335	0.262	0.207	0.165	0.133	0.088
7	0.425	0.400	0.376	0.354	0.333	0.314	0.296	0.279	0.210	0.159	0.122	0.095	0.059
8	0.376	0.351	0.327	0.305	0.285	0.266	0.249	0.233	0.168	0.123	0.091	0.068	0.039
9	0.333	0.308	0.284	0.263	0.243	0.225	0.209	0.194	0.134	0.094	0.067	0.048	0.026
10	0.295	0.270	0.247	0.227	0.208	0.191	0.176	0.162	0.107	0.073	0.050	0.035	0.017
11	0.261	0.237	0.215	0.195	0.178	0.162	0.148	0.135	0.086	0.056	0.037	0.025	0.012
12	0.231	0.208	0.187	0.168	0.152	0.137	0.124	0.112	0.069	0.043	0.027	0.018	0.008
13	0.204	0.182	0.163	0.145	0.130	0.116	0.104	0.093	0.055	0.033	0.020	0.013	0.005
14	0.181	0.160	0.141	0.125	0.111	0.099	0.088	0.078	0.044	0.025	0.015	0.009	0.003
15	0.160	0.140	0.123	0.108	0.095	0.084	0.074	0.065	0.035	0.020	0.011	0.006	0.002
16	0.141	0.123	0.107	0.093	0.081	0.071	0.062	0.054	0.028	0.015	0.008	0.005	0.002
17	0.125	0.108	0.093	0.080	0.069	0.060	0.052	0.045	0.023	0.012	0.006	0.003	0.001
18	0.111	0.095	0.081	0.069	0.059	0.051	0.044	0.038	0.018	0.009	0.005	0.002	0.001
19	0.098	0.083	0.070	0.060	0.051	0.043	0.037	0.031	0.014	0.007	0.003	0.002	0
20	0.087	0.073	0.061	0.051	0.043	0.037	0.031	0.026	0.012	0.005	0.002	0.001	0
25	0.047	0.038	0.030	0.024	0.020	0.016	0.013	0.010	0.004	0.001	0.001	0	0
30	0.026	0.020	0.015	0.012	0.009	0.007	0.005	0.004	0.001	0	0	0	0
40	0.008	0.005	0.004	0.003	0.002	0.001	0.001	0.001	0	0	0	0	0
50	0.002	0.001	0.001	0.001	0	0	0	0	0	0	0	0	0

Appendix B. Present Value of an Annuity of $1 for n Years, Discounted at Rate k

Percent

Period	1%	2%	3%	4%	5%	6%	7%	8%	9%	10%	11%	12%
1	0.990	0.980	0.971	0.962	0.952	0.943	0.935	0.926	0.917	0.909	0.901	0.893
2	1.970	1.942	1.913	1.886	1.859	1.833	1.808	1.783	1.759	1.736	1.713	1.690
3	2.941	2.884	2.829	2.775	2.723	2.673	2.624	2.577	2.531	2.487	2.444	2.402
4	3.902	3.808	3.717	3.630	3.546	3.465	3.387	3.312	3.240	3.170	3.102	3.037
5	4.853	4.713	4.580	4.452	4.329	4.212	4.100	3.993	3.890	3.791	3.696	3.605
6	5.795	5.601	5.417	5.242	5.076	4.917	4.767	4.623	4.486	4.355	4.231	4.111
7	6.728	6.472	6.230	6.002	5.786	5.582	5.389	5.206	5.033	4.868	4.712	4.564
8	7.652	7.325	7.020	6.733	6.463	6.210	5.971	5.747	5.535	5.335	5.146	4.968
9	8.566	8.162	7.786	7.435	7.108	6.802	6.515	6.247	5.995	5.759	5.537	5.328
10	9.471	8.983	8.530	8.111	7.722	7.360	7.024	6.710	6.418	6.145	5.889	5.650
11	10.368	9.787	9.253	8.760	8.306	7.887	7.499	7.139	6.805	6.495	6.207	5.938
12	11.255	10.575	9.954	9.385	8.863	8.384	7.943	7.536	7.161	6.814	6.492	6.194
13	12.134	11.348	10.635	9.986	9.394	8.853	8.358	7.904	7.487	7.103	6.750	6.424
14	13.004	12.106	11.296	10.563	9.899	9.295	8.745	8.244	7.786	7.367	6.982	6.628
15	13.865	12.849	11.939	11.118	10.380	9.712	9.108	8.559	8.061	7.606	7.191	6.811
16	14.718	13.578	12.561	11.652	10.838	10.106	9.447	8.851	8.313	7.824	7.379	6.974
17	15.562	14.292	13.166	12.166	11.274	10.477	9.763	9.122	8.544	8.022	7.549	7.102
18	16.398	14.992	13.754	12.659	11.690	10.828	10.059	9.372	8.756	8.201	7.702	7.250
19	17.226	15.678	14.324	13.134	12.085	11.158	10.336	9.604	8.950	8.365	7.839	7.366
20	18.046	16.351	14.877	13.590	12.462	11.470	10.594	9.818	9.129	8.514	7.963	7.469
25	22.023	19.523	17.413	15.622	14.094	12.783	11.654	10.675	9.823	9.077	8.422	7.843
30	25.808	22.396	19.600	17.292	15.372	13.765	12.409	11.258	10.274	9.427	8.694	8.055
40	32.835	27.355	23.115	19.793	17.159	15.046	13.332	11.925	10.757	9.779	8.951	8.244
50	39.196	31.424	25.730	21.482	18.256	15.762	13.801	12.233	10.962	9.915	9.042	8.304

Percent

Period	13%	14%	15%	16%	17%	18%	19%	20%	25%	30%	35%	40%	50%
1	0.885	0.877	0.870	0.862	0.855	0.847	0.840	0.833	0.800	0.769	0.741	0.714	0.667
2	1.668	1.647	1.626	1.605	1.585	1.566	1.547	1.528	1.440	1.361	1.289	1.224	1.111
3	2.361	2.322	2.283	2.246	2.210	2.174	2.140	2.106	1.952	1.816	1.696	1.589	1.407
4	2.974	2.914	2.855	2.798	2.743	2.690	2.639	2.589	2.362	2.166	1.997	1.849	1.605
5	3.517	3.433	3.352	3.274	3.199	3.127	3.058	2.991	2.689	2.436	2.220	2.035	1.737
6	3.998	3.889	3.784	3.685	3.589	3.498	3.410	3.326	2.951	2.643	2.385	2.168	1.824
7	4.423	4.288	4.160	4.039	3.922	3.812	3.706	3.605	3.161	2.802	2.508	2.263	1.883
8	4.799	4.639	4.487	4.344	4.207	4.078	3.954	3.837	3.329	2.925	2.598	2.331	1.922
9	5.132	4.946	4.772	4.607	4.451	4.303	4.163	4.031	3.463	3.019	2.665	2.379	1.948
10	5.426	5.216	5.019	4.833	4.659	4.494	4.339	4.192	3.571	3.092	2.715	2.414	1.965
11	5.687	5.453	5.234	5.029	4.836	4.656	4.486	4.327	3.656	3.147	2.752	2.438	1.977
12	5.918	5.660	5.421	5.197	4.988	4.793	4.611	4.439	3.725	3.190	2.779	2.456	1.985
13	6.122	5.842	5.583	5.342	5.118	4.910	4.715	4.533	3.780	3.223	2.799	2.469	1.990
14	6.302	6.002	5.724	5.468	5.229	5.008	4.802	4.611	3.824	3.249	2.814	2.478	1.993
15	6.462	6.142	5.847	5.575	5.324	5.092	4.876	4.675	3.859	3.268	2.825	2.484	1.995
16	6.604	6.265	5.954	5.668	5.405	5.162	4.938	4.730	3.887	3.283	2.834	2.489	1.997
17	6.729	6.373	6.047	5.749	5.475	5.222	4.988	4.775	3.910	3.295	2.840	2.492	1.998
18	6.840	6.467	6.128	5.818	5.534	5.273	5.033	4.812	3.928	3.304	2.844	2.494	1.999
19	6.938	6.550	6.198	5.877	5.584	5.316	5.070	4.843	3.942	3.311	2.848	2.496	1.999
20	7.025	6.623	6.259	5.929	5.628	5.353	5.101	4.870	3.954	3.316	2.850	2.497	1.999
25	7.330	6.873	6.464	6.097	5.766	5.467	5.195	4.948	3.985	3.329	2.856	2.499	2.000
30	7.496	7.003	6.566	6.177	5.829	5.517	5.235	4.979	3.995	3.332	2.857	2.500	2.000
40	7.634	7.105	6.642	6.233	5.871	5.548	5.258	4.997	3.999	3.333	2.857	2.500	2.000
50	7.675	7.133	6.661	6.246	5.880	5.554	5.262	4.999	4.000	3.333	2.857	2.500	2.000

Glossary

Accelerated depreciation

Any *depreciation*[1] that produces larger deductions for depreciation in the early years of a projects's life.

Acceptance criterion

Any minimum standard of performance in investment analysis (cf. hurdle rate).

Accounting income

An economic agent's *realized income* as shown on financial statements (cf. economic income).

Accounting rate of return

A figure of investment merit, defined as average annual cash inflow divided by total cash outflow (cf. internal rate of return).

Accounts payable (payables, trade payables)

Money owed to suppliers.

Accounts receivable (receivables, trade credit)

Money owed by customers.

Accrual accounting

A method of accounting in which *revenue* is recognized when earned and expenses are recognized when incurred without regard to the timing of cash receipts and expenditures (cf. cash accounting).

---

[1]Words in italics are defined elsewhere in the glossary.

Acid test (quick ratio)
A measure of *liquidity,* defined as *current assets* less inventories divided by *current liabilities.*

Aftertax cash flow
Total cash generated by an investment annually, defined as profit after tax plus depreciation, or equivalently, operating income after tax plus the tax rate times depreciation.

Allocated costs
Costs systematically assigned or distributed among products, departments, or other elements.

Annuity
A level stream of cash flows for a limited number of years (cf. perpetuity).

Asset turnover ratio
A broad measure of asset efficiency, defined as net sales divided by total assets.

Bankruptcy
A legal condition in which an individual's or company's assets are assumed by a federal court official and used to pay off creditors.

Benefit-cost ratio
Profitability index.

β-**risk** (systematic risk, nondiversifiable risk)
Risk that cannot be diversified away.

Bond
Long-term publically issued debt.

Bond rating
An appraisal by a recognized financial organization of the soundness of a *bond* as an investment.

Book value
The value at which an item is reported in financial statements (cf. market value).

Break-even analysis
Analysis of the level of sales at which a firm or product will just break even.

Business risk
Risk due to uncertainty about investment outlays, operating cash flows, and salvage values without regard to how investments are financed (cf. financial risk).

Call option
Option to buy an asset at a specified exercise price on or before a specified maturity date (cf. put option).

Call provision
Provision describing terms under which a bond issuer may redeem bond in whole or in part prior to maturity.

Capital
The amount invested in a venture (cf. capitalization).

Capital budget
List of planned investment projects.

Capital consumption adjustment
Adjustment to historical cost depreciation to correct for understatement during inflation.

Capital rationing
Fixed limit on capital which forces company to choose among worthwhile projects.

Capitalization
The sum of all long-term sources of financing to the firm, or equivalently, total assets less current liabilities.

Cash accounting
A method of accounting in which changes in the condition of an organization are recognized only in response to the payment or receipt of cash (cf. accrual accounting).

Cash budget
A plan or projection of cash receipts and disbursements for a given period of time (cf. cash flow forecast, cash flow statement, pro forma forecast).

Cash cow
Company or product that generates more cash than can be productively reinvested.

Cash flow
The amount of cash generated or consumed by an activity over a certain period of time.

Cash flow cycle
The periodic transformation of cash through *working capital* and fixed assets back to cash.

Cash flow forecast
A financial forecast in the form of a *sources and uses statement.*

Cash flow from operations
Cash generated or consumed by the productive activities of a firm over a period of time; defined as profit after tax plus *noncash changes* minus noncash receipts (cf. cash provided by operations).

Cash flow principle
Principle of investment evaluation stating that only actual movements of cash are relevant and that they should be listed on the date they move.

Cash flow statement
A refinement of a *sources and uses statement* in which related sources and uses are grouped under various headings such as *cash provided by operations,* cash provided from external financing, etc.

Cash provided by operations
All cash generated or consumed by the productive activities of a firm over a period of time, *including* changes in current assets and liabilities required to support changing sales volumes (cf. cash flow from operations).

Certainty-equivalent
A guaranteed amount of money which a decison maker would trade for an uncertain cash flow.

Close off the top
Finance jargon meaning to foreclose the possibility of additional debt financing.

Collection period
A ratio measure of control of *accounts receivable,* defined as accounts receivable divided by credit sales per day.

Common shares
Common stock.

Common-size financial statements
Device used to compare financial statements, frequently of companies of disparate size, whereby all balance sheet entries are divided by total assets and all income statement entries are divided by net sales.

Common stock (common sharesstock)
Securities representing an ownership interest in a firm.

Compounding
The growth of a sum of money over time through the reinvestment of interest earned to earn more interest (cf. discounting).

Conglomerate diversification

Ownership of operations in a number of functionally unrelated business activities.

Constant-dollar accounting

System of inflation accounting in which historical-cost items are restated to adjust for changes in the general purchasing power of the currency (cf. current-dollar accounting).

Constant purchasing power

The amount of a currency required over time to purchase a stable basket of physical assets.

Consumer price index (CPI)

An index measure of inflation equal to the sum of prices of a number of assets purchased by consumers weighted by the proportion each represents in a typical consumer's budget.

Contribution to fixed cost and profits

The excess of *revenue* over *variable costs*.

Conversion ratio

Number of shares for which a *convertible security* may be exchanged.

Conversion value

Market value of shares investor would own if he or she converted one convertible security.

Control ratio

Ratio indicating management's control of a particular current asset or liability.

Convertible security

Financial security which can be exchanged at the holder's option for another security or asset.

Correlation coefficient

Measure of the degree of comovement of two variables.

Cost of capital (opportunity cost of capital, hurdle rate, weighted-average cost of capital)

Return on new, average risk investment company must expect to maintain share price. A weighted average of the cost to the firm of individual sources of capital.

Cost of debt

Yield to maturity on debt; frequently after tax, in which event it is one minus the tax rate times the yield to maturity.

Cost of equity
Return equity investors expect to earn by holding shares in a company. The expected return forgone by equity investors in the next best, equal risk opportunity.

Cost of goods sold (cost of sales)
The sum of all costs required to acquire and prepare goods for sale.

Coupon rate
The interest rate specified on interest coupons attached to bonds. Annual interest received equals coupon rate times the *par value* of the bond.

Covenant (protective covenant)
Provision in a debt agreement requiring the borrower to do, or not do, something.

Coverage ratio
Measure of financial leverage relating annual operating income to annual burden of debt (cf. times interest earned ratio, times burden covered ratio).

Cumulative preferred stock
Preferred stock containing the requirement that any unpaid preferred dividends accumulate and must be paid in full before common dividends may be distributed.

Current asset
Any asset which will turn into cash within one year.

Current-dollar accounting
System of inflation accounting in which historical-cost items are restated to adjust for changes in the price of specific item (cf. constant-dollar accounting).

Current liability
Any liability which is payable within one year.

Current portion of long-term debt
That portion of long-term debt which is payable within one year.

Current ratio
A measure of *liquidity,* defined as current assets divided by current liabilities.

Days sales in cash
A measure of management's control of cash balances, defined as cash divided by sales per day.

Debt (liability)
An obligation to pay cash or other goods or to provide services to another.

Debt capacity
The total amount of debt a company can prudently support, given its earnings expectations and equity base.

Debt-to-assets ratio
A measure of *financial leverage,* defined as debt divided by total assets (cf. debt-to-equity ratio).

Debt-to-equity ratio
A measure of *financial leverage,* defined as debt divided by shareholders' equity.

Default
To fail to make a payment when due.

Default premium
The increased return on a security required to compensate investors for the risk the company will default on its obligation.

Deferred tax liability
An estimated amount of future income taxes that may become payable from income already earned but not yet recognized for tax reporting purposes.

Delayed call
Provision in a security which gives the issuer the right to call the issue but only after a period of time has elapsed (cf. call provision).

Depreciation
The reduction in the value of a long-lived asset from use or obsolescence. The decline is recognized in accounting by a periodic allocation of the original cost of the asset to current operations (cf. accelerated depreciation).

Dilution
The reduction in any per share item (such as earnings per share or book value per share) due to an increase in the number of shares outstanding either through new issue or conversion of outstanding securities.

Discount rate
Interest rate used to calculate the *present value* of future cash flows.

Discounted cash flow
The method of evaluating long-term projects, which explicitly takes into account the time value of money.

Discounted cash flow rate of return
Internal rate of return.

Discounting
Process of finding the present value of future cash flows (cf. compounding).

Diversifiable risk
That risk which is eliminated when an asset is added to a diversified portfolio (cf. β-risk).

Diversification
The process of investing in a number of differing assets.

Dividend payout ratio
A measure of the level of dividends distributed, defined as dividends divided by earnings.

Earnings (income, net income, net profit, profit)
The excess of revenues over all related expenses for a given period.

Earnings per share
A measure of each common share's claim on earnings, defined as earnings available for common divided by the number of common shares outstanding.

Earnings yield
Earnings per share divided by stock price.

EBIT
Abbreviation for earnings before interest and taxes.

Economic income
The amount an economic agent could spend during a period of time without affecting his or her wealth (cf. accounting income).

Efficient market
A market in which asset prices instantaneously reflect new information.

Equity (owners' equity, net worth, shareholders' equity)
The ownership interests of common and preferred stockholders in a company; on a balance sheet, equity equals total assets less all liabilities.

Equivalence
Concept which states that two cash flows occurrring at different times are of equal value if the cash flow occurring sooner can be converted into the later cash flow by investing it at the prevailing interest rate.

Expected return
Average of possible returns weighted by their probability.

Figure of merit
A number summarizing the investment worth of a project.

Financial accounting standards board (FASB)
Official rule-making body in accounting profession.

Financial flexibility
The ability to raise sufficient capital to meet company needs under a wide variety of future contingencies.

Financial leverage
Use of debt to increase the expected return and the risk to equity (cf. operating leverage).

First-in, first-out (FIFO)
A method of inventory accounting in which the oldest item in inventory is assumed to be sold first (cf. last-in, first-out).

Fisher effect
Proposition that the nominal rate of interest should approximately equal the real rate of interest plus a premium for expected inflation (cf. real amount, nominal amount).

Fixed cost
Any cost which does not vary over the observation period with changes in volume.

Fixed-income security
Any security which promises an unvarying payment stream to holders over its life.

Forcing conversion
Strategy in which a company forces owners of a convertible security to convert by calling the security at a time when its call price is below its conversion value (cf. call provision, convertible security).

Frozen convertible (hung convertible)
Convertible security which has been outstanding for several years and which cannot be forced to convert because its *conversion value* is below its call price (cf. forcing conversion).

Funds
Any means of payment. Along with cash flow, funds is one of the most frequently misused words in finance.

Gains to net debtors
Increase in debtor's wealth due to decline in purchasing power of liabilities.

General creditor
Unsecured creditor.

Gross margin percentage
Revenue minus cost of goods sold divided by revenue.

Hurdle rate
Minimum acceptable rate of return on investment (cf. acceptance criterion, cost of capital).

Historical-cost depreciation
Depreciation based on amount originally paid for asset.

Income
Earnings.

Income statement (profit and loss statement)
A report of a company's revenues, associated expenses, and resulting *income* for a period of time.

Inflation premium
The increased return on a security required to compensate investors for expected inflation.

Insolvency
The condition of having debts greater than the realizable value of one's assets.

Internal rate of return (IRR)
Discount rate at which project's *net present value* equals zero. Rate at which funds left in a project are *compounding* (cf. rate of return).

Internal sources
Cash available to a company from *cash flow from operations.*

Inventory turnover ratio
A measure of management's control of its investment in inventory, defined as *cost of goods sold* divided by ending inventory, or something similar.

Inventory valuation adjustment
Adjustment to historical-cost financial statements to correct for the possible understatement of inventory and *cost of goods sold* during inflation.

Investment bank
A financial institution specializing in the original sale and subsequent trading of company securities.

Investment value
Value of a *convertible security* based solely on its characteristics as a fixed-income security and ignoring the value of the conversion feature.

Last-in, first-out (LIFO)
A method of inventory accounting in which the newest item in inventory is assumed to be sold first (cf. first-in, first-out).

Liability
An obligation to pay an amount or perform a service.

Liquid asset
Any asset that can be quickly converted to cash without significant loss of value.

Liquidation
The process of closing down a company, selling its assets, paying off its creditors and distributing any remaining cash to owners.

Liquidity
The extent to which a company has assets that are readily available to meet obligations (cf. acid test, current ratio).

Liquidity ratio
Any ratio used to estimate a company's *liquidity* (cf. acid test, current ratio).

Market line (securities market line)
Line representing relationship between *expected return* and *β-risk*.

Market value
The price at which an item can be sold (cf. book value).

Monetary asset
Any asset having a value defined in units of currency. Cash and accounts receivable are monetary assets; inventories and plant and equipment are physical assets.

Multiple hurdle rates
Use of different *hurdle rates* for new investments to reflect differing levels of risk.

Mutually exclusive alternatives
Two projects which accomplish the same objective, so that only one will be undertaken.

Net income
Earnings.

Net monetary creditor
Economic agent having *monetary assets* in excess of *liabilities*.

Net monetary debtor
Economic agent having *monetary assets* less than *liabilities*.

Net present value (NPV)
Present value of cash inflows less present value of cash outflows. The increase in wealth accruing to an investor when he or she undertakes an investment.

Net profit
Earnings.

Net sales
Total sales revenue less certain offsetting items such as returns and allowances and sales discounts.

Net worth
Equity, shareholders' equity.

Nominal amount
Any quantity not adjusted for changes in purchasing power of the currency due to inflation (cf. real amount).

Noncash charge
An expense recorded by an accountant not matched by a cash outflow during the accounting period.

Nondiversifiable risk
β-risk, systematic risk.

Operating leverage
Fixed operating costs which tend to increase the variation in profits (cf. financial leverage).

Opportunity cost of capital
Cost of capital.

Opportunity cost
Income forgone by an investor when he or she chooses one action opposed to another. Expected income on next best alternative.

Option
See *call option, put option.*

Over-the-counter market (OTC)
Informal market in which securities not listed on organized exchanges trade.

Owners' equity
Equity.

Paid-in capital
That portion of *shareholders' equity* which has been paid-in directly as opposed to earned profits retained in the business.

Par value
An arbitrary value set as the face amount of a security. Bondholders receive par value for their bonds on maturity.

Payables period
A measure of a company's use of trade credit financing, defined as accounts payable divided by purchases per day.

Payback period
A crude figure of investment merit and better measure of investment risk, defined as the time an investor must wait to recoup his or her initial investment.

Perpetuity
An *annuity* that lasts forever.

Plug
Jargon for the unknown quantity in a pro forma forecast.

Portfolio
Holdings of a diverse group of assets by an individual or a company.

Preferred stock
A class of stock, usually fixed income, which carries some form of preference to income or assets over *common stock* (cf. cumulative preferred stock).

Present value
The present worth of a future sum of money.

Price-to-earnings ratio (P/E ratio)
Amount investors are willing to pay for $1 of a firm's current earnings. Price per share divided by earnings per share over the most recent 12 months.

Principal
The original, or face, amount of a loan. Interest is earned on the principal.

Private placement
The raising of capital for a business through the sale of securities to a limited number of well-informed investors rather than through a public offering.

Pro forma statement
A financial statement prepared on the basis of some assumed events that have not yet occurred.

Profit center
An organizational unit within a company that produces revenue and for which a profit can be calculated.

Profit margin
The proportion of each sales dollar that filters down to *income*, defined as income divided by *net sales*.

Profits
Earnings.

Profitability index (benefit-cost ratio)
A figure of investment merit, defined as the *present value* of cash inflows divided by present value of cash outflows.

Protective covenant
Covenant.

Public issue (public offering)
Newly issued securities sold directly to the public (cf. private placement).

Put option
Option to sell an asset at a specified exercise price on or before a specified maturity date (cf. call option).

Quick ratio
Acid test.

Range-of-earnings chart
Graph relating *earnings per share* (EPS) to earnings before interest and taxes (EBIT) under alternative financing options.

Rate of return
A general term meaning yield obtainable on an asset.

Ratio analysis
Analysis of financial statements using ratios.

Real amount
Any quantity which has been adjusted for changes in the purchasing power of the currency due to inflation (cf. nominal amount).

Realized income
The earning of income related to a transaction as distinguished from a paper gain.

Retained earnings (earned surplus)
The amount of earnings retained and reinvested in a business and not distributed to stockholders as dividends.

Return on assets (ROA)

A measure of the productivity of assets, defined as *income* divided by total assets. A superior but less common definition includes interest expense and preferred dividends in the numerator.

Return on equity (ROE)

A measure of the productivity or efficiency with which shareholders' equity is employed, defined as *income* divided by *equity.*

Return on investment (ROI)

The productivity of an investment or a profit center, defined as *income* divided by *book value* of investment or *profit center* (cf. return on assets).

Residual income security

A security which has last claim on company income. Usually the primary beneficiary of company growth.

Residual profits

An alternative to *return on investment* as a measure of *profit center* performance, defined as *income* less the annual cost of the capital employed by the profit center.

Revenues

Sales.

Rights of absolute priority

Specification in bankruptcy law stating that each class of claimants with a prior claim on assets in liquidation will be paid off in full before any junior claimants receive anything.

Risk-adjusted discount rate (cost of capital, hurdle rate)

A *discount rate* which includes a premium for risk.

Risk aversion

An unwillingness to bear risk without compensation of some form.

Risk-free interest rate

The interest rate prevailing on a default-free bond in the absence of inflation.

Risk premium

The increased return on a security required to compensate investors for the risk borne.

Sales (revenue)

The inflow of resources to a business for a period from sale of goods or provision of services (cf. net sales).

Secured creditor

A creditor whose obligation is backed by the pledge of some asset. In liquidation, the secured creditor receives the cash from the sale of the pledged asset to the extent of his or her loan.

Securities and Exchange Commission (SEC)
Federal government agency that regulates securities markets.

Semistrong-form efficient market
A market in which prices instantaneously reflect all publically available information.

Senior creditor
Any creditor with a claim on income or assets prior to that of *general creditors*.

Sensitivity analysis
Analysis of impact on a plan or forecast of a change in one of the input variables.

Shareholders' equity
Equity, net worth.

Shelf registration
Experimental SEC program under which companies can file a general-purpose prospectus describing their possible financing plans for up to the next two years. This eliminates time lags for new public security issues.

Simulation (Monte Carlo simulation)
Computer-based extension of *sensitivity analysis* that calculates the probability distribution of a forecast outcome.

Sinking fund
A fund of cash set aside for the payment of a future obligation. A bond sinking fund is a payment of cash to creditors.

Solvency
The state of being able to pay debts as they come due.

Sources and uses statement
A document showing where a company got its cash and where it spent the cash over a specific period of time. It is constructed by segregating all changes in balance sheet accounts into those that provided cash and those that consumed cash.

Spontaneous sources of cash
Those liabilities such as accounts payable and accrued wages that arise automatically, without negotiation, in the course of doing business.

Spread

Investment banker jargon for difference between the issue price on a new security and the net to the company.

Statement of changes in financial position

A financial statement showing the sources and uses of working capital for the period.

Stock

Common stock.

Stock option

A contractual privilege sometimes provided to company officers giving the holder the right to purchase a specified number of shares at a specified price and for a stated period of time.

Standard deviation of return

A measure of variability. The square root of the mean squared deviation from the *expected return.*

Striking price (exercise price)

The fixed price for which a stock can be purchased in a call contract or sold in a put contract (cf. call option, put option).

Strong-form efficient market

A market in which prices instantaneously reflect all information public or private.

Subordinated creditor

A creditor holding a debenture having a lower chance of payment than other liabilities of the firm.

Sunk cost

A previous outlay that cannot be changed by any current or future action.

Sustainable growth rate

The rate of increase in sales a company can attain without changing its profit margin, assets-to-sales ratio, debt-to-equity ratio, or dividend payout ratio. The rate of growth a company can finance without excessive borrowing or a new stock issue.

Times burden covered

A *coverage ratio* measure of *financial leverage,* defined as earnings before interest and taxes divided by interest expense plus principal payments grossed up to their before-tax equivalents.

Times interest earned
A *coverage ratio* measure of *financial leverage,* defined as earnings before interest and taxes divided by interest expense.

Trade payables
Accounts payable.

Underwriting syndicate
A group of *investment banks* that bands together for a brief time to guarantee a specified price to a company for newly issued securities.

Unrealized income
Income earned but for which there is no confirming transaction. A paper gain.

Variable cost
Any expense that varies with sales over the observation period.

Volatility
β-risk.

Warrant
A security issued by a company granting the right to puchase shares of another security of the company at a specified price and for a stated time.

Weak-form efficient market
A market in which prices instantaneously reflect information about past prices.

Weighted-average cost of capital
Cost of capital.

With-without principle
Principle defining those cash flows which are relevant to an investment decision. It states that if there are two worlds, one with the investment and one without it, all cash flows that differ in these two worlds are relevant and all cash flows that are the same are irrelevant.

Working capital (net working capital)
The excess of current assets over current liabilities.

Working capital cycle
The periodic transformation of cash through current assets and current liabilities and back to cash (cf. cash flow cycle).

Yield to maturity
The *internal rate of return* on a bond when held to maturity.

Index